Sometimes A Great Nation

Sometimes A Great Nation

WILL CANADA BELONG TO THE 21st CENTURY?

Peter C. Newman

The great nations
have always acted
like gangsters
and the small nations
like prostitutes . . .

— Stanley Kubrick

Canadian Cataloguing in Publication Data

Newman, Peter C., 1929-

Sometimes a great nation

ISBN 0-7710-6750-X

1. Canada – Politics and government – 1963-   .*
I. Title.

FC609.N49 1988   971.064   C88-094146-4
F1034.2.N49 1988

Printed and bound in Canada by
T. H. Best Printing Company Limited

McClelland and Stewart
The Canadian Publishers
481 University Avenue
Toronto, Ontario
M5G 2E9

For Roy Abraham Faibish,
Canada's conscience in exile

Acknowledgements

Most of the pieces in this collection, here in slightly edited form, were first published in *Maclean's*, the *Financial Post, Canadian Geographic, City and Country Home, Saturday Night*, and the *Globe and Mail*. I am grateful to their publishers for allowing me to reproduce these assignments. This book was edited by Janet Craig, Martin Lynch, and Camilla Newman.

By the same author:

Contents

PART THREE

Power Politics

PART FOUR

Departures

EPILOGUE

Sometimes A Great Nation

FOREWORD

Sometimes A Great Nation

THIS IS ONE JOURNALIST'S DISTILLATION of the jumble of incidents and events that marked Canada's passage between the promising autumn of 1973 and the perilous summer of 1988. The collection of occasional pieces that follows – most of them written overnight for looming deadlines – is a selection from the nearly one thousand dispatches I wrote during those fifteen years. The book is divided into six categories: *Wild Years in the Peaceable Kingdom, Heroes, Power Politics, Departures, Business Watch*, and *Diversions*. Except for *Diversions*, which deals with more personal pursuits, most of these articles stalk the tentative heroes and closet villains who populate these northern latitudes. By exploring the handful of metaphors that cut across the often contradictory private and regional interests that characterize our national psyche, I have tried to show how Canada has been built on dreams as well as appetites.

This country was put together not only by bloodlines, kin, and tradition but by tides of newcomers of every stock, creed, and persuasion, united mainly in their will to embrace an unknown world more promising than the one they were leaving behind. Keeping that optimism intact has not been easy, but most of the dreams have survived, as they have for me. I arrived at the impressionable age of eleven, escaping the Nazis goose-stepping across Europe. Though it was only sanctuary we sought, my family and I soon felt we had entered the most special land on earth. If at times I and others who came here in similar circumstances seem a little too earnest in defending things Canadian or worrying about the future of our adopted land, it's because of the bitter lessons we learned in Europe, where the vigorous independence of our once-free home countries was indivisible from individual freedom.

Canada's founding peoples – the Indians and Inuit, the French, Scots, English, and United Empire Loyalists – bearing diverse historical memories of their own, see their country through the distorting glass of entrenched ethic, habit, and accommodation. We New Canadians tend to view our adopted land in a kind of glowing light, as an unsoured society with the potential of realizable ideals. Alone among the Western world's industrialized nations (Canada ranks seventh in that august company), this country is not yet crystallized but still in the process of becoming – something that was true of the United States in the 1880s and of Europe long before that. Most Canadian hierarchies are open to anyone regardless of racial credentials or origins; let my decade and a half as editor of Canada's largest newspaper (the *Toronto Star*) and most influential magazine (*Maclean's*) attest to that. Many of us who came here by choice can exercise an option denied in our lands of birth: to question and criticize those in authority. Because no officially sanctioned Canadian Dream exists, we can bitch about this country and adore it at the same time.

It's a mood that sets us apart from citizens of the United States, where the American Dream continues to circumscribe its true believers and bedevil its malcontents. The distinction between the American melting pot and the Canadian mosaic remains our single most important national characteristic. Here, most of us – the country's founding races, plus the Europeans, Asians, West Indians – arrived trailing our own roots, now firmly transplanted into fertile new ground. What makes Canada so special is the unwritten compact that bigotry will not be condoned (except in every small-town pub) and that instead of abusing one another we can almost always talk out our problems and sometimes even our prejudices. It's vital that we never lose hold of this fragile but essential quality: that everyone is permitted to live and let live, allowed to curse the politicians while loving the land, to debate endlessly the meaning of our national existence while living it day by day.

MY CRITICS ACCUSE ME of being more concerned with people than with policies, and they're right. Events evolve from the interplay of personalities with circumstance, but it is the way men and women in positions of influence act and react to those events that really counts. Without intimate glimpses into their lives, history would not only be duller but also incomplete. It is the anecdotes and piquant asides that reveal why individuals under pressure behave as they do. If fairly and accurately reported, such day-to-day epiphanies can bring to life a whole era.

In that context, my quest has been not so much for a holier-than-everyone leader (my past attempts at canonization have generally backfired), or even for some great cause, as for an ideological position free of hidebound philosophies. Being actively Canadian (as opposed to just living here) requires a pragmatic progression of choices about what to believe in. Among the mainstays of my faith is the notion that it is essential to preserve the relatively gentle society on *this* side of the 49th parallel. We must reject the seductive but fatal assumption at the source of the American way of life: the gospel that more is better and that progress, efficiency, and monetary gain should be the ultimate goals of human activity. It ain't necessarily so.

I also think that a greater slice of decision-making powers should be shifted directly to the people. Governing should take on a deeper meaning than the exchange of favours among various platoons of power brokers who keep the system flowing, mostly in their own direction. In the current partisan environment, Canada's major political parties are little more than organized appetites for power, temporary alliances of regional and economic interests used to frame the issues around which elections can be fought. During more than a quarter-century of political reporting, I failed to discover any fundamental differences between Liberals and Conservatives – except, perhaps, that Liberals tend to fish from the sterns of rented rowboats while Tories prefer casting their lures off docks, encouraging the fish to come to them. (My research also revealed that Conservatives usually prefer twin beds, which may explain why there are more Liberals.) I once tabulated the platform pledges of the three national parties over the past ten election campaigns. The promises they made were remarkably similar, varying only in their degree of distributing largess with the taxpayers' dollars: the Tories promised handouts to voters from birth to death; the Liberals, from womb to tomb; the Socialists, from erection to resurrection.

Politics in this country too often becomes an unfolding of miscalculations, so that a leader's best chance of long-term achievement is through inadvertence. Watching the antics of our parliamentarians, it is easy to adopt the sour outlook of George Bernard Shaw in one of his *Prefaces*: that "if people cannot have what they believe in, then they must believe in what they have."

BY MID-1988 WE HAD ARRIVED at one of those rare junctures in Canadian history when we could sense the continuity of an age being cut. What comes now will be different from what came before. We may be due for one of those turning points that compress perspectives, redistribute regional allegiances, and bid amen to political dynasties.

It was the combined effect of Brian Mulroney's adamant free trade initiative plus his Meech Lake Accord and tax reform package that triggered the sea change. These and other trends represent nothing less than a rewriting of the social contract between Canadians and their government. We have no choice now about accepting what Norman Mailer tagged the "law of life, so cruel and so just, that one must grow or else pay more for remaining the same."

This will be particularly difficult because for too long we have lacked the momentum that flows from people feeling common cause with their national institutions. The fun has gone out of Canadian politics. Many voters are beginning to feel like Gene Hackman in an obscure but brilliant movie called *Night Moves*. It's the story of a spiritually exhausted private detective who spends most of his time watching football on TV, drinking a little, and complaining a lot. At the start of the film, Hackman is in pretty good form, declaiming visions of living and governing as contests that can be won, but his illusions gradually evaporate. He concludes that life and politics are exactly like all those interminable games he's been watching. "Nobody wins," he says to no one in particular. "One side just keeps losing slower than the other."

Canada's most serious dilemma at the moment is not the paralysis of parliament, not the potential renewal of French-English confrontation if the Meech Lake constitutional initiative fails, not even the outcome of the Great Free Trade Debate. It is the growing disbelief that anything significant can be done to resolve the nation's problems through political action. This demands collective will and individual passion, which have rarely been mobilized by any political leader.

Lacking the political unity that can foster effective consensus, we must devise a new and more contemporary way of seeing our country and ourselves. Canada must be re-invented.

THE ONE INDISPUTABLY GREAT ASPECT of this particular nation-state is its size, and the most astounding aspect of its history has been its survival imposed on that enormous hunk of geography. Few land masses of such outrageous dimensions can withstand the tensions of democracy. The stresses and strains of stretching the rule of law across 88 degrees of longitude and 42 degrees of latitude virtually guarantee inefficient central government. With so many built-in checks and balances needed to accommodate vastly differing regional aspirations, change is bound to be slow and painful. While local identity is at the heart of each region's consciousness, so much emphasis has been placed on such differences that critics have condemned these hearth-and-home emotions for preventing us from having a national culture. "The paradox of the cultural life," observed John Grierson, father of Canadian documentary cinema and founder of the National Film Board, "is that there are no capitals of culture. Every church, however local, is holy ground, and equally so." It's true. Unity and identity are separate qualities, and one does not subtract from the other.

Canada may always remain what Keith Spicer, editor of the *Ottawa Citizen*, called "this archipelago of envies," but that's partly because we live in the world's most awkwardly designed country. Where else is there a nation 5,780 miles long by 200 wide, with twenty-six million inhabitants scattered along a series of abandoned canoe routes? Spiritually, even those who dwell on our wilder shores live near "The Border." This unwieldy dispersal of our population decides the nature of Canadian life; it affects everything we do in that we have to deal with small numbers of people scattered over enormous distances. The ratio of transportation costs to eventual market price is complex enough to deal with in terms of commodities, but it is much more difficult in terms of transmitting ideas, culture, and emotions from east to west, from north to even more north, and back again. There is so much more to geography than space. Even if few Canadians budge north of their summer cottages (and even if most Torontonians still suffer nosebleeds west of the Humber River), Marshall McLuhan was right when he postulated our unique relationship with nature:

"We go outside to be alone, and we go inside to be with people – a pattern that is antithetic not only to Europeans, but to all other cultures whatever."

That gut-link to the outdoors is reflected not only in our psyches but in our looks. Historian William Kilbourn once observed that "outnumbered by the trees and unable to lick them, a lot of Canadians look as though they had joined them – having gone all faceless or a bit pulp-and-papery, and mournful as the evening jackpine round the edges of the voice, as if something long lost and dear were being endlessly regretted." Dale Benson, location manager for the beef opera *Rocky IV*, was asked why he chose to shoot the movie in Vancouver. His down-to-earth reason for picking British Columbians to portray rugged Soviet citizens watching Sylvester Stallone beating their hero to a pulp? "Californians look too pretty," he explained. "You people look like you've really lived."

It is the streak of nordicity in Canadians that makes us look and feel that way. "Because of our origin in the Northern frontier," wrote historian W. L. Morton, "Canadian life to this day is marked by a Northern quality; the line which marks the frontier from the farmstead, the wilderness from the baseland, the hinterland from the metropolis, runs through every Canadian psyche." Even though most Canadians think the Precambrian Shield is a birth control device, territorial integrity (holding on to our northern turf, that is) remains our strongest sustaining myth. We happily give away our energy sources and minerals at rock-bottom prices and sell off the most profitable parts of our secondary manufacturing sector. But let a Yank demand one drop of our water or sail through the North West Passage, and we go ape. That's why Arctic sovereignty, fishing rights, and acid rain (or, for that matter, Quebec separatism, which was perceived by most English Canadians as a threat to the physical continuity of our reach from sea to sea) have become such hot issues.

If geography is destiny (and it probably is), the most apt physical analogy for our psychological status as a nation was a bit of theatre that took place in August 1969. An artist named William Vazan drew a crescent line by walking along a sandy beach at low tide in P.E.I. while another artist walked a similar curved line along Vancouver Island's western shore. "Of course," said Vazan, "when the tide changed, the water erased my crescent line – but for most of a day we had Canada in parentheses." Phyllis Webb, a poet who lives on Saltspring Island, B.C., was delighted: "When I read that story . . . something joyfully tumbled over in me. Those wild men on the beaches – from sea to shining sea – had made a witty, imaginative, sardonic statement about Canada, and they'd created, if not an art, at least an event. Canada is a whole bundle of parentheses, and emotionally we are all caught in the embrace of those inhibiting arms. . . ." We are indeed. (Besides, as comedian Dave Broadfoot pointed out, "The world needs Canada. If Canada wasn't there, the Chinese could sail right across and invade Denmark.")

Much of our inferiority complex stems from feeling dwarfed by our geography. British poet Rupert Brooke rhapsodized about Canada's "unseizable virginity," and American critic Edmund Wilson despaired: "How can one get hold of such a country? How can one think of such space in terms of human meaning?" Six time zones gird the prodigious dimensions of the Canadian subcontinent: when it is a dusky 4:30 p.m. in Newfoundland, church bells are pealing high noon across the Yukon. Canada is larger than China, with a population smaller than Ethiopia's. Less than 7 per cent of Canada's landscape is actually settled, and to carve even that sliver out of the wilderness was a Homeric epic, a silent battle against the cold and the wind and the rocks. Most of our hinterland broods silent and inaccessible, an empty land filled with wonders. "This country," novelist Morley Callaghan mused, "has been like a woman waiting at a window of an old house at a crossroads. She is an ageless, wild, hard beauty. Men riding by come to her in the night. They use her, but never really possess her. They leave her and ride on, afraid of her fierce domination over them, knowing they can't handle her; she leaves them feeling small . . . so she is like the old woman who lived in a shoe; she has had so many children she doesn't know what to do . . . none want to claim her and call her 'Mother'."

Besides geographical elephantiasis, climate has been a favourite scapegoat for Canadians' sense of inferiority – our six months of winter and six months of bad sledding. I have always found it difficult to accept that being cold applies to the heart and soul as it does to fingers and toes. Even if only Outer Mongolia has a colder capital city than Ottawa, our central heating should have eliminated winter as a prime source of ennui. (Many are cold, but few are frozen.) The best thing to do is enjoy the brisk weather and play some hockey. "We are in between the world's superpowers, skating in circles at centre ice," wrote Doug Beardsley in his evocative *Country on Ice.* "Yet this fact need not lead us to the defeatist attitude that at times dominates the Canadian will. It can also be a clarion call to play the game with the reckless abandon of the crazy Canuck that represents the most positive side of our national character: we have 'the spirit' to draw on."

Another reason why – apart from the effects of geography and climate – Canadians have evolved such a splendid inferiority complex may be the natural legacy of living in a country that, as the New Brunswick poet Alden Nowlan put it, "has no history – only a past." According to this myth, Canada was born without ever having been conceived. With little economic logic or the fulfilment of any manifest destiny, we are supposed to have just sort of simmered up – an incongruous potpourri of losers from foreign wars and mercantile extravagances left out to dry in the long wash of history. Not so. As Al Hochbaum, that magnificent naturalist and artist from Delta, Manitoba, once observed, "Memories dim. They must be refreshed; history is no more than memories refined." Exactly. We define ourselves not so much by what we see or hear but by what our memories cannot let go. And being Canadian means having no shortage of such memorable experiences.

Certainly, we may be a loose federation of wildly diverse regions on the very margin of the civilized world. But there is a quiver of common intent that can be counted on across this country – as any prime minister who has abused his mandate or tried to direct our national destiny in undesirable directions can testify.

We don't have enough history only if "history" is measured in blood. That there has never been a war of Canadian origin, that only two of our politicians (Thomas D'Arcy McGee in 1868 and Pierre Laporte more than a century later) were assassinated, and that our fiercest rebellion – Louis Riel's brave stand on behalf of Métis river rights – took only an estimated seventy-two lives, have been paraded as marks of inadequacy and national immaturity. Surely the opposite is true.

We even have a fascinating share of prehistory, though too few Canadians are aware of it. Almost everyone has heard of the haunting stone structures at Stonehenge in Britain, but few realize that our

Indians' forefathers were also erecting their medicine wheels for astronomical purposes in early times. Serpent Mound near Peterborough, Ontario, for example, is an 1,800-year-old ceremonial site, and there are others across Canada that are far older. In Newfoundland, Viking settlements date back at least a thousand years; in southwestern Ontario, excavated longhouses show that permanent communities of five thousand people thrived before Columbus set sail, and sophisticated cultures had developed in the Queen Charlotte Islands long before that. We may not have medieval castles, but we have forts equally unique in their construction, and, of course, the log cabin. The castle symbolized power and wealth for a few, but the early Canadian log cabin represented for many a combination of hope, belief, and determination – the basic ingredients that made Canada possible.

IF SURVIVAL HAS BEEN our most noteworthy achievement, as Margaret Atwood and other savants have claimed, so be it. Survivors are the winners in almost any game. Toronto novelist and broadcaster Harry J. Boyle had it right when he praised "the soul-sharpening satisfaction that comes from being a survivor." And we have survived with dignity, if not with joy. Becoming a Canadian never required conversion to a burning new faith, or even a salute, since we had no distinctive flag during the first ninety-eight years of our existence. Founded on individual allegiance instead of social compact, Canadian nationhood proceeded so slowly that it took thirty-eight years after Confederation in 1867 for the other provinces to join – except Newfoundland, of course, which waited another half century just to be sure.

Settlement of Canada's West and North was distinguished not by shootouts, vigilantes, or posses but by the entrenched presence of governmental and corporate authority. Pierre Berton recalls his father telling him that on the Canadian side of the border during the Klondike Gold Rush, a man could lay down his pack or a sack of gold in the middle of the trail and return in a week knowing no one would have touched it. The North West Mounted Police enforced order so emphatically in Dawson that you could be arrested for fishing on a Sunday. At the Alaskan port of Skagway, by contrast, "Soapy" Smith ruled over a northern Gomorrah in which nothing was sacred and every form of crime and corruption flourished unabated. (Canadians' respect for law and order has endured. In 1979, for instance, when a train spill released chlorine gas over the Toronto suburb of Mississauga, the largest peacetime evacuation in history ensued, with a quarter-million people having to leave their houses. Their homes and businesses were deserted for a week, yet the crime rate dropped.)

The most important agency in moulding Canada's formative mentality was the Hudson's Bay Company, as I discovered in my research into its history. Its factors and factotums impressed the Company's operational code on the frontier, emphasizing cautiously progressive pragmatism, an aversion to risk-taking, and the notion of moderation as not just a safe course between extremes but a secular mandate on how to conduct one's life. Most important, the HBC traders converted much of the upper half of North America into a company town writ large, in which men and women displayed individuality and imagination at their own risk. The first HBC forts were the ultimate expression of what the literary critic Northrop Frye has dubbed "the garrison mentality." Frye described these small communities as "surrounded with a physical or psychological 'frontier,' separated from one another and from their American and British cultural sources: communities that provide all that their members have in the way of distinctively human values, and that are compelled to feel a great respect for the law and order that holds them together, yet confronted with a huge, unthinking, menacing, and formidable physical setting."

During the HBC's first half-century, military skirmishes transformed its outposts into garrisons in more than a metaphoric sense, and later, as they softened into trading towns, very little changed. The prevailing ethic remained deference to authority inside the ramparts and deference to nature beyond them. This orderly attitude, rooted in collective survival rather than individual excellence, coloured what most people did – and, especially, didn't do. It stressed life's sombre virtues – the notion that there is nothing more satisfying than a hard day's work well done, that the good man always earns more than his keep. In dramatic contrast to the shotgun individualism of the American West, the idea was to be careful, to be plainly dressed, quiet-spoken, and, above all, close with one's money and emotions. Flashes of pleasure and moments of splendour had to look accidental, never planned. Sparse of speech but swift in action, the tight-lipped Orcadians and Highlanders who ran the Company stores had temperaments ideally suited to Canadian pioneering: a meld of persistence and self-sufficiency. Intellectually armed by the Shorter Catechism, those durable Scotsmen made up in loyalty and moral fibre what they lacked in creativity and exuberance.

The incense of all that deference lingered over Canada long after the Hudson's Bay Company declined into commercial purgatory. You could immediately spot a Canadian at any gathering: he or she was the one who automatically chose the most uncomfortable chair. It was all part of our national affinity for discomfort and self-denial. This tendency to kowtow became to the Canadian psyche what yeast is to bread-making: without its curious catalytic effect, Canadians felt reduced to a doughy mess. We learned to excel in making the worst of bad situations, underestimating our individual and collective worth, living out Earle Birney's dire diagnosis of Canada as "a high-school land, frozen in its adolescence." Fearing disorder more than oppression, we dribbled away our self-esteem and patrimony in the revolutions we did not launch, the risks we failed to take, the acts of daring we managed to avoid. We became Don Quixotes in parkas singing *a cappella* blues.

Our prevailing attitude was all too reminiscent of the story about two jazz fans who once approached Duke Ellington on the street, vaguely aware he was a musical great but not certain which one.

"Hey, man," one of them demanded, "ain't you the Duke?"

"Baby," was the reply, "I'm whoever you want me to be."

All too often, we have been who and what outsiders wanted us to be. In allowing foreign aspirations to define indigenous goals, we became citizens of a country for others to build their dreams on. Henry James complained about "the complex facts of being an American." Being a Canadian was simple: deference was our state religion, prostration our national posture. (We even practised dishonesty with ingratiating overtones: while Revenue Canada estimated that billions of dollars in federal revenues had gone unreported through deliberate tax evasion, Ottawa also revealed that 91 per cent of those fraudulent returns were filed exactly on time.)

Our patterns of diffidence are not hard to document. The last time Canadians had to defend their soil was in the War of 1812, when the Americans offered to free us from the burdensome yoke of the British motherland. Horrified, we fought them off and eventually repelled the would-be liberators, staunchly declaring that we wanted to remain colonials. Ever since, we have secretly suspected that no one has tried to conquer us because we were not worth invading.

The quintessential Canadian statesman of this colonial period was Mackenzie King, who ruled us longer than anyone else, had the sex life of a gnat, never took a political chance, and on a 1949 visit to his good friend John D. Rockefeller Jr. was so fastidious that he took along six spare shoelaces. ''The most successful politician in our history resembled a bald Queen Victoria and for recreation talked to spooks,'' the iconoclastic painter Harold Town once remarked.* More recently, Olympic speed skater Gaetan Boucher explained why he competed in the American, not the Canadian, way. ''The attitude most Canadians have is not really right,'' said he. ''They come up to you and ask, 'You were tenth, eh? Well, that's not too bad.' But it is. Compare that with the Americans. They do everything to win, not to finish tenth.''

Unable to figure out whether we were the least of the great powers or the greatest of the small powers, we decided, in the smug afterglow of the Second World War, to become something we called a ''middle power.'' We sent contingents of peace-keeping soldiers into trouble spots where they would be shot at, mauled, and manhandled but not permitted to return fire or retaliate in any way. It was perfect casting. Out of that dazzling display of diffidence grew our reputation as world-class fall guys. It meant, for one thing, that Canadian passports became an invaluable commodity; having one immediately identified its bearer as harmless. Several of the most senior Soviet spymasters (including such major players as Robert Soblen, Colonel Rudolf Abel, and Gordon Lonsdale, who obtained the plans of Britain's nuclear submarines) operated on Canadian passports. Olaf Rankis, executive vice-president for security and intelligence at Gordon Liddy & Associates, the Miami firm that supplies mercenaries to various industrial groups, once confessed, ''I always travel wearing a red maple leaf pin in my lapel. Nobody hates the Canadians.'' When Michael Valpy of the *Globe and Mail* was in Ghana, he interviewed a senior American diplomat who

---

*He then added a dig at the RCMP Musical Ride for good measure: ''Our finest national spectacle consists of a group of police in red coats charging at nothing with spears.''

revealed that U.S. State Department personal security courses advise anyone due for a hazardous posting not to look too obviously American. "They tell us to try to look Canadian," he admitted. "We're supposed to fade into the background and say 'oot' and 'aboot'."

In this self-deprecating mood, which seems to have peaked during the late Seventies, the only real mark of acceptance – the validation not only of any Canadian's dreams and ambitions but of his or her self-worth – came from the United States. We were the country cousins awed by the new Roman Empire. A crude expression of our genus envy was Donald Sutherland's comment in a 1981 *Playboy* interview. "Canadians are so incredibly insecure," he said. "Somewhere in the psyche, every single Canadian has a feeling that people in the United States have some kind of visceral, cultural and life experience he does not have. If you're Canadian, you think about a person from the States as the brother who went to sea, caught the clap and made a million dollars in Costa Rica or Hong Kong."

Only in Quebec was there a spirit of self-determination, a deeply personal romantic mythology that eventually emerged as political power. French Canadians discovered that a vibrant politics requires a vibrant culture. It was the poets, painters, writers, and singers of Quebec who gave the people enough self-confidence to push René Lévesque into office. Not until the mid-Eighties did English-Canadian culture catch up with this refreshing breakthrough.

Typically, it was an expatriate American, the writer Joyce Carol Oates (then living near Windsor, Ontario), who best defined English Canada's former state of irresolution. Renée Maynard, one of her heroines who emigrates from the United States, is baffled by her new compatriots and wonders why Canadians are always mocking their own cities, their own universities, their own music and galleries. Renée wonders if they are deliberately testing her . . . "but no, they were sincere enough." At about the same time Edmund Wilson, the American critic who had rhapsodized about the talents of Morley Callaghan, was appalled to discover that instead of strengthening the novelist's Canadian reputation, his comments aroused the fury of our academics and reviewers. It was only the boldest of domestic critics who dared praise any Canadian work. When Lorraine Monk published her splendid *Between Friends/Entre Amis*, Peter Swann in his unashamedly favourable review admitted that in a rash moment of enthusiasm he had broken the first law of Canadian life. "This," he conceded, "decrees that we denigrate every good thing we do, take a negative stance toward every Canadian achievement, nitpick to death anything positive, starve anyone with talent and drive out anybody who dares show cultural or artistic leadership or excellence." Swann's song of praise ended with an apology to Lorraine Monk and her collaborators for thus tempting Canadian fate: "I fear that they now will be struck down in their prime. . . ." Marshall McLuhan alone maintained his poise in the customary critical slaughter of our best writers' works (including his own) while they became the darlings of New York's literary bigwigs. "I experience a great deal of liberty here in Toronto," McLuhan cooed. "I wouldn't get that in the States, because I'm taken quite seriously there. The fact that Canadians don't take me seriously is a huge advantage. It makes me a free man."

Treading water became our national sport, and we loved poking fun at ourselves.

"Why does a haircut in Canada cost eight dollars?"

"Two bucks for each corner."

The music critic Larry Le Blanc described the most popular Canadian singer of the day with the quip: "If you close your eyes and think of a naked Anne Murray, parts of her always come up airbrushed." *People* magazine dismissed the songbird as "coming across like a Madonna of Sunnybrook Farm." Andrew Malcolm, the *New York Times* correspondent who wrote a marvellous book on the Canadian character, concluded that "the only way to get a Canadian to praise his or her country is to announce you are an American, and then criticize Canada unmercifully. Sometimes even that wouldn't do it."

HEROES REFLECT THE NATIONS that anoint them, and Canada is no exception. Latin countries tend to pick leaders who spend most of their time on balconies, waving at befuddled mobs. The British have been reduced to worshipping the generals, admirals, and crafty traders who ran the Empire when most of the continents were tinted rosy red. The Americans, requiring heroes as a constant reminder of their capacity for love, manufacture idols as quickly as they tear them down. This tendency to whip up adolescent crushes and cravings over even the most mundane public figures was never more evident than in *Time*'s choice of Ronald Reagan as its 1980 Man of the Year. Reagan was portrayed as a mixture of John Wayne and Mother Teresa. The magazine's cover story gushed on about his face – "ruddy, in bloom growing younger by the second" – and his voice as having been "decorated by a florist." That a voting majority of Reagan's four kids hardly spoke to him was dismissed by the assertion that he "gets along better with grown-ups" and, anyway, "Reagan bears much of the aspect of an adorable child himself."

Canadian heroes – the few we have deigned to recognize – have mainly been lost explorers, slyly hoping they would discover a shortcut to Cathay around each river bend. Except for Louis Riel, few of our deities have represented ideals and were rarely central to their time or place. There is little consensus on who Canada's cultural heroes are (mine include Ralph Allen, Harry J. Boyle, John Grierson, Bruce Hutchison, Arthur Irwin, Hugh MacLennan, Abraham Rotstein, and Patrick Watson) except for the painters who belonged to the Group of Seven. Most Canadians assume that the Group of Seven was led by Tom Thomson – an authentic Canadian hero because he drowned at the height of his career – but in fact he died three years before the Group was formed.

There are some curious lapses in our choices. The St. Malo navigator Jacques Cartier is credited with the modern "discovery" of Canada and widely hailed, but the Genoa merchant-adventurer John Cabot made his landfalls in Newfoundland and Cape Breton thirty-seven years earlier. The only memorials to Cabot are the trail looping around a Cape Breton peninsula and the plaque on a drafty baronial tower on Signal Hill in St. John's, better known as the location for some of Guglielmo Marconi's early transmissions. If Cabot had only landed in what is now the United States he would have been even more famous than Christopher Columbus, who is accepted as America's discoverer (and has an annual holiday named after him) though he did not, of course, even sight the coastline of the North American continent. There is additional irony in the Marconi connection. In 1902, the Laurier government made $80,000 available to Marconi so that he could build his wireless radio station, turning its back on Reginald Aubrey Fessenden from the Eastern Townships of Quebec, who had invented voice transmissions as opposed to Marconi's Morse code.

Fessenden was the first to transmit voice messages – for the U.S. Weather Bureau – broadcasting from his laboratory at Cobb Island on the Potomac to a receiving station at Arlington, Virginia.

James Wolfe, Louis Joseph de Montcalm, and Isaac Brock are more appropriate Canadian heroes, since they died in battle without knowing the outcome, but the memory of our most daring privateer, Antoine Laumet *dit* de Lamothe Cadillac, is perpetuated only by the American car industry. Canada's epics – the magnificent journeys of the *voyageurs*, the building of the Canadian Pacific Railway, the *St. Roch*'s sailing through the North West Passage – have exemplified the anonymous courage and collective endurance of its participants rather than individual acts of heroism. "The unfettered individual and the rebel extolled, so common to the American experience, have little meaning for Canada," historian Frits Pannekoek has noted. "It was not Walsh who saved the West but Walsh and the North West Mounted Police, it was not Van Horne who built the railway but Van Horne and the navvies, and it was not Dumont who was the rebel but Dumont and the Métis."

In our peculiar way we do not mark the birthday of Sir John A. Macdonald, our founding prime minister, but celebrate Queen Victoria's birthday long after it has been forgotten in the mother country. Even our treatment of genuine war heroes is shabby. The legend of Victoria Cross winner W. A. "Billy" Bishop, who shot down seventy-two enemy planes in a mere twenty-three weeks of operational flying, has been tarnished by a haphazardly researched film documentary. Heirs of the best-known Canadian flying ace of the Second World War, George "Buzz" Beurling, sold his medals through a three-line classified ad. At present, ours are the only armed forces in the world with no decorations for bravery under fire, though there exist two civilian medals awarded by the Governor General.

The most conspicuous heroic Canadian of recent times was, of course, Terry Fox, the young British Columbia athlete who hobbled as far as he could across this country in 1981. He qualified as the quintessential Canadian hero-victim, being pinned with the Order of Canada on his deathbed. Similarly, Norman Bethune was not truly confirmed in his heroic status until he died in 1939 (from neglecting a cut finger after operating on an infected patient) during Mao's guerrilla fighting. At another level, we did not particularly celebrate

Ambassador Ken Taylor's heroism in smuggling six U.S. diplomats out of the Ayatollah's reach until he appeared on the cover of *Time*. Ottawa then exacted revenge on the unconventional diplomat by not offering him an appropriate posting after his stint as Consul-General in New York, forcing his resignation.

A *BEAU SABREUR* WHO APPROACHED heroic stature in the period covered by this book was Pierre Elliott Trudeau. Certainly no Canadian felt neutral about him. He came at us like the chivalrous echo of a more gallant age – his intelligent, skull-formed face, shimmering wit, and Gallic shrugs promising release from the national stupor that had typified the reigns of his predecessors. Canadians were at first captivated by this unusual man who promised that government could be a way of sharing in the passions of our age.

If he didn't accomplish everything we had hoped, it was mainly because during most of his time in office Trudeau functioned more as a head of state than as the leader of a nation. Along with Charles de Gaulle, he seemed to believe that a man's *grandeur* grew in direct proportion to his aloofness, yet he also became a master practitioner of the cheap and cynical tricks of politics. Posing alternately as carefree swinger or earnest technocrat, he remained emotionally crippled, a dandy in aspic.

Still, Trudeau did upset the applecarts of interest groups that had shared for generations the political power that counted, rendering them impotent with one cold gaze or colder action. In the treatment of his cabinet, his caucus, his party, and even his own office staff, the prime minister remained outside the traditional behaviour patterns of his trade. He governed the country like the headmaster of a rigorously administered private school, ruling by fear and keeping everyone – not excluding the electorate – permanently insecure. He transformed himself into a presidential figure.

No group of Canadians grew angrier with Trudeau than the business community. Behind the discreet rustle of *Financial Posts* and *Wall Street Journals* being folded meticulously in the reading rooms of their exclusive lunching clubs, Canada's business elite found it difficult to pronounce the prime minister's name without an accompanying expletive. They weighed his every ad lib with deep suspicion and, more seriously, moved significant lumps of disposable funds outside the country. In my own ramblings through Establishment ranks, I remember Charles Rathgeb, an amateur balloonist who was then head of Canadian Comstock International, telling me about a dinner attended by two of Canada's richest men, Toronto industrialists Nelson Davis and John A. "Bud" McDougald. When the after-dinner chatter got around to politics, Davis suggested that since the prime minister was well known for his daredevil antics and loved to show off his sense of adventure, Rathgeb ought to take Trudeau ballooning. "Chuck," Davis suggested, with appropriate nudges and winks, "I'll give you a cool million if you take that man across Lake Ontario to Rochester in your balloon – and give him a little shove when you're halfway." McDougald, then head of Argus Corporation, jumped into the exchange with ill-concealed glee: "You've just made *two* million!"

Rathgeb, feeling a little uncomfortable because the two megacapitalists seemed to mean it, countered: "How will I get picked up?"

"Don't worry," came the answer. "We'll have lots of parachutes and lots of boats, but none for our friend from Ottawa."

Trudeau's governing ideology could best be explained by the existentialism of French philosopher Jean-Paul Sartre – that "man invents himself through exercising his freedom of choice." This is what Pierre Trudeau was really all about: a man creating himself through authentic political acts. He liked to pretend that he espoused the hang-loose philosophy of Saint Thomas ("Trust the authority of your senses") Aquinas, but he acted more like G. Gordon Liddy, the Watergate burglar-patriot, who wrote in his autobiography: "I made myself precisely who I wanted to be." No matter how much his friends and critics speculated about which great thinkers influenced Trudeau most, the answer was always the same: himself. He became his own brains trust, and his self-proclaimed superiority prompted jokes at his expense. A story going the rounds had two Ottawa wags meeting and one asking the other:

"Did you hear about Trudeau's accident?"

"No. What happened?"

"Well, he was out for his morning walk . . . when he got hit by a motorboat."

In the end, there was about Pierre Trudeau's stewardship (examined in more detail in the essay entitled "The Man in the Iron Mask") a brand of bored sophistication that made it a lot less than poignant to part with the pleasure of his company. During his sixteen years in office, he had become the lightning rod for nearly everybody's dissatisfactions. I remember watching with fascination a trucker at a motel near Red Deer, Alberta, who had lost seventy-five cents in a soft-drink machine. He squared off and kicked the thing. Nothing happened. He shook it nearly off its hinges. No luck. Then he stood back, glared at the offending contraption, and through clenched teeth cursed: "God damn Trudeau anyway!"

"What really did Trudeau in," reflected Professor Edgar Friedenberg of Dalhousie University, "was what Canadians called his arrogance. He knew how to lose gracefully, and sometimes did; but he didn't know how to look like a loser, or a man who thought he was no better than anybody else. He shouldn't have had to; there isn't a living statesperson with a comparable grasp of world affairs, or as enlightened a conception of statecraft. Canadians might be able to accept that level of sheer competence from Gretzky, but not, for sixteen years, from a prime minister. Mr. Mulroney, it appears, will present few problems in this respect."

UNLIKE MOST MODERN CANADIAN TORIES, who have historically exercised an unerring instinct for their own jugulars, Brian Mulroney came to office determined to reconcile the warring factions of the Conservative party. This he achieved, and his great electoral sweep of 1984 was not, as Havelock Ellis once complained about the outcome of a British election, "merely the exchange of one nuisance for another."

Behind those Gucci eyes there still lurks the small-town boy from Baie Comeau who grew up with no money and less privilege. Neither rebel nor reactionary, Mulroney probably comes as close as anyone to personifying his party's label of being a true Progressive Conservative – which in itself is a contradiction in terms, like uncontested divorce, jumbo shrimp, postal service, hamburger steak, or military intelligence. An unusual mixture of old- and new-style campaigner, Mulroney is no ideologue or intellectual. He is a labour lawyer, unfettered by political dogma, committed mainly to a kind of functionalism that measures policies by how well they might work and how many votes they might win. His great failing, of course, has been wanting to be loved instead of respected. Sometimes, making enemies is essential. (When Voltaire was on his deathbed, an attending priest asked whether he was ready to renounce the Devil. The great French sage looked surprised, then shook his head. "This," he whispered, "is no time to make new enemies.")

It is much too early to arrive at any definitive judgement of the Mulroney record (which I plan to explore in a future book), but the emerging paradox of his regime is that although he has been portrayed as the ultimate opportunist, his major policy commitments – free trade, the Meech Lake Accord, tax reform, and the defence build-up – are highly volatile political initiatives with grievous short-term risks. What Mulroney seems to be gambling on is an unusual perception of the Canadian political structure.

WHENEVER CANADIAN SOCIETY IS EXAMINED, it is in terms of its identity crisis, bicultural problems, or agonies as a pygmy nation in thrall to one or another overdeveloped empire. The country is rarely viewed through the prism of its status as one of the world's most successful capitalist states. Yet that's what we are – a capitalist society run by clusters of interlocking elites. The businessmen's credo is a collection of attitudes rather than any carefully conceived theology, but it does follow a catechism of sorts. The actions of all men and women, the orthodox believe, are governed by the marketplace. That faith in the supply and demand mechanism as an arbiter of human activity is the starting point of the Mulroney government's policy options.

Though their popularity with ordinary voters subsequently sagged, the PCs' economic agenda was set before they took office. Ottawa had collected only three small budgetary surpluses in the preceding three decades. Twenty-one years of Liberal rule had left the national treasury $180 billion in the hole. During the Trudeau years, federal expenditures moved the public debt from less than $1,000 per capita in 1968 to more than $6,000 in 1984. The federal deficit of $576 million on total expenditures of $13 billion jumped to $30 billion on spending of $100 billion – though no one seemed particularly better off.

Faced with such narrow fiscal discretion in the public sector, Mulroney moved to reactivate private spending in the hope that employment would be created without massive inputs from the federal treasury. Amazingly, the policy worked. Since 1984, we have consistently led the industrialized world in job creation and, with adjustment for the purchasing power of currencies, Canada achieved the second-highest per capita income of any major economy, ahead of both Japan and West Germany. Manufactured goods amount to more than two-thirds of our exports, and we have become a serious source of international investment capital, at least four billion dollars a year. Despite some soft commodity prices, our gross national product has since 1984 expanded faster than that of any other country. The most recent edition of *Fortune*'s "International 500" includes thirty-five Canadian companies, the fourth-highest total on the list. We have grown fully competitive with American industry, racking up an $82-billion surplus on merchandise trade in the past four years. "Canadians have little to feel inferior about," Conrad Black trumpeted in the last of his *Globe and Mail* columns. "This is a great country capable of competing with Americans or anyone else. . . . Precisely those who are most antagonistic and contemptuous towards the United States are those who would perpetuate an irrational fear of that country and a puny self-image of this one."

What if Conrad Black is right?

LIVING NEXT TO THE UNITED STATES has been reminiscent of an old-fashioned marriage, with the husband insisting, "If you do exactly what I want, dear, we'll have a really good time." Or, to switch metaphors, the Americans think of us (if they think of us at all) as an attic in their mansion. Attics tend to be taken-for-granted storage spaces somewhere up there, occasionally essential but a topic of concern only if they are the source of strange noises or cold draughts. If and when free trade is implemented, we will be moving down from the attic into American living rooms, or at least into their pantries. That is good reason to be very nervous. We will find ourselves thrown into the much tougher world of the international marketplace, having to make our way through Darwinian swamps of unfettered competition where survival of the fittest and the fastest is all that counts.

The problem with having the United States as a neighbour is that it's a nation whose imperialism is an all-pervasive force of nature. "It envelops us as a mist, penetrating every sphere of our cultural, political, economic and social environment," according to University of Toronto political economist Abraham Rotstein. "For that very reason we seem to feel powerless, unwilling and unable to achieve the perspective necessary for an appraisal of our situation. It sometimes seems as superfluous to ask what should be done about the Americanization of this country as it is to ask what should be done about the weather.'' While we continue to fuss about survival, the Americans identify their past and future with the great notions spelled out in their founding documents – the Declaration of Independence, the Constitution, and the Bill of Rights. These were the acts that shattered feudal land laws, gave the individual supreme sanction to pursue happiness, and set loose the forces that still prompt every American to expect an ever-increasing standard of living, not as a hope but as a *right*. These aspirations constitute very much more than idle theories in the minds of political science majors or decorous ramblings of the Daughters of the American Revolution. Thomas Jefferson believed in the freedom of each new generation to rediscover itself, and that's why the United States is in a state of perpetual revolution.

In confronting the United States we must accept the proposition that we are dealing with what Arnold Toynbee called the American Empire, a sentiment reflected as far back as 1776 in Thomas Paine's dictum: ''The cause of America is in great measure the cause of all mankind.'' The late Senator Kenneth Wherry picked up the anthem when he chirped to his Nebraska followers: ''With God's help we will lift Shanghai up and up, ever up, until it's just like Kansas City!''

THIS IMPERIALISTIC WRIT TO SWALLOW the world is the context in which we are planning to enter a free trade area with the Americans. The prospect of being part of a five-trillion-dollar economy stretching from the North Pole to the Rio Grande is alluring, but the risks are enormous. In the past we could afford the luxury of not having to choose between surrender and resistance to the magnetic pull of the American Dream on the basis of economic considerations. We were the resource storehouse to the free world, and everyone wanted what we had. That is no longer true, and, equally important, all of the other major industrialized countries are joining or have joined trading blocs that will give their domestic manufacturers access to markets of a hundred million people or more. By 1992, for example, Western Europe expects to be so thoroughly integrated that it will be using a common currency. For Canadians to reject the free trade pact strictly on the grounds of its undoubted threat to Canadian sovereignty is too simplistic. The alternative – trying to preserve a vanishing status quo – could be even worse. (My favourite quote of the entire free trade controversy was an interjection during the House of Commons debate on April 28, 1987, about economic decision-making, when NDP financial critic Michael Cassidy exclaimed: ''We are held back because of irresponsible decisions made in foreign boardrooms – decisions which should have been made right here in Canada!'')

What bothers me most about the free trade deal – apart from its cultural dimensions – is its energy aspect. The former PC federal energy minister (now justice minister) Ramon Hnatyshyn was dead right when he declared in 1979: ''Free trade in energy with the Americans is like wife-swapping with a bachelor.'' There is little doubt that this was the Reagan administration's bottom-line reason for entering into the free trade negotiations in the first place. U.S. energy experts predict that declining domestic production will raise America's current 25- to 30-per-cent dependence on petroleum imports to 50 to 60 per cent by 1995. Philip Verleger Jr. of Washington's Institute for International Economics estimates that the value of U.S. petroleum imports will rise from $44 billion in 1985 to $130 billion by 1995. Free access to Canadian energy sources – lock, stock, and oil barrel – would fuel the American industrial machine for the foreseeable future. Even when we start to run out of our own oil, under the terms of the treaty, Canada must provide ''proportional access to the diminished supply'' without price discrimination. Our energy exports would not, of course, be limited to oil. One reason Quebec Premier Robert Bourassa supports free trade is that it would allow him to sell immediately three billion dollars' worth of Manicouagan and James Bay power to New England over ten years. Precisely such an arrangement was blocked by Ottawa's National Energy Board in June 1986.

Apart from these and many other specific aspects of the deal, its fundamental weakness is that we are entwining our destiny with a trading partner heading for the skids. While the demise of the British Empire took more than three-quarters of a century to become apparent (as annual increases in productivity dropped below those of its industrial competitors), the decline in American productivity is proceeding at least three times as fast. Between 1979 and 1986, the U.S. investment rate has been the second-lowest in the industrialized world, and the rate of growth in net output per worker has averaged only 0.4 per cent a year – the lowest of any industrialized state. The cumulative U.S. national debt amounted to $645 billion from the time the *Mayflower*'s starboard lookout first sighted the Plymouth shores to the day Ronald Reagan became president. By the time his term expires, the burdensome national debt load will have tripled. Any nation faced with such astronomical fiscal liabilities must take drastic remedies. If, by the time those draconian but essential cures are put into effect, our economy has been folded into that of the United States, we could be mortally infected.

Economic union between the two countries would dismantle the tariffs that still encumber the $160 billion in annual trade across the U.S.-Canadian border, giving our manufacturers access to a quantum jump in potential customers. But at the same time, American factories would be swamping our domestic markets with their output, taking advantage of the built-in price differential of their longer production runs. More seriously, future industrial expansion would almost certainly take place south of the 49th parallel because the four main factors that go into deciding where to produce any item – climate, social service costs, proximity of market, and cost of labour – would clearly favour U.S. locations. Canada's only long-term experience with free trade supports this pessimistic conclusion. Our agricultural implements industry, which has had duty-free access to the United States since 1944, transferred its production facilities south of the border and has since disappeared. Fifteen years ago, Canadian firms still controlled 12 per cent of the North American tractor market; now the percentage is so small it can barely be calculated. This has happened despite the fact that at last count there were nearly two million tractors requiring periodic replacement on Canadian farms. While the agricultural implement business is highly cyclical (in five- and seven-year spurts), Canadian farmers purchase an average of two billion dollars' worth of tractors and implements a year. Except for a Winnipeg plant now owned by Ford, we no longer make any farm tractors or combines. The last major Canadian-owned facility, Massey Combines Corporation, at Brantford, Ontario, declared bankruptcy in 1988.

FREE TRADE'S GREATEST BENEFIT has already been achieved. In the process of debating what we might have to surrender, we discovered what we already have.

At what remains a subconscious level, Canadians have begun to resolve their traditional self-doubts and instead of searching for a national identity are putting into practice their separate ones. At the same time, we have realized the American experience we once so envied cannot be sustained by a country that tosses up a succession of such scrap-iron leaders as Richard Nixon, Gerald Ford, Jimmy Carter, and Ronald Reagan. Fond of Americans as individuals, we feel increasingly alienated from their society. We're no longer jealous. We can see in our country – and not in theirs – the continued possibility of realizing our true potential. Comparing ourselves with other nations, it's easy now to see how attractive, egalitarian, and relatively gentle our society still is and how full of promise is our future. There is a kind of inbred conservatism in us – a caution, an even keel, that suddenly seems vital to preserve.

We are people with little talent for excess. Most of us would rather be Clark Kent than Superman. Our cities remain oases of relative civility on a continent where most urban areas are armed camps. And that may be the element in the free trade mix that might cause us to draw back: fear. Not fear of economic competition or vestiges of our vaunted inferiority, but an innate sense of alarm that somehow the disturbing verities of American society will permeate our own daily lives. "I am not naive about Canada," says Harry J. Boyle, "but the hidden forces in American society for all kinds of dark and dangerous practices are real and make our warts and blemishes look puny. At the moment, humane political forces somehow seem to scratch through. But there is a very narrow margin of political strength in America holding back the tides of a particular form of fascism. There is probably a better name for it, but it is regressive and has roots in the fact that a minority can hold up the majority on such things as guns. In spite of the horrible examples of such apparatus of government as the Dies committee, the ghosts of McCarthy still stalk the bureaucratic halls of agencies such as the CIA and FBI."

Whether we can steel ourselves to take on such fanaticism remains an open question, but the fallout from the free trade pact has already taken hold, allowing us to appreciate the contrast between what we've been able to preserve in the northern half of North America and what others have lost. Imperceptibly, but in a very real way, we are jettisoning our colonial mentality, perceiving ourselves in terms of our own rather than imported values.

No one has as yet articulated precisely how the prevailing mood is changing, but as if by prearranged signal many Canadians have become fed up with the inferiorities that have held our psyches so firmly captive in the recent past. Not since frontier days has there been such a surge of self-reliance, such a determination by individuals of all ages, sexes, and most circumstances to strike out on their own and exercise more control over their lives. Most of us feel vibrantly alive, veins humming with adrenalin as we begin to assert ourselves. At the same time, the traditional sources of authority are losing their clout. How can we hold in awe, for example, the chartered banks, where we once deposited our money and our consciences, when they turn out to have invested our hard-earned savings in such grounded high-fliers as Brazil and Dome?

Ours remains a putty culture, yeasty yet penetrable, but the new generation moving into power is full of ginger, set on getting things done. These men and women no longer believe, as did their cowering predecessors, that history was made across the sea, that business acumen and know-how exist only beyond our borders, or that the best we can manage here is a pale imitation. (The conquest of any nation takes place not on battlefields or in boardrooms but within the soul of its people and the minds of their leaders. The choice between surrender and resistance is dictated not by material resources or available manpower but by this state of psychological abdication – essentially the admission that something is lacking in the victim that the conqueror might supply.)

Having rejected these exhausted verities, we have come to appreciate that Canada is no mere accident of history or some earnest valedictorian's hazy dream. What we have here is a daily miracle of a country. We have settled a subcontinent, attained high standards of comfort and orderliness, and have contributed more than our share to the defence of freedom in two world wars. Compared with most other nations, our power structure is not rigid; the excitement of new frontiers and new perceptions beckons only a horizon away.

THERE ARE NO MAGICAL WINDOWS through which to proclaim the future. The Laurier prediction that the 20th century would belong to Canada never did come true because we behaved as if we still belonged to the 19th. The next century will not belong to any nation east of Hawaii, as the world's economic centre of gravity shifts ever westward to the Pacific Basin. The real question is whether Canada will belong to the 21st century. Looking back over the last fifteen years – as portrayed in the pages that follow – it seems to me that we are finally growing up. The essential element of that newfound adulthood is that we stop asking ourselves who we are. We may lack a homogeneity of purpose, but our nationality exists because Canada exists. It is the same emotion once described to me by the late Will Ready, a Welsh poet and essayist who was chief librarian at McMaster University: "Wales rings in my mind like a bell in an underwater belfry. I am of Wales and everything I write and dream about is framed in that Welsh context."

A variation on this theme was the testimony of Dr. J. H. Maloney, former minister of development for Prince Edward Island, before a CRTC hearing about regional alienation and identity. "Certainly in the Maritimes," he said, "there has been no loss of identity. We're very sure of that. In Prince Edward Island if anybody ever said he was alienated, I would say: 'You are not alienated. I can tell you exactly who you are; you are the illegitimate son of your Aunt Mary. . .'"

That's it. One by one, we can create the sum of our national identity. Canada is a collection of twenty-six million characters in search of an author.

After feeling for more than a century that being Canadian was a journey rather than a destination, we have arrived at last. We have attained a state of delicious grace which allows us to appreciate that what's important is not so much *who* we are but *that* we are – that sometimes a large nation can become a great one.

Peter C. Newman
Cordova Bay, British Columbia
September 10, 1988

PART ONE

Wild Years in the Peaceable Kingdom

The Seventies, Eighties – and Beyond

WHAT FORMS THE PERCEPTION of any decade, what gives urgency to the expectations of its survivors and allows its participants a rationale for their actions, is some deeply shared common experience. It was the excitement and agony of the Second World War that formed the Forties, the somnambulism of prosperity that symbolized the Fifties, the nerve-wrenching detonations of social, sexual, and political change that shook us up during the Sixties. Now, we suddenly find ourselves in the final year of the Seventies, looking back on a tumble of events that adds up to no discernible pattern or structure.

Yet the legacy of the Seventies may be even more formative than the afterbirth of the pulsating Sixties. A decade ago, we merely altered our lifestyles; ten years later we may be on the verge of transforming the way we are governed.

The real victim of the Seventies was not so much Pierre Trudeau as the traditional Canadian approach to government as a royal court conducted by a self-selected hierarchy dedicated mainly to its own perpetuation. Imperceptibly, a new style of populism has emerged, based on no recognizable ideology, whose roots are the simple but universal conviction that governmental authority at all levels is overstepping its proper boundaries.

In the final year of the decade, this new brand of politics still remains a mood in search of a movement, representing a decline of faith in middle-of-the-road solutions and the arithmetics of compromise more than any drastic shift to the right. But its objectives are clear: that politicians must stop treating voters as objects that can be bought with their own money at quadrennial auctions called election campaigns; that some way must be found to alleviate the desperation of the young, burdened by the shallowness of the education system and the frustrations of a narrowing job market; that the murderous effects of inflation on consumer prices and fixed incomes must be arrested – and soon.

So far, the most obvious outcrop of this new political temper has been the wave of protest against a scale of spending by the federal government that has seen Ottawa's gush of expenditures rise to nearly one billion dollars a week. But the issue runs very much deeper.

What is becoming increasingly apparent is that political power is about to be assembled and harnessed in new and unpredictable ways. By the end of the Eighties, most of our legislatures, federal and provincial, will have undergone one of those rare, historical convulsions that every so often redistribute the coalition of political forces that keeps democracies alive and functioning.

—1979

❄   ❄   ❄

PERHAPS THE EVENTS that best bracket the decade suddenly ending – one claim we can hold on to as proof that the Seventies weren't just the Fifties in a leisure suit – were the departure and return of Jacques and Louise Cossette-Trudel from their exile in France. It was during the closing months of 1970, after all, that this ardent couple and their half-dozen colleagues brought the nation to its knees when, as members of the Front de Libération du Québec, they kidnapped James Cross, the British trade commissioner in Montreal, and ordered the broadcast of revolutionary tracts. Nearly a decade later, they came back and ordered a club sandwich.

Between the Cossette-Trudels' departure and their homecoming both the province they tried so violently to "liberate" and the country they hoped to humiliate had altered more radically than they could ever have imagined. Only a decade ago Canadians were aglow with post-Expo spirit. We had a freshly minted leader in Pierre Trudeau, a cool man in a hot world maintaining a sense of inner repose and outward excitement, reminding us all that we were a young nation with unexploited possibilities, inviting Canadians to share in his quest for "a just society." The Mounties and their musical ride were still our finest ambassadors. We counted for something in world councils; the OECD in Paris proclaimed that our economic future had few limits. Sir Wilfrid Laurier's erstwhile pledge about Canada and the twentieth century seemed about to be fulfilled. In Quebec, on January 17, 1970, Robert Bourassa, then billed as a reformer, became leader of the Quebec Liberal party and 102 days later swept the polls on a straight federalist ticket.

Now, on the tremulous edge of the Eighties, René Lévesque's government, which shares the Cossette-Trudels' objectives, if not their methods, is firmly ensconced in power and has risked a plebiscite on its separatist intentions. The intractable tandem phenomena of high unemployment and rising inflation are draining our economic vitality.

The Seventies have been a witch's brew of a decade. As stealthily as a thief in the night whose silent passing leaves a sense of disquiet rather than the grief of stolen treasures, the decade robbed us of the natural optimism that once anchored the Canadian character. It was during the Seventies that we began to turn in on ourselves, to shut out most of the rest of the world, to doubt our collective aptitude to survive and our individual capacity to deal with the forces of social, economic, and political dissension threatening the country's future.

The historians will probably reduce the Seventies to a marginally significant period of transition. But for those of us who lived through it, the decade signalled less a time of transformation than the end of something. And what was ending was the delicate but durable consensus that has kept Canadians together. Our national symbols – the RCMP chief among them – have been debased, and while existing public institutions, social ethics, and individual values were being challenged and abandoned on all sides, no new ones were being established or embraced.

The Canadian genius for compromise and conformity, the willingness of people to subjugate their regional interests and personal feelings for the sake of the national interest, was dead or dying. By this, the last, decisive year of the decade, we no longer had, as we could

45

once believe, merely two solitudes but rather two dozen million solitudes, based on the distemper of our individual discontents. It's as if a centre of action had broken down in each one of us – as if we were living through a spasm of history in which society no longer shaped personalities, but men and women preferred to plot their own personal journeys to self-fulfilment. This produced a laid-back generation of narcissists, less interested in life than in lifestyles, caught up in their private chemistries to the exclusion of national concerns. We became preoccupied with surface appearances, symbols that might somehow reassure us that regardless of the rest of the country, we were still "All right, Jack!"

This self-indulgent attitude disconcerted the politicians, who couldn't decide whether they should switch from pretending to be agitators to pretending to be statesmen. They became neither and lost their mandates in the process. The Left fragmented itself into confusion and impotence; the Right co-opted the political Centre. Among our party leaders (including provincial premiers elected before 1970) only Pierre Trudeau survived the decade still in office, if not entirely in power, a poignant reminder of his – and our – shattered hopes.

A great deal happened during the Seventies, but not much seemed to change. Unlike the Sixties, it was a decade that never managed to spawn any generational voices of its own. The young grew up separately, sharing few hot causes or cold exiles, dropping back to draw their ideals from the smugness of the sleepy Fifties.

Building on the activist momentum of issues imported from the United States, the Sixties generation went on a psychic rampage, permanently shaking the very foundations of Canadian society by challenging its collective faith in the Protestant ethic, questioning the worship of compromise as an essential ingredient in social change. Dr. Vivian Rakoff, chief of psychiatry at Sunnybrook Hospital in Toronto, saw the Seventies as a period of evaluation and reminiscence: "We have the sense of having come through a firestorm."

THE SIXTIES SHORT-CIRCUITED all our nervous systems. Richard Rovere of *The New Yorker* tagged it "this slum of a decade," but for most of those who formed its youthful vanguards (marching to Ernest Hemingway's dictum that whatever makes you feel good *is* good) the memories are not all downers. Their daze of puberty turned into a binge of sensuality, with promiscuity, marijuana, and the pseudo-military couture of revolution becoming symbols of their defiance and rejection of middle-class values. Suddenly it seemed as if all of Canadian society had reorganized itself around the problem of getting kids safely through the teen-age years. Youth was all we wrote, sang, and talked about. In 1969, John Lennon made a pilgrimage to Toronto's Varsity Stadium to stage Woodstock-North, a match-lit affair dedicated to peace, love, and international understanding. Nine years later, the Canada Jam rock festival at Mosport was distinguished only by the amount of beer consumed. Today's fourteen- to twenty-four-year-olds have turned superachievers, bucking for the twenty-odd places reserved for Canadians in the frosh year of the Harvard Business School.

At the same time, the age thirty-plus survivors of the Sixties have long since turned in their buckskins, commando berets, and combat boots for jogging suits, have cut their hair, and now get their rushes from darting into health-food stores, watching "M*A*S*H" reruns, and "maximizing their potential" inside the corporate pyramids they had once vowed to dislodge. Bob Bossin, best of the Sixties campus activists, who was instrumental in setting up Toronto's Free University, has moved out of extra-parliamentary politics to practise his banjo as a member of Stringband.

Prompted by the excesses of their American counterparts, Bossin and his shock troops hoped to overturn the system, detonating a revolution that would create a radically different Canadian society. Instead, we got Joe Clark, "King of Kensington," and Cuisinarts.

During the Sixties, only the young enjoyed a "lifestyle"; now everybody does. The Sixties girl wore blue jeans and peasant blouses, let her hair grow long and natural, dabbled in drugs and group gropes, had an active sex life, and adopted the birth-control pill. The archetypal Woman of the Seventies wears boots the year round, has rediscovered nail polish and purple lipstick, forsaken the natural look for permed curls, and still leads an active sex life, though she's less certain about which contraceptives to use. (To accommodate one of her whims, the cosmetics makers recently came up with makeup specifically designed to stay on in bed.)

More important, the only political movement to survive the Sixties has been feminism. Men in the early Seventies went into huddles as women reached out for a larger number of society's command posts. (Cowards went "unisex.") Flora MacDonald would never have made a significant run for the Tory leadership, Barbara Frum, Jan Tennant, and Valerie Elia would not have become star broadcasters, and Canada's abortion laws would never have been changed had it not been for the women's movement. Feminism made sex a political issue, and that's where there was the most impact – between the sheets.

The Sixties male talked about alternatives, wore denim and T-shirts, had shaggy hair, smoked pot, and "encountered." His Seventies counterpart has converted to the values of upward mobility and determined that he must dress and smell the part. (In 1978, male cosmetics worth an estimated $100 million were sold in Canada.) Sunbeam even has a special dryer called Li'l Red Devil designed for men to take along on business conferences. The kind of vanity that was once the private preserve of salon dandies now embraces male peacocks who are fervently masculine. The changing style in men (to suit the ideal contemporary women) is most noticeable in the switch from the thin-lipped neurotic movie heroes of the Fifties (James Dean, Montgomery Clift, John Garfield) through the sensitive but alienated idols of the Sixties (Jack Nicholson, Dustin Hoffman, and George Segal) to the current crop of witty guys (Richard Dreyfuss, Kris Kristofferson, and Jon Voight), who don't treat women like daffodils or buddies but can handle their new equality with competence and conviction.

If the Seventies had an anthem, it was the nihilistic two/four beat of the disco. The free-floating gyrators of the Sixties have been replaced by cool automatons who flaunt their desire under the strobes in a sexually charged choreography that reduces sensuality to its crudest mechanical form. "Disco," wrote Andrew Kopkind in *New Times*, "affirms the 'unreal' Seventies, emphasizing surfaces over substance, mood over meaning, body over mind, going out over staying in."

A vibrant domestic film industry was born during the Seventies, but most Canadians still went to American movies and the big box-office smashes of the decade featured a mean shark (*Jaws*) and cartoon characters (*Star Wars* and *Superman*). Rock musicians became cultural heroes, and even Canadians, usually slow on the entrepreneurial uptake, got the message by fielding such groups as Rush, Trooper, Chilliwack, CANO, Klaatu, and Harmonium.

It was O.J. Simpson who popularized the word "superstar," and it was superstars like O.J. who made sports the biggest money-making entertainment around, with a lot of youngsters who grew up shooting pucks on ice ponds in Saskatchewan suddenly finding themselves in executive salary ranges. At the same time, it was big business (through overexpansion) that diluted the quality of the game, creating an unwieldy league that produced maybe a dozen good hockey nights per season. Reggie Jackson and Charles O. Finley kept baseball alive, but tennis and squash emerged as the decade's fastest-growing sports.

The great Canadian saga of the Seventies was the power shift westward that followed the 1973 OPEC price hikes, which began to move the centre of gravity of Canadian corporate decision-making out of the economic, political, and cultural nexus of the Toronto-Montreal-Ottawa corridor toward Alberta.

"Cowboy" was the epithet used by the barons of Bay Street when they first encountered Calgary's newly influential entrepreneurs, even if, like Bob Blair, they had been educated at Choate, the American Establishment's very own prep school, and Queen's University. The new paladins who ran Alberta didn't exactly conform to the suave mid-Atlantic patricians who still dominate Toronto's boardrooms. But neither were they Marlboro men with bank accounts who paraded their anti-intellectual biases. Their conversation was peppered with the technological patois of their trade. Life in the New West combined creative conservatism with big-buck ostentation and the open optimism of the frontier.

The gas-and-oilionaires such as Bob Blair, Jack Gallagher, Jack Pierce, Bill Richards, Rob Peters, and Arne Nielsen represented an important new configuration in the Canadian power structure. "Now we can do anything anyone out of New York or Houston or London can do," Blair proclaimed. "There's a clear movement of financial power away from Toronto and Montreal into Western Canada." The worth of Western Canada's conventional hydrocarbon energy potential had been estimated at sixty-five billion dollars.

The central figure in this tilt of authority westward was Peter Lougheed, who made his definitive pronouncement on the subject during the 1976 Conservative leadership contest by demanding, "Why should I want to run Canada when I already run Alberta?" Sheik Yamani, the oil minister from Saudi Arabia, sensed the length of the premier's reach while visiting the province in mid-1978 to study its tar sands prospects. At a private Government House reception there came an awkward moment when he stared deeply into Peter Lougheed's face and announced to a hushed gathering, "You really *do* have blue eyes!"

IN TERMS OF OUR PLACE in the world, most of us have fond memories of the early Seventies as a time when the Canadian dollar was still a serious currency. Yet it was a harsh decade, crammed with kidnappings, wars, and the spectacle of the United States being ruled by an ambitious and paranoid man of dismal wit whose downfall allowed us to participate vicariously in the high drama of an event that never really touched us. We watched the Watergate embarrassments being unveiled, numbly gazing at the final bloodletting and horrors of Da Nang, Saigon, and Cambodia, concluding that however bad things might be at home we were damn lucky not to be as corrupt or disingenuous as the awful Americans. We had come through our testing time with the imposition of the War Measures Act; we had already taken a cynical turn of our own. And so again we attempted to escape from the outside world, longing to recreate simpler times by retreating to the comforting absolutes of hearth and home. It was not to be.

At the edge of the Eighties, we stand at a moment in Canadian history that may yet change all of our lives and citizenships. The continuing disintegration of authority at the centre may yet turn the Eighties into the most decisive decade of them all. Our once peaceable kingdom has become a strange new land, its future as unpredictable as a hailstorm.

—1979

❄   ❄   ❄

AS THE FIRST YEAR of the twentieth century's ninth decade ended, the lenten tedium and oppressive conformity of Canadian life had vanished. With all the fervour of born-again agnostics, Canadians in every region, occupation, and economic circumstance spontaneously and angrily challenged their governments, their bosses, and their banks. By year-end, the craving for order and obedience, historically so

50

dominant in this peaceable kingdom of ours, had been replaced by confusion reminiscent of the swaying bleachers at a Stones concert.

The widening dichotomy of trust between the governors and the governed no longer was limited to the radical young or the financially strapped. Pent-up resentment of authority burned across the land, with ordinarily placid middle-class citizens accusing the politicians of lies and damned lies. Only the most faithful of retainers still believed that national problems had political solutions.

Besieged federal parliamentarians responded by throwing up such mind-blowers as the National Energy Program, Eugene Whelan, and a brand-new constitution covered with beaver tracks. The politicians' fatuous pronouncements continued slithering off Ottawa's photocopiers like limp herring. But no one paid attention. While Pierre Trudeau was levitating in a space all his own, Joe Clark succeeded in giving banality a bad name. Ideology was dying, and authenticity became an overrated virtue.

It was a bruising process, a time of anarchic impulses and lost touchstones.

What really took place was the unruly passage from an acceptance of closed-shop authority to a militancy that questioned most traditional power groupings. The once-smug citizens of a once-smug country staged a coup d'état against the notion of having the big personal decisions made for them by self-selected hierarchies. It happened not only in governments but also in business, union ranks – and families.

It was Pierre Trudeau who inadvertently set off the process. His insistence on drafting a new charter of rights prompted voters to re-examine past dues, present entitlements, and absent powers. In gaining their own constitution, Canadians came of age in a curiously uncharacteristic way.

It was not pride of independence that dominated the national conscience of a country about to be untied from Mother Britannia's apron strings. It was a scream of defiance against usurious interest rates and spirit-crushing inflation. Unemployment in Canada had created a horde of jobless greater than the ranks of the country's entire armed services during the Second World War. What should have been a time of national celebration turned sour.

Protests and strikes grew commonplace. Instead of obediently following march organizers, the frustrated men and women who took part in the demonstrations eyed their own leaders with the wariness of starving foxes.

Cecil Taylor, militant boss of the United Steelworkers' local that led a seventeen-week strike against Stelco Incorporated and cost it seventy million dollars in lost profits, was shouted down as he was announcing the victorious settlement at Hamilton's Ivor Wynne Stadium. When his members started setting the building on fire by lighting copies of the new contract, Taylor adjourned the meeting with the taunt: "If you want to light fires, I'll be at the union hall this afternoon. You can burn that down!" The 100,000 angry workers Dennis McDermott organized and led to Ottawa on Grey Cup weekend set their own bonfires on Parliament Hill, and the Canadian Labour Congress chief threatened that next time he would forcibly take over parliament itself.

No one seemed immune from this mood of spreading sedition. Convicted kidnapper and FLQ revolutionary Jacques Rose was hailed with two standing ovations at the policy convention of the Parti Québécois in Montreal, while René Lévesque's pleas for provincial sovereignty, based on some lingering association with Canada, were postponed. In response, Alex Paterson, a mild-mannered Montreal lawyer and co-president of the province's English-speaking Positive Action Committee, huffed, "The mood of our community has shifted from reason to hostility, from moderation to calls for civil disobedience, from hope to a search for new solutions."

Violence was becoming a habit. Vandalism cost Toronto schools about one million dollars, while in Halifax the murder rate doubled, with reported rapes up by 40 per cent. More than two million Criminal Code offences were committed across the country during 1981. In formerly placid backwaters such as Ontario's Bruce and Grey counties, hooded and armed farmers, infuriated by high interest rates, threatened bankers, particularly those of the Commerce, which raked in an unprecedented 61-per-cent profit increase.

The revolutionary spirit flourished everywhere. Only Ruhollah Khomeini remained unperturbed, contemplating the legacies of terror. Even though Iran under his bloody stewardship had butchered or deposed two presidents and four prime ministers, the Ayatollah maintained that what gave his country stability was the speed with which its leaders could be replaced. The grisly killings of Anwar Sadat of

52

Egypt and Ziaur Rahman of Bangladesh (and the attempted assassinations of Ronald Reagan and Pope John Paul II) underlined the vulnerability of the international order. By year-end, invasions and insurrections had created more than ten million refugees, with new victims from Guatemala and Nicaragua swelling the ranks of the dispossessed from Pakistan, Somalia, and the Sudan. Cuba exported its revolution by maintaining 50,000 soldiers in Angola, Ethiopia, and the Yemens. The United States sold Pakistan $3.2 billion worth of arms – even though that country (with Libya's support) had moved farther in its atomic bomb development than Iraq had before the Israeli bombing on June 7.

Such thunder of distant apocalypse was matched at home by dour predictions that North America during 1981 had moved into a major recession, the worst since the economic blight of the Thirties. Paper losses on the Toronto Stock Exchange alone amounted to more than twenty billion dollars, and businesses across the country were going bankrupt at the rate of twenty-five hundred a month. Stockbrokers' Christmas cards were featuring gallows humour, such as this verse sent out by Toronto's Loewen, Ondaatje, McCutcheon & Company, poking fun at Finance Minister Allan MacEachen:

> Our spending programs are a hit
> So let's forget the deficit.
> Let's make sure that no one mentions
> Or thinks about our indexed pensions.

While MacEachen's enterprise-destroying budget attracted most of the criticism, it was the Bank of Canada's drum-tight monetary policy that deserved more of the blame by raising interest rates to an unprecedented peak of 23 per cent. Governor Gerald Bouey (who won *his* war on inflation by accepting a 1981 salary increase to $104,500) admitted that unemployment was "disagreeable and unpleasant" but stubbornly stuck to the monetarist-style diktats that helped increase it. His approach was all too reminiscent of the barb delivered to the November conference of British Conservatives at Blackpool by Robert Jones, one of the party's activists: "They tell us that monetarism is only a theory. Perhaps then they should try jumping off the Blackpool Tower. Gravity is only a theory."

Hardest hit was the North American automobile industry, its Canadian branches suffering from protracted layoffs. The prestigious Moody's Investors Service took the unheard-of step of downgrading the credit rating of General Motors Corporation, long the symbol of America's industrial strength, after third-quarter earnings showed a net operating loss of $468 million. GM's Canadian subsidiary managed to find a new market by shipping 13,500 Chevrolet Malibus to Iraq, where they were used for partial compensation to widows of soldiers killed in the interminable war with Iran.

While Toronto retained its dominance as the country's leading financial centre, industry, money, and people continued shifting westward. So much so that during the pre-game banter at the Grey Cup game in Montreal, Ontario Premier Bill Davis casually suggested to Alberta Premier Peter Lougheed that they make a little wager: Ontario's budgetary deficit (one billion dollars) against the Alberta Heritage Fund (nine billion dollars). With a half-time score for the Ottawa Rough Riders of 20–1, Davis thought he had it made, but Lougheed (whose Eskimos won in a 26–23 squeaker) never did take the bet.

Corporate cannibalism flourished throughout the year, with companies worth twenty-seven billion dollars (representing one-fifth of all stocks listed on the Toronto Stock Exchange) being swallowed up in mergers and acquisitions. To divert themselves from the burden of all the sombre economic and political news, Canadians took up fads, new and old, some spilling over from the United States and Japan. Rubik's Cubes and Sony Walkmans became ''must'' items for the urban chic, who started sending each other Strip-A-Grams and gift certificates for fitness-dance classes. Jelly beans came in with Ronald Reagan, the Rolling Stones were back on the road, a pacifist wave was sweeping Europe, and Toronto's Four Seasons Hotel was judged the third best in North America (and twenty-fourth in the world). The best news of 1981 was that in June, after 109 episodes, ''Charlie's Angels'' finally halted production; the year's non-news event was that Brooke Shields lost a court decision to halt publication of nude photos of herself.

Canadians drank more beer than usual (eighteen and a half gallons each), and recreational bicycling became our fastest-growing sport. It wasn't a vintage year for whooping cranes: out of twenty-five eggs, three chicks reached the flight stage and of these, only two survived. Poodles remained Canada's favourite dogs. The most significant book published in 1981 was the *Encyclopedia of Music in Canada*, while the U.S. best-seller lists sparkled with such gems as Alexandra Penney's *How to Make Love to a Man*, which the *Washington Post* dismissed in a one-line review: "So much for lying back and thinking of England."

If 1981 had an appropriate swan song, it may have been the one-man exhibit of a hundred Canadian flags painted by Toronto artist Charles Pachter. "I discovered something magical about that image," he says. "I turned something banal into something mysterious. But more than one of my flags is staggering halfway down the pole, all knotted up against itself, which represents the whole feeling of pent-up frustration and tension in this country." In some of Pachter's final canvases the red maple leaf has torn away from its moorings. It is an angry emblem, not soaring with pride but plummeting in free fall like a spent rocket. "There's no question my show is documenting something that's going on in this country – a pulling apart – the tearing away at the strings trying to hold us together."

—1981

AS 1983 BEGAN, PIERRE TRUDEAU was winging across Southeast Asia on a seven-nation tour, hustling Canadian subway cars, sawmills, and Dash-7s. Twelve months later he was on yet another world swing, this time peddling his brave but vaguely worded peace plan. The trips and their different impulses bracket the bizarre twelve months just past. Our earlier preoccupation with the need for jobs has given way to concerns even more sombre. The hunger of January was for economic recovery; the longing of December was for human survival.

Suddenly our domestic divisions seem irrelevant, not because they have been resolved but because of the loom of mushroom clouds on our mental horizons. The delicate political consensus by which this country has historically been governed was never programmed to deal with the insanity of nuclear war. The peace movement spent 1983 operating largely outside our existing political institutions, but its message governed much of our popular consciousness.

On the world stage, Trudeau's disarmament mission amounted to no more than a cameo appearance. Many Ottawa critics saw his trips as a vain attempt to rescue his faltering domestic leadership. Anything to get out of town. In the strange calculus of disarmament negotiations, authority depends on how much each participant is willing to throw into the pot. Under Trudeau's stewardship, Canada became the only democracy in world history to disarm itself voluntarily. His crusade thus became a lost cause.

The international incident that revealed our real standing in the world was the October 25 U.S. invasion of Grenada. We are the senior Commonwealth nation in the hemisphere, spending $150 million a year on foreign aid in the Caribbean – and yet when the Americans decided to wade ashore, they notified our external affairs department an hour *after* their landing and only sixty minutes before we could read all about it in the *New York Times*.

Even if, during his occasional 1983 visits to Canada, Trudeau spasmodically lapsed into affability, his string was clearly running out. In office for most of a generation, he has surpassed the unpopularity of his predecessors, who at least managed to hold on to most of the middle-class vote that has always been the Liberals' strength. It was the loss of this stolid political base during 1983 that drove the Liberals even lower in the Gallup polls, triggering the process of political succession. On June 11, when Brian Mulroney won the leadership of the Tories on a steamy fourth ballot, the balance of power swung to his party.

One of the great disillusionments of 1983 was that we turned out to be living in a paper world. There was a time when few contracts seemed more hallowed than bank loans. But if you were big enough – Dome, say, or Massey, Brazil or Argentina – you could roll your debts over, with interest added to principal, and no one seriously expected that promises of repayment would ever be honoured.

In the United States the political scene continued to be dominated not so much by Ronald Reagan the man as by the outdated mentality he tried to impose on the world. It was vintage Fifties Hollywood – every good guy a John Wayne, every woman a pug-nosed dream. Reagan differed from other U.S. presidents not because he was such a hard-shelled conservative but because he was so pushy about it. The huge budgetary deficit notwithstanding, during most of 1983 the United States enjoyed sustained economic growth with tolerable inflation. By year end the Democrats, still searching for a modern reincarnation of the Roosevelt magic – F.D.R.'s charm and Eleanor's balls – seemed ready to settle for the abstract decency of Walter Mondale, thus guaranteeing Reagan's re-election.

The stock market soared for most of the year, and stockbrokers turned fat margins, but the industry itself was being assaulted by the chartered banks, led by the Toronto-Dominion, offering discount trading services. The effect was so devastating that only one seat on the Toronto Stock Exchange was sold in 1983 – at a bargain-basement rate of fifty thousand dollars, less than the going rate for Toronto taxi licences. The TSE took the unprecedented step of advertising its seats for sale, but there were no takers. Inside the corporate world, the hard lessons long recognized in individual households were finally being learned. The reigning 1983 buzz-phrase was ''Let's bare-bone it,'' as overheads were cut and executives' liquid lunches turned to Inniskillin instead of Château Lafite.

Ontario placed three renegade trust companies under a yet-to-be-justified trusteeship, but the business story of the year was the nearly two billion dollars wasted by Montreal's Canadair in trying to develop a saleable executive jet. (Anybody in the business knowns that corporate honchos prefer Gulfstream IIIs '''cuz you can stand up in the potty.'') Sequestered in their pseudo-Tudor offices, most of Canada's chief executive officers failed to comprehend the new economy over which they were presiding. The trouble was that unlike Japan, where eighty top private-sector presidents resigned because they had not met their sales targets, business in Canada continued to be run by the same tired gang of uninspired number-crunchers whose idea of experiencing an epiphany was to nibble finger-sandwiches at receptions for superannuated bank chairmen in their favourite haunt, the Toronto Club.

Two separate societies were evolving. The great paradox was that more businesses failed and more were started than in any previous year. Some towns and regions boomed; others stagnated. We were in transition between one kind of economy and another. Computers, which had influenced the design of almost everything, produced at least one great flub. The Boeing 767, first of the new-generation jets designed by computers, was tested for 176 fail-safe procedures – everything except how much fuel it takes to fly past Gimli.

Most provincial premiers tried to adjust to the computer age with grants and new education facilities, but their activities had yet to yield much payback. Most radical among them was William Bennett of British Columbia, who rewrote the social contract for Pacific coast Canadians, undermining the sedate populism that has been this country's prevailing political mode. Instead of repudiating him, British Columbia's silent majority blessed his efforts – and every other government went on notice to copy him.

In Quebec, René Lévesque tried desperately to rally members of his cabinet (those out on bail or not holidaying) into giving the province reasonable government. At the same time, Robert Bourassa's resurrection was guaranteed to turn patronage into Quebec's national sport. The new Liberal leader was yet again busily plotting how to protect himself against his instinct for duplicity.

As the year ended in confusion, Canadians were perplexed about their individual and collective futures. The desperate circumstances called for a grand act of mischief, and Edmonton artist Peter Lewis was glad to oblige. An understudy of Salvador Dali and student of the successful chain of signal fires strung from Scotland to the Channel Islands in celebration of Prince Charles's wedding, Lewis organized individuals and chambers of commerce to build bonfires across Canada and the United States for 1986. The fire pattern, in the shape of a dove and olive branch, was planned as a group project, stretching through six provinces and twenty-three states. "The dove's tail connects Ottawa and Washington," Lewis explained. "The fires will run as far as southern Oklahoma, north to Moosonee, with the beak at English Bay in Vancouver. All 4,500 fires will be intervisible. The dove in its entirety should be photographed by the nice folks at NASA from the space shuttle. We have a potential audience of 800 million. Why be local when you can be global?"

Like the masked dancers at the Duchess of Richmond's gala ball before the Battle of Waterloo, Lewis's bonfires seemed an ideal way to capture this ambiguous moment of suspended annihilation.

—1983

CANADA'S HEADLINE WRITERS and sonorous anchor voices spent 1985 regurgitating the absurdities of our submerged banks and barfy tuna. But beneath the surface of Canadian society the earth began to move.

For the first time since the Great Depression of the Thirties, signals of class polarization were identified by the professional pulse-takers of Canadian public opinion. Allan Gregg, chairman of Decima Research Limited, reported, "The most significant trend we picked up during the year right across Canada is a growing and potentially dangerous class disparity, in terms of response to common behavior. This is not a question of class definition but the beginning of class-based thinking."

This phenomenon found its most immediate expression on the federal scene: the rich sidestepped participation in the political process, and the poor felt powerless to influence it. That meant the important core of middle-class values – essential to the Canadian experience – was being eroded. Canadians have in the past prided themselves on belonging to one of the world's few classless societies, with most of us categorizing ourselves as adherents of what George Orwell termed "the lower, upper-middle class." The egalitarian impulse that first forged a new nationality across the top half of the North American continent is under intense pressure.

For many of us, that may be a disquieting thought; for Brian Mulroney it could mean a political lynching. Here is a prime minister elected mainly because his pragmatic style and thousand-watt smile suggested he might be able to reconcile the country's social and economic interests. But instead of being benign burghers ready to set aside individual concerns for the sake of the national good, we have become a hard-bitten crew of canny crofters, more concerned with protecting our own turf than improving our neighbours' lot.

That tight-fisted attitude has become most apparent in the backlash to Ottawa's tentative pokes at the gargantuan deficit left by Pierre Trudeau. Everyone, it seems, agreed that federal funding had to be slashed, so long as not a penny of the cuts came out of their own pockets. Demands for deficit reductions remained as strong as resistance to the means of achieving them.

In such tendentious times, polarization of the haves and have-nots, the tensions among geographical regions, and even the conflict inside families were growing worse. The blighting economic recession of the early Eighties turned Canadians' anger on the Trudeau and Clark governments, blaming not the process but the people in charge. When Mulroney swept to power, most voters were pleased that they had changed the players and expected their problems to be resolved. But with the Alberta bank bail-outs, the tuna affair, and all the other things that went wrong, the conclusion was that it isn't the people who are to blame but the system itself.

In the face of such widespread and exponentially multiplying dis-illusionments, governments – including the provincial administrations of British Columbia, Alberta, Saskatchewan, Manitoba, New Bruns-wick, and Prince Edward Island, all facing elections during the next twelve months – were caught in a trap. With widening class disparity making any kind of operational consensus increasingly difficult to achieve, the temptation for elected politicians was to do very little, so that voters would at least not have anything new to get riled about. Yet "doing nothing" proved to be an equally certain prescription for defeat, because an inactive government inevitably falls victim to the popular assessment that it is not a viable agent of change and therefore deserves to be turfed out.

By the mid-1980s Canada was in a dangerously fractious mood. Even those Canadians fortunate enough to be part of the good life were feeling uneasy, certain there were potentially more benefits to be gained than they were already enjoying. Selfishness, for a growing segment of the population, became Canada's official religion.

The event that crystallized that and all the other stirrings of disquiet was the mid-year federal budget. This ill-conceived document seemed to broadcast a signal that the government was sanctioning the dismal notion that there was nothing wrong with the rich getting richer while the poor grew poorer. The fact that old-age pensions were cut back while millionaires were allowed to claim tax-free capital exemptions for their old masters and their young mistresses reinforced the incipient class-structure split. The perception that Ottawa had turned against the old and the needy crumpled the government's numbers ratings, causing one of the steepest drops in popularity since that sort of poll was first taken. The barriers to social and economic advancement were becoming institutionalized.

And so, at mid-decade, Canada was caught in a peculiar bind. The economic indicators were pointing up, and, compared to most other countries, Canada was a land sprouting with more opportunities than it was cursed with problems. Still, many Canadians were beginning to feel that the solution to what was troubling them could not be found within orthodox politics.

That essential middle ground between smugness and despair was growing dangerously narrow.

—1986

PART TWO

Heroes

Wayne Gretzky

HOCKEY HAS BECOME A CELEBRATION of violence, greed, and macho posturing. So much so that the elbow to the chin and knee to the groin seem to have been sanctified as the sport's most essential instruments.

Sportscasters with hairy forearms and strident voices seem constantly to be invading the TV screen, telling us more than we want to know about each player's stud line, mid-season scoring total, and beer endorsements. The sport that rightly claims to be the only true Canadian invention has become what the late Ralph Allen, a former editor of *Maclean's*, called "a double-barrelled exercise in delinquency – the juveniles on the ice; the adults in the expensive seats up above."

An exception to all this is Wayne Gretzky, the shy Edmonton Oiler who almost never allows a week to go by without rewriting the record books. His modest style, subtle dash, and relaxed confidence add up to a touch of magic on the ice. It's magic to watch him sneak the puck behind some hapless goalie's back; magic to see him stickhandling his way across the blue line; magic to observe him outmanoeuvring his opponents instead of trying to elbow, slash, or board them.

In his best-selling celebration of the Oilers, *The Game of Our Lives*, Peter Gzowski advanced the notion that Gretzky may be the beneficiary of a delayed time-frame mechanism that calms down his view of the action around him, allowing him to anticipate and react at a speed out of sync with that of his opponents. What separates Gretzky from his peers, wrote Gzowski, "may well have nothing to do with physical characteristics but be a matter of perception, not so much of what he sees but how he sees it, and how he absorbs it.''

There is something very Canadian about the Oilers' centre super-star. Having to handle mobs of adoring women and almost two million dollars a year in pocket money hardly seems to have turned his head. ''I just feel lucky to be one of the 420 guys who get to play in the NHL,'' says he.

Gretzky has in the past been written off as a prodigy about to be exposed as a kid who got lucky. He is not. He is as fine a hockey player as this country has ever produced and is in the process of becoming a genuine hero to a nation that badly needs one.

—1982

Terry Fox on Film

F EW CANADIAN BUSINESSES have more richly earned as shoddy a reputation as the film industry. Touted as the mirror of our identity and the high road to fortune for tax-shelter-happy dentists, it wiped out its investors, did nothing to define the nation, and spawned a motley crew of deal-makers whose taste was all in their mouths.

Into this wary, weary climate comes *The Terry Fox Story*. The movie, much like Fox himself, overcomes more than one seemingly insurmountable obstacle to reach its objectives. It may well be the best, and it is certainly the most Canadian, of the many weak attempts we've had at making a decent indigenous movie.

Eric Fryer, the cancer amputee who portrays Fox, is totally believable. At first, Fox (in the movie, as in real life) is alone, with no fanfares or support systems. The journey starts with the simple ceremony of sticking his artificial foot into the Atlantic at Cape Spear in eastern Newfoundland. Doggedly, he begins to hobble the eight thousand kilometres home. In the harsh morning light, huddles of well-wishers in tiny Newfie outports coalesce, as luminous as figures in a Renoir painting. There's a lame Patrick Watson, in a brilliant cameo shot, hobbling out to deliver an obscene benediction.

Inexorably and almost imperceptibly, Fox's pilgrimage develops its own field of force. The kid begins to draw crowds and media groupies. The movie's pace takes off when Fox is joined by Bill Vigars, a Canadian Cancer Society official (Robert Duvall). A noble-looking man with a devilish countenance, Vigars turns the lonely trek into a "Marathon of Hope."

The film has serious flaws. The music, by Bill Conti, is modified Muzak more suitable to afternoon TV soaps. What this film needed was some hard-edged, early-era Lightfoot or the evocative funk of Vangelis. The indoor lighting is poor throughout, and the first thirty minutes threaten to turn the film (literally) into a sleeper.

The Terry Fox of this movie is no hero – just an athletic kid angry that he has six short months to live. The undeniable courage is there, but he can't work up the nerve to break the news to his father that he intends to run across Canada. When his mother tells her husband for him, the response is a flat and very Canadian "When?"

What raises this film beyond its pedestrian potential is the camera work of Richard Ciupka. The cinematographer who shot *Atlantic City*, Ciupka captures subtle shifts in landscape and quality of light as plot and character move across the country, from Newfoundland in April to Ontario in deep summer. The last mists of morning in a Quebec field, the mauve evenings on the road, the lush farmlands of the St. Lawrence Valley are less a backdrop than the movie's main theme. Canada becomes a land to flee across: every village a destination, every town a landmark. Yet there is an austere chill in the land across which Fox struggles – a parallel but very different texture from Ingmar Bergman's Sweden or Richard Attenborough's India.

By the time Fox approaches Thunder Bay at the end of his run, he is alone again, still nourished by that invisible current of anger that dominated his brief life. But, alone or not, he has become what he wanted to be, and in the one soliloquy allowed him by script-writer Edward Hume he pronounces his own epitaph: ". . . life is about reaching out to people and having them touch you back."

Terry Fox was determined to run across the country "from telephone pole to telephone pole." His ordeal has been authenticated by this ninety-eight-minute film, which manages to suspend disbelief without romanticizing his odyssey.

—1980

Jack McClelland

A T THE HEIGHT of a recent publishing season, when bookstores in Western Canada started running out of copies of my second volume of *The Canadian Establishment*, Jack McClelland reacted in typical style. Instead of loading the boxes of books aboard a train or cargo aircraft, he hired half a dozen trucks and dressed their drivers in rented tuxedos. I was never quite certain what the ultimate purpose of this exercise was meant to be, since no one except McClelland himself – who waved off the convoy with exaggerated formality and a dash of bravura gestures – paid the slightest attention to the strange caravan snaking its way across country.

But it was vintage McClelland, and I was reminded of this small incident when it was announced that, after twenty-nine years at the operating helm of his publishing house, McClelland is assuming less onerous duties as chairman of the board. It is a pleasure to use the occasion of this change in his status to pay tribute to my friend and publisher, a man who almost single-handed Canadianized our book industry and gave the country its first indigenous popular literature in the process.

His publicity ploys and promotion gimmicks have gilded the McClelland legend, such as his annual skating appearance on the rink in front of Toronto City Hall, where he handed out free Canadian paperbacks to anyone who confessed that reading was his or her pleasure.

But to those of us who are his authors, and we number half a thousand strong, Jack McClelland has been very much more than a good promoter and a great publisher. He is, above all, a sensitive and shrewd editor, spotting the weaknesses in a sentence, paragraph, page, or book, writing casual fix-notes that magically resolve literary blocks. More than that, he is what all authors need when facing the terror of blank pages and blanker minds: an understanding friend who appreciates the essential loneliness of our craft. He will do anything for his authors, not excluding the arrangement of abortions or bail.

A surprisingly modest individual (and closet war hero as commanding officer of a motor torpedo boat), McClelland is an irreplaceable and irrepressible natural resource. But at times his sense of the ridiculous runs away with him. When a certain lady, whose chauffeur's uniform I had described as matching the bottom of her swimming pool, took my words to the Supreme Court of Ontario, McClelland did not take kindly to her lawsuit. It was only with great difficulty that our lawyer convinced him not to appear in the judge's august chambers dressed in a white toga, prepared to bear witness that its colour matched the bottom of his Jacuzzi. Now, *that's* a loyal publisher.

—1982

Hugh MacLennan

IF THE CANADIAN EXPERIENCE boasts a spiritual town crier – the Boswell of our aspirations and afflictions – it has to be Hugh MacLennan, the Montreal novelist. His writing is saturated with wisdom, humour, and tenderness, setting down the awesomely terrifying truth about people discovering each other too little and too late. MacLennan is at his best chronicling slow lives. His books are almost pathological examinations of men's and women's feelings, portraying their distances, their subconscious protection of each other, the kindness and the pain that accompany their separateness. The truth he reveals is not in the least sensational. Just truth.

His unfashionable view of literature is that it must do more than assert life as a meaningless accident. Once asked how he picks his themes, MacLennan replied, "They pick me. You get things through the pores." Released from the novelist's bonds of plot and characterization, MacLennan the essayist succeeds in portraying what Edmund Wilson, the dean of U.S. literary critics, once called "a point of view surprisingly and agreeably different from anything else I knew in English: a Canadian way of looking at things."

MacLennan has described the *Reader's Digest* as "the Kraft cheese of literature" and Mackenzie King as "this sly, ponderous, soft-footed Presbyterian leprechaun with the emotional development of a ten-year-old mother's boy and the political vision of the Vicar of Bray." He wrote about the American takeover of Canadian resources as "a seduction in which the lady keeps murmuring that she can't help herself," and said of Pierre Trudeau that "the light in his eyes was a Gioconda light of such subtle and curious intensity, I doubt if even the painter of Mona Lisa herself could have captured it.''

Now completing his eighth novel, MacLennan still teaches literature at McGill, dividing his days between a modest downtown Montreal apartment and his country retreat in North Hatley. Haunted by human transiency, he jealously guards his anti-British bias by viewing the world through a staunchly Celtic heritage. ''A Celt,'' he explains, ''has a dog-whistle sound that an Anglo-Saxon simply doesn't get.'' Contemptuous of ivory tower esthetes, whose books he dismisses as ''poetry of the menopause,'' he believes that a writer must be engaged with the issues of his time, echoing D.H. Lawrence's dictum that ''the novel treats the point at which the soul meets history.''

The author of *Two Solitudes* is not optimistic about Canada's future: ''Politics are very advanced if they're forty years behind the reality of the times. What's happening in Quebec now is very possibly part of the decline of the West. Civilizations just die. The Sixties was the first decade when the West consciously entered the post-Christian era. Some fibre went out of us.''

Perhaps. But these essays establish that nothing has gone out of Hugh MacLennan. He is the master of Canadian prose.

—1978

Pierre Berton

WRITING," NOVELIST J.P. DONLEAVY once complained, "is turning one's worst moments into money." Pierre Berton operates on exactly the opposite impulse, turning into eminently marketable prose the best of his feelings about his country, his family, his friends, and his many special interests. His craft glows with a sense of celebrating its author, so that his twenty-fifth book seems as vital and tantalizing as his first.

He is, of course, very much more than a writer, having gained equal fame as a raconteur, television star, newspaper columnist, magazine editor, army of one, and accessory before the fact in countless causes. In a country where everyone tries desperately to keep quiet, Pierre Berton believes in making noise.

He is a big man with large appetites; his body language can be deafening. Probably my favourite memory of the Berton brand of bombastic beastliness is of sitting, some time during the late Fifties, in an office at *Maclean's* being used by Robert Thomas Allen, the humorist. We were quietly comparing notes about the dastardly habits of people who insist on remaining disenchanted with the brilliant first versions of our manuscripts when Berton, who was then the magazine's managing editor, burst through the door, gave Bob Allen a prolonged blast about the hopelessly despicable nature of what he had written, and wheeled out again. Allen was crushed. In one of those moments of lucid pathos that sometimes illuminate human contact, he looked up at me and whimpered, "Who does that man think he is, *Pierre Berton?*"

If not exactly a limousine liberal, Berton is a sucker for underdogs of every variety and has been known to pledge his undying loyalty to the NDP from a Princess telephone on the side of his pool at his Kleinburg mansion. But it is as a popular historian that his name and reputation will survive. He has mastered the art of making ordinary events glow with excitement, suffusing his books about the Canadian past with the retroactive ring of truth. When he describes what a hundred professional historians have written about before him, Berton makes it sound, if not exactly like re-inventing the wheel, at least like rediscovering the flat tire.

He has survived those critics of Canadian literature, especially of the academic variety, who model themselves on a species of fish that populates certain jungle streams in Brazil – tiny but innumerable, their whole head is in their teeth; they can remove the flesh from a man's bones in minutes. Berton has not merely survived his critics, he has bested them. Every writer has within himself a single source which nourishes what he is and what he has to say. In Pierre Berton, that invisible wellspring has become a gusher that never runs dry.

Here is a Western Canadian of special gift and high style, opinionated, even intransigent, yet unmarked by the gloomy introspection of his calling. He liberated himself early from the narrowing vanities that leave most Yukoners standing where they began. He left home young, made his own way, creating himself in the process. That creation is today one of the most interesting and important Canadians of his generation.

—1982

Bruce Hutchison

BACK IN 1967, when Expo was lighting up Canada's hopes and Montreal's skyline, Lester Pearson lent his prime ministerial suite in the Habitat apartment complex to Dean Acheson. The former U.S. secretary of state immediately invited his old friend Bruce Hutchison to share the luxurious penthouse, and the two families had a whacking good time touring the Fair. Their only distraction occurred when a bright-eyed Englishwoman spotted Acheson, instantly identified him as Anthony Eden, and demanded an autograph. Acheson signed the British statesman's name with a flourish, later explaining that he couldn't bear to disappoint a loyal subject of the Queen. What impressed Hutchison most of all was that they were constantly being smuggled into exhibits through back doors reserved for VIPs while the crowds lined up in front. "This," Acheson whispered to him at one point, "this is privilege, and privilege is wicked. Still, you learn to endure it."

It's this world of political privilege that Hutchison, now editorial director of the *Vancouver Sun*, portrays in his memoir, *The Far Side of the Street*. It's a world in which the boundaries between the reporter and his subjects often meld into friendship and mutual admiration, as they comfort each other with their faith in the reasonableness and political tractability of man. This has always been Hutchison's turf, and he has occupied it with distinction and literary grace. His talent is to draw large conclusions from small events. His style, despite some purple patches, helps obliterate the distance that usually separates the non-fiction writer from his subjects, so that the reader is never in the position of having to watch Hutchison watch the politicians who populate his book. "I write," he confesses, "because in a lifetime of at least 2,000 years, as time should be reckoned, I may have learned something about the world and, within it, a Canada now gone and quite unbelievable to most of its contemporary inhabitants, together with certain men who made and unmade it, their consequences, good and bad, still unknown today."

Most of Hutchison's reminiscences concern themselves with the six Canadians who have occupied the prime ministership in his time as a journalist. Each profile advances his thesis that assumption of this country's highest political post reshuffles the elements in a man's character so that he becomes both a part of and contributor to the mystique that surrounds the office.

It's Hutchison's remarkable ability to evoke character studies out of the flash glimpses he gives into the important people he knew that raises this volume from a fascinating autobiography into an important reflection of his time. There's the wife of William Aberhart, the Social Credit premier of Alberta, sitting beside her husband at cabinet sessions, knitting energetically like Dickens's harridan at the Paris guillotine, and whispering reprovingly, "Now, now, William!" whenever her husband lost his temper; Charles Ritchie, Canada's former high commissioner to the United Kingdom, doing an imitation of himself, with wild gestures and shrill sound effects, during his ceremonial approach to Queen Elizabeth's throne in shoes suddenly glued to the palace floor by wads of discarded chewing-gum; Robert Kennedy who, in Hutchison's private company, turns out to be a "quiet man of small stature, neatly whittled face, cool manner, and soft speech."

Only occasionally do Hutchison's personal feelings colour his narrative, sometimes through the mouth of Dot, his late wife and soul mate. He recalls a Washington dinner during which Dean Acheson and George Ball had conducted an outrageous debate about the grandeur and burden of American power while the rest of the guests listened in silent awe. Finally, Dot Hutchison couldn't stand it any longer and interrupted the boastful titans. "What," she demanded, "is going to happen when you Yanks get too bloody big for your britches?"

—1976

Robertson Davies

ROBERTSON DAVIES, MASTER OF MASSEY COLLEGE, once wrote a play called *Fortune My Foe*. In it, one of his leading characters exclaims, "God, how I have tried to love this country . . . I have given all I have to Canada – my love, then my hate, and now my bitter indifference. But this raw, frostbitten place has worn me out and its raw frostbitten people have numbed my heart."

Whether or not this cry comes from the heart of the author himself it is hard to tell, but there are those close to him who believe that Robertson Davies, like so many artists bred here, has always found Canada hard to endure if impossible to flee. Still, because of his background and education (he was born into the Upper Canadian upper class, the son of a family of newspaper owners and Liberal senators and educated at Upper Canada College and Oxford's Balliol), his enormous, intensive, and varied talents as a writer, and his genius for civilized eccentricity, he has been able to respond to his alienation from country in a manner that's uniquely his own.

In effect, he has created a kind of non-Canada within our chilly boundaries, making out of Massey College at the University of Toronto an intellectual haven for himself and a clutch of post-graduate scholars who come there to pursue their serious ends. Inside its elegant walls he moves among his Junior Fellows in their gowns, looking quite magnificent in a necromancer's beard, living in the Master's Lodge, presiding once a month at High Table, sniffing snuff out of Aram's horn, sipping claret, responding with superb indifference to all charges that the college is snobbish, anachronistic, sexist, and maybe even absurd. (There are no souls on ice at Massey College.)

If these trappings were all he was master of, the media and the masses of students beyond the college's quad (Massey has 84 fellows, the university that shelters it has 19,526) might be justified in making mock of Davies's mannerisms. But the Master has played a splendid joke on his detractors. In the past two years – after writing twenty-one novels, plays, and works of theatrical criticism that brought him mild approval at home and little notice abroad – he has made an international reputation for himself as a writer that places him beyond Canada, if still of it, beyond the radical rage of student newspaper editors, beyond angry feminists, high on the pinnacle where he's always dwelt in spirit.

When his novel *Fifth Business* was published in 1970 it was accorded an international critical response that boggled Davies's acquaintances. ("My God," said a fellow professor, "it's fulfilling Rob's sanest dreams.") The *New York Times* called it "a marvelous enigmatic novel, driven by an irresistible force," *The New Yorker* said it was elegant, *Esquire* saw it as being "as masterfully executed as anything in the history of the novel." Saul Bellow claimed it had taught him much, John Fowles looked on with admiration, and the *Toronto Star* said it was bored.

When I repeated these comments to the Master in his study one afternoon, he merely looked mildly pleased, though he was willing to allow that his new novel, *The Manticore*, was also "quite all right" according to his English, American, and Canadian publishers as well as the Literary Guild and the Book-of-the-Month Club. He then went on to talk with a spirit, style, and erudition that were entirely expected and with a generosity and a certain sweet self-mockery that were not. What follows are excerpts from our conversation:

If Britain had never been invaded by the Normans, it is quite likely that the position of women would be splendid now, and would have been splendid for the last fifteen hundred years. The Normans brought to England the Roman law and the attitude of the Roman Catholic church toward women, which tended to downgrade them in one way while exalting them through the figure of the Virgin in another way. But under the old Celtic law that had prevailed in Britain and under old Saxon law, women inherited equally from their fathers. They could have divorce upon showing good reason, and good reason was cruelty, madness, sexual incapacity. They could, when they were divorced, take their property back from the marriage, and they could marry again without any difficulty whatever, and they had a well-recognized and honourable place in society. But as soon as they came under the dominance of Roman law and the Catholic church, women had an awful time that continued right up to 1882, when the Married Women's Property Act was passed. I have a very high regard for women. I am very fond of women. I admire them, and think they have extraordinary qualities which are not at all like the predominant male qualities.

The world is burdened with young fogies. Old men with ossified minds are easily dealt with. But men who look young, act young, and everlastingly harp on the fact that they are young but who nevertheless think and act with a degree of caution that would be excessive in their grandfathers are the curse of the world. Their very conservatism is second-hand, and they don't know what they are conserving.

I think of an author as somebody who goes into the marketplace and puts down his rug and says, "I will tell you a story," and then he passes the hat. And when he's taken up his collection, he tells his story, and just before the denouement he passes the hat again. If it's worth anything, fine. If not, he ceases to be an author. He does not apply for a Canada Council grant.

Because I am a Canadian, I couldn't really live anywhere else. I have had chances to do so and have never given it serious consideration. I belong here. To divorce yourself from your roots is spiritual suicide. The expatriate, unless he is really a rather special kind of person, is very unhappy. I just am a Canadian. It is not a thing which you can escape from. It is like having blue eyes.

I tell my class of graduate students, "Keep your ears open to the promptings of your destiny and don't worry too much if you and your destiny do not agree about what you should have and when you should have it. Happiness is always a by-product. It is probably a matter of temperament, and for anything I know it may be glandular. But it is not something that can be demanded from life, and if you are not happy you had better stop worrying about it and see what treasures you can pluck from your own brand of unhappiness.''

I'm always urging architects to bring a whisper of magnificence, a shade of lightheartedness, and a savour of drama into the setting of our daily lives. How long is it since any Canadian architect has included a secret passage in a new house? The building inspector would no doubt insist that it be equipped with electric light, drainage, and an air-changing system.

I feel that people will eventually have to come back to getting their serious information from print. When you see TV and film, you're seeing what is primarily a work of art. It is calculated to catch and hold your attention by the arts of theatre. Now when you are reading a report or anything like that, you can stop, you can consider, you can contradict. You can check your information and you can make notes. You can't do any of these things with the theatrical arts and it's wrong to be hoodwinked into taking them as information. They are entertainment.

I don't think I would ever write a book with what anybody would call pornography in it because I feel that pornography is a cheat. It is an attempt to provide sexual experience by second-hand means. Now sex is a thing which has to be experienced first hand, if you are really going to understand it, and pornography is rather like trying to find out about a Beethoven symphony by having somebody tell you about it and perhaps hum a few bars. It's not the same thing. Sex is primarily a question of relationships. Pornography is a do-it-yourself kit – a twenty-second best.

I am very interested in the condition of sainthood. It is just as interesting as evil. What makes a saint? You look at the lives of some of the very great saints and you find that they were fascinating people. Just as fascinating as great criminals or great conquerors. Most saints have been almost unbearable nuisances in life. Some were reformers, some were sages, some were visionaries, but all were intensely alive, and thus a living rebuke to people who were not. So many got martyred because nobody could stand them. Society hates exceptional people because such people make them feel inferior.

The English influence in Canada has not, I think, in general been a happy one. We have been patronized by the English and they have taken us for granted. No people in the world can make you feel so small as the English, and they have, I think without ever being conscious of it, made many of their dominions feel small. We are the good daughter who stayed at home to help mother. We did it in 1776. We did it in 1812. The good daughter who stays home ends up by being taken for granted by mother, and that is what happened to us. My background is not English; it is Welsh and Dutch, and I look at the English with a fairly cold eye. I am fascinated by them, because I want to see what makes them tick, but I am fascinated by them as a Spaniard in the third century might have been fascinated by Rome. England is on the slides, and I want to see what happens.

The American influence on Canada is again a strange and ambiguous one, but the Americans are much more influenced by England than they pretend. I don't believe in historical parallels, but when Rome was at its pinnacle the most prestige-lending possession a Roman could have was a Greek secretary. At this moment the most prestige-lending thing you can have in New York is an English secretary. Britain has reached the secretarial level of decline. You look at American magazines and their booze and their classic clothes and their shoes and all those things are still advertised in English terms; when they really want to build something up there is a saddle, or Anne Hathaway's cottage, or a Guardsman plastered on it, to give it prestige. This is fascinating. But it is the sign of a country that is becoming a symbol of the past.

Canada demands a great deal from people and is not, as some countries are, quick to offer in return a pleasant atmosphere or easy kind of life. I mean, France demands an awful lot from her people, too, but France also offers gifts in the way of a genial, pleasant sort of life and many amenities that we don't regard as important here and have done little to create. Canada is not really a place where you are encouraged to have large spiritual adventures.

I don't think we're particularly eager to look for the Canadian identity because many people are afraid of what they may find. They fear it will not be a very flattering picture. You have got to get rid of a lot of the Shadow side of your nature before you come to the reality of it. The Shadow is the inferior side, the unacknowledged evil. And Canada is scared of her Shadow.

A lot of people complain that my novels aren't about Canada. I think they are, because I see Canada as a country torn between a very northern, rather extraordinary, mystical spirit which it fears and its desire to present itself to the world as a Scotch banker. This makes for tension. Tension is the very stuff of art. Plays, novels – the whole lot.

—1973

Margaret Atwood

BECOMING A METAPHOR is never easy, and Margaret Atwood, with her wintry eyes and corrugated hair, tries hard to conceal herself in her books, leaking information in bits and pieces, fortifying instinct with detail and publishing the results.

Her *Life Before Man* is populated with heroines and anti-heroes driven by the conviction that they must attempt to become major characters in their own lives. Women such as Lesje Green (half Lithuanian and three-quarters Jewish), who discovers that risking your life is less important than risking your soul. Men such as Nate Schoenhof, who has given up his law practice to carve toy rocking-horses but never quite realizes that the forces that drove his ambitions didn't come out of the same faucet as those that control his emotions. In typical Atwood fashion, all her characters meet their come-uppance, torturing one another with ancestry, drowning themselves in a kind of existential quicksand.

It is in the architecture of her prose that Atwood's novels achieve their power. She can build whole chapters around the difference between a pause and a silence, call down laughs as sharp as thunderclaps, yet never waste a phrase or thought. Her art is rooted in an ability to step back from herself, calibrate her characters' emotions, acknowledge the absurdity of life, and then create comedy out of hurt or vice versa. She understands that love, however precipitate, inevitably casts its partners back into the loneliness that first disposed them to each other – until their isolation becomes intolerable and they are driven back together, more needy than before. "Dreams are not bargains," she reminds us. "They settle nothing."

Even when Atwood occasionally slips into girlish chatter or tries too hard to turn her scenes into symbolic crossword puzzles, her flaws become a signature, like uneven threads in a handmade wall-hanging. Her writing has always been an exploration of the reality in which she lives; in the process, she has helped provide us with a sense of place. "I don't think Canada is 'better' than any other place," Atwood once wrote, "any more than I think Canadian literature is 'better'; I live in one and read the other for a simple reason – they are mine, with all the sense of territory that implies. Refusing to acknowledge where you come from is an act of amputation. By discovering your place you discover yourself."

Life Before Man may not be *the* great Canadian novel, but it is an important book. Margaret Atwood is one of those rare writers with the agitating voice of a born truth-teller.

—1979

Mordecai Richler

Only three weeks earlier, when tubes had been curling in and out of him everywhere like surgical spaghetti, Dr. Morty Zipper had gently pressed his hand and asked, "Can you hear me, Josh?"

In response, Joshua had blinked his eyes.

"You're lucky to be alive."

"I'll be the judge of that," Joshua thought.

THAT'S A FAIRLY TYPICAL PASSAGE from Mordecai Richler's latest best seller.

Like Richler's previous novels, it is the chronicle of a Montreal man-child's sexual misadventures, vocational follies, and inevitable come-uppances. What gives Richler's prose real bite is its deep and sometimes painful probe into the Jewish soul. His distorting exaggerations and flights of fancy aside, Richler's acidic sallies capture both the agony and the joy of being Jewish in Canada.

Even though some of their best friends may be WASPs, Canada's estimated 300,000 Jews exist in a world unto themselves. ("I was just born a Hebe like some guys come into this world with a clubfoot or a stammer," one of Richler's characters complains.) Being Jewish, unlike being a Canadian rooted for generations in French or British traditions, means remaining constantly in flight and flux, searching for a warm glow of security others may take for granted.

The presumption of strangers who view the Jewish community

through a veil of preconception and prejudice is one of omnipotence; the fact is one of frailty. It's all a question of assumed legitimacy. The upwardly mobile WASP has a clear choice: either he accepts the pleasures and burdens of reaching for authority and takes the chance of being corrupted by it, or he risks powerlessness and irrelevance.

Most thoughtful Jews don't feel they have that luxury. They operate on the principle that the guarantee of their continued freedom in Canada depends on how effectively they can make their public and private interests coincide. That's why contributions by Jews to so many of the country's cultural and philanthropic institutions run proportionately far above their numbers.

They are among this country's most valuable citizens, warm, generous, and amazingly productive, proud if slightly insecure about being Canadian. Or, as Mordecai Richler would have it: "Canadian-born, he sometimes felt as if he were condemned to lope slant-shouldered through this world that confused him. One shoulder sloping downwards, groaning under the weight of his Jewish heritage . . . the other thrust heavenwards, yearning for an inheritance, any inheritance, weightier than the construction of a transcontinental railway, a reputation for honest trading, good skiing conditions."

—1980

R. A. D. Ford

AT A TIME WHEN MOST OF CANADA'S public servants are neither behaving as servants nor giving a damn about the public, it's a pleasure to pay tribute to an individual who has decorated Ottawa's payroll for forty years.

Robert Arthur Douglas Ford, who has just officially retired as Canada's ambassador to the Soviet Union, has long been Canada's most distinguished representative abroad, having spent the past sixteen years in Moscow, nine of them as dean of the diplomatic corps. In his sparsely furnished second-floor embassy apartment on Starokonyushenny Pereulok, he held court to visiting diplomats, businessmen, journalists, and other wayfarers, ever willing to share his finely honed appreciation of the Kremlin's subtleties and intrigues. To have been briefed by Ford – as I was during my last trip to Moscow a year ago – was not just to obtain first-hand information about Soviet intentions but to get a *feeling* for what the Russian people were thinking.

This was possible because Ford – who first came to Moscow as the embassy's chargé d'affaires in the early Fifties and returned as ambassador in 1964 – not only spoke Russian but had mastered the language to a degree that his poetry was published in U.S.S.R. journals. This allowed him unique entry into the forbidden world of the Soviet intellectual elite. His translations into English of Pasternak, Esenin, and Akhmadulina became standard texts. (An accomplished linguist, Ford has also translated poetry from French, Portuguese, and Serbo-Croatian.)

Ford is remarkable for the equanimity with which he faces his contest against muscular atrophy, which hit him at twenty, when he was given a year to live. He is able to walk only a few yards at a time with the help of a complicated set of crutches, his face a mask of agony. Mortality is a constant companion in his poetry. "Now I can talk freely because death is in bed with me," he writes. "That is the advantage of knowing death young. It has a vast familiarity." It was both a mark of respect and a concession to his handicap that he was the only non-member of the Soviet presidium allowed to use elevators inside the Kremlin.

His own slim volumes of verse (one of which won a Governor General's Award) are a tally of dissolving forms, faceless walkers, unrequited love. "Ford," the critic Miriam Waddington once wrote, "is absolutely honest without being confessional, and completely unsentimental. He often has awkward moments, but never false ones."

—1980

Claude Ryan

THE INTELLECTUAL SEARCHES for truth; the politician seeks power. Which is why so few great thinkers make good politicians, and vice versa. But occasionally circumstances throw up a rare individual who combines within himself both these contrary strains, and the most impressive example is Claude Ryan, the former editor of *Le Devoir*, who was elected to lead Quebec's Liberal party.

Ryanmania never swept the province, but at a time when Quebec's pro-Canada organizations had collapsed, he not only nursed a battered and corrupt political organization back to vigorous health but won solid endorsement for his view of federalism. After a rocky start Ryan ran party affairs from a nondescript beige office on the corner of a nondescript street in Montreal's east end, exuding the incandescent Gallic wisdom that is his trademark. His nose, like some ancient compass needle, swings toward the visitor, the hooded eyes probing hidden intentions; his cheeks are etched with fatigue lines, giving his face the topography of Quebec's electoral map.

Instead of chronicling the news, he's making history, and it isn't easy. He has toured eighty-five ridings in the past six months and out of all those midnight rides has emerged a much tougher man. No one owns him. "I'm not trying to resolve any problems with pious invocations," he says. "I feel optimistic because I have faith in serious work. That's the great difference that separates me from some of our friends in both the Parti Québécois and the press. They expected me to come out from on top as the guy who had a message to deliver from Mount Ararat. I said, 'No, I'm going down to the ground where the people are, and from there we'll see the seeds we plant prosper and bear fruit.' I enjoy a greater margin of freedom than most political leaders because I'm in control of more information on party affairs.''

There is an existential air about Claude Ryan's every move, and it's easy to believe that his future is Canada's future – that this unusual politician embodies the kind of cultural duality without which this country will not survive.

—1979

Ken Taylor

C ANADIAN HISTORY has always reminded me of cheddar cheese. It's not smelly and gooey like French Camembert, not full of fascinating holes like Swiss Emmentaler, nor sensuous like Danish Blue. It's just solid, occasionally tasty, but mainly a bit flaky. That's why our history books chronicle the adventures of a most unlikely set of heroes. They're a sparse company made up mostly of adventurers and explorers blundering through muskeg, confident they were really on their way to discovering the fabled treasures of India and China. The few politicians who have managed to qualify as genuine heroes – Sir John A. Macdonald, Sir Wilfrid Laurier, and J.S. Woodsworth – have found themselves having to carry an absurd consignment of symbolic freight.

Now, with a courageous act as sudden and unexpected as tracer fire, it turns out that at least one of our diplomats is cast straight out of a rerun of "Mission: Impossible." Our ambassador to Iran, Kenneth Taylor, harboured six American diplomats and carefully stage-managed their escape.

This runs counter to the image that exists of our thousand-member diplomatic corps. Cultivated, clever, and cordial, they seem at least from the outside to be men and women with passions as dry as winter leaves, living out careers that consist largely of scribbling unread *aides-mémoire*, conducting each other on incestuous *tours d'horizon*, and sipping Kir at National Day receptions. Instead of practising the blunted skills of "honest brokers," they have perhaps been spending their spare time reading John le Carré and, when called upon, can act with all the derring-do of George Smiley at his best.

We can all walk tall basking in the borrowed glory of Ambassador Taylor's achievement. His brand of heroism touches something real and worth emulating. It serves as a reminder that there may be unused and undiscovered qualities lurking somewhere in each of our psyches that, given the appropriate circumstances, might produce an equivalent act of courage.

We have been handed the opportunity for a second look at the whole business of being Canadian: the chance to make a quiet tally of how much there is in this country's emphasis on individualism, freedom of expression, and basic good sense that's worth preserving. There is a bit of Ken Taylor in all of us.

—1980

Eric Kierans

H E IS IN HIS SEVENTY-SECOND YEAR now and his eyes have the permanently bleached look of poached eggs, but Eric Kierans, the socialist-millionaire who has influenced Canadian politics at many levels, still enjoys challenging the established order of things.

When I called on him recently at his spacious home on one of the fashionable dead-end streets that line Halifax's North West Arm, he was particularly exercised about the prospect of Canada becoming the Manchuria of the Eighties – a supplier of unprocessed resources to manufacturing nations that garner most of the jobs.

"Our place in any kind of global system controlled by the United States is going to be merely as a supplier of raw materials," he complains. "We are being ground right into a mould. What happened at international summits like the one at Williamsburg, Virginia, is that the Western democracies pledged themselves to integrate fiscal and commercial policies, and that means monetary and trade policies as well. In other words, they're building an economic pyramid with us as a Manchuria in one corner."

Kierans, an ardent nationalist, laments the fact that he had to sell the Montreal glue factory he owned to an American multinational. He tried for four years to find a Canadian buyer, but every domestic bid was at least a third below competing British, European, and U.S. offers. Instead of trying to revive the dormant Foreign Investment Review Agency, Canada, he feels, should adopt the equivalent of a 1916 Swedish law that prevents outsiders from investing in capital enterprises without special acts of Parliament; that law has kept foreign ownership in Sweden down to less than 6 per cent. By throwing the economy open to free trade at the same time, the Swedish government has protected its citizens from abuses by domestic monopolies.

Kierans would never advocate free trade between Canada and the United States because, as he says, "they'll break the arrangement they make a thousand different ways." He thinks the Americans would have trouble competing (fairly) with any other nation because of their high overhead costs (mainly the huge Pentagon budgets) and the fact that U.S. citizens take for granted that they should enjoy the world's highest standard of living.

"One thing people in this country will have to accept," he predicts, "is that the standard of living all around the Western world is going to be lower for everyone. What we're going to see is the final destruction of that old shibboleth about governments intentionally favouring the rich because they are supposed to be the ones who save and invest. That's all crap, because most profits are reinvested internally, not for public purposes."

He is equally dubious about politicians who preach that the solution to our enduring unemployment problem is to go high tech, pointing out that the entire thrust of sophisticated technology is to displace white- and blue-collar workers. "To say that investment in technology will produce the jobs that Canada needs and wants is to say that such investors are philanthropists. They are not."

"The Mulroney government lost me right at the beginning, for two reasons," he says. "I had an open mind until I found out that Mulroney was increasing his cabinet to forty. That's a Tower of Babel. The new ministers will not want to sit in a room smoking cigarettes; they're going to create large bureaucracies, start meddling, and find new ways of interfering in the economy. The other thing, of course, was when Mulroney said Canada was open for business. That almost made me sick, because we have been the most wide-open country in the world to everybody – otherwise so much of Canada wouldn't be owned by others."

Kierans, who served in several key portfolios in the Lesage government before leaving Quebec to enter the federal scene and become a junior minister and a senior influence within the Trudeau cabinet, is most worried about Canada's 1.3 million unemployed. He believes there may be a hard core of 10 per cent of Canadians without work for the rest of the century. In economic terms, they have been declared redundant. Says Kierans: "This group is socially stillborn, they're born into a society that has nothing for them to do, that has nothing to make their living viable. This has gone on throughout history, and as a result we've had wars to clean it up."

Just about the only politician Kierans feels optimistic about is Robert Bourassa, the Liberal leader in Quebec. "He's a different guy altogether now," Kierans insists. "We were on some panels together during the referendum debate, and he was just beautiful. He is not going to make any more silly mistakes and is more a federalist than he ever was." Kierans has just spent most of a productive decade teaching economics at McGill and Dalhousie universities and is currently scholar in residence at the Institute for Research on Public Policy. He loves living on the tidewater of the Atlantic and in a way is returning to his roots: he started his business career as a commercial traveller in the Maritimes during the Thirties.

What haunts Eric Kierans – along with a growing number of other thoughtful Canadians – is that the dilemmas faced by this country now run so deep that they will not be resolved without some drastic structural reforms in the economy and correspondingly fundamental changes in the benign human nature that once defined the Canadian character.

—1985

David Lam

WHEN MIKE HARCOURT, the extrovert socialist then mayor of Vancouver, was presiding over the official opening of the Dr. Sun Yat-sen Classical Chinese Garden, he inadvertently blew the cover of British Columbia's most secretive – and most interesting – philanthropist. After going on about the horticultural wonders of the only authentic classical Chinese garden ever built outside China, Harcourt ended his oration with a flourish: "We all want to thank David Lam for his one-million-dollar anonymous gift that made this great project possible."

Lam has been a shadowy but heavyweight presence in West Coast real estate for years. His Canadian International Properties Limited has funnelled an estimated $500 million of Hong Kong funds into North America, and even though he is slowing down he negotiated sales and purchases of buildings worth $100 million during 1985.

What makes Lam stand out, not only among his fellow Chinese but also within the bleak philanthropic climate of the whole Canadian Establishment, is his determination to give away about five million dollars a year. His recent creative donations include one million dollars to the University of Victoria to help create a Centre for Pacific Rim Studies; one million to establish the David Lam Management Research Library at the University of British Columbia; one million to help expand Regent College, a theological seminary in downtown Vancouver; one and a half million to help fund social and theological studies in Hong Kong; and many other smaller projects, such as helping to fund the Vancouver Police Centennial Museum and sending the Vancouver Symphony Orchestra on a tour of Japan.

Not since the Koerner brothers arrived on Canada's west coast from Czechoslovakia in the late Thirties has a newcomer to British Columbia given away so much money and used it to such good effect.

"I always judge a person by what he does with his money," Lam told me in a rare interview. "And what I try to do is not just duplicate or substitute what governments should be doing but contribute in ways that will help modernize our thinking, because if the mind changes, everything changes." One example of this technique is Lam's sponsorship of a series of medical and philosophical seminars in Hong Kong later this year. "If I can reach a handful of intellectuals," he said, "say just twenty-seven people, one day, when Hong Kong is swallowed up by China, they will be scattered. But it is like sowing a seed which may blossom, keeping alive and spreading new ideas, including Christianity."

David Lam's father was born in a village 190 kilometres northeast of Hong Kong, the son of a teacher who was converted to Christianity and became the village's Baptist pastor. Lam's father moved to Hong Kong, where he put his nine children through university. After graduating from a Chinese college, David took an MBA degree from Temple University in Philadelphia. He later returned to join Hong Kong's Ka Wah Bank, becoming its chief executive officer after ten years. In 1967, after seventeen years at the bank, he felt that he had gone as far as he could in Hong Kong, and wanting to afford his three daughters a safer sanctuary, Lam moved to Canada. He was forty-four years old and not rich, but he fell in love with Vancouver and opened a real estate office. His former Hong Kong contacts enlisted him as a channel for investing their flight capital. He insisted that they lend him enough money to buy a piece of each real estate deal on his own account.

Apart from that very solid financial beginning, Lam's success was based on applying what amounts to Confucian ethics to real estate, which hardly ever happens in the raucous world of Vancouver's flippers. "Luck and my Chinese philosophy told me enough is enough – don't go for the last dollar," he says. "Because I always felt that I would rather lose a deal and a commission than lose a friend, many of my clients are now my friends – and many of my friends are my clients. I always pay slightly more than the market and charge slightly less – so I always seem to have waiting lists for my buildings.'' His greatest coup was buying and selling the Insurance Exchange Building in downtown San Francisco at a twenty-three-million-dollar profit. That cash was put aside to finance his David and Dorothy Lam Foundation. ''I didn't need that kind of money,'' he recalls. ''I was already enjoying life 100 per cent.''

''The Chinese in Canada have come through a lot of suffering and discrimination, and yet we feel a very useful part of the community,'' says Lam. ''I want to modernize the thinking of both the Chinese and the Canadians through the exchange of Christian and Oriental philosophies and religions. Harmony is the key – with yourself and with nature.''

Lam's hidden agenda is to enhance the image of the Chinese community, to set an example that his compatriots, several of whom could well afford to do as he does, should follow. ''I carry this burden, that I want Canadians to recognize that the Chinese in this country are not a liability,'' he said. ''Otherwise, I would be quite happy just sailing and digging my garden.'' To a close friend who was with him when the Dr. Sun Yat-sen Garden was being fêted, Lam was more direct. ''If I were building a Jewish Garden,'' he remarked, ''I could have got the money raised ten times over. And even though there are more Chinese in Vancouver who are richer than the Jews, I can't get any money out of them.''

In his own quiet way, David Lam is trying to redress the balance.

—1986

Moses Znaimer

TELEVISION ENTERTAINMENT in this country has traditionally been polarized between the intellectual pretensions of the CBC and the cynical money-machine approach of CTV, leaving little room in the middle for those rare birds, the independent entrepreneurs. The most interesting of these prodigies, who not only thrives on originality but has made it pay, is Toronto's Moses Znaimer.

His community station, CITY TV, recently moved into new headquarters featuring so many innovations that a curious team of notetakers from ABC in New York were early visitors and Japanese technicians flew in for a look. Inside a renovated, turn-of-the-century Gothic edifice on Queen Street West, Znaimer has done away with conventional studios. Reports come from the working environment of reporters' desks and flow through thirty-eight transmission ports known as hydrants into a central control room. Not only does this save money but it does away with the artificial atmosphere of most TV studios.

"MuchMusic," another of Znaimer's brainwaves, which now has a national audience of 1.3 million including that of its French offspring, "*MusiquePlus*," is already being broadcast from a storefront studio that allows passersby to watch and occasionally participate. "I'm interested in making real contact with the community," Znaimer told me. "We are, as far as I know, the first television facility set up to receive genuine interactivity from our public. If I can take a picture of somebody, shake their hand, create some kind of commitment or connection, I've got a viewer who will stick."

CITY recently extended its broadcast reach into southwestern Ontario, despite some serious doubts from the CRTC whether anyone in the province's agricultural belt would be interested in Znaimer's boogie-style programming. The theory he advances to justify his claim that the standard demographics no longer apply runs like this: "It's not that everybody in Toronto is inherently hip and that everybody in, say, Woodstock, is inherently hick. It's that some people in Woodstock are hip and some people in Toronto are hick – it's a frame of mind that has little to do with geography. There are many farmers turning on CITY because they think of themselves as being progressive, more vital, a little younger, a little more optimistic – all the things that define our style."

A more creatively daring Znaimer enterprise is his worldwide franchising of the play *Tamara* by Toronto's John Krizanc. In what Znaimer calls a "living movie," actors are spread through a suitable mansion, performing several simultaneous story lines that reconstruct a 1927 weekend in the home of Italian poet Gabriele D'Annunzio. Originally a smash hit in Toronto, it has been playing in Los Angeles for almost three years, opened in Mexico City last December, and is due to open in New York this fall. It will probably spawn sister companies in Paris, London, and Budapest.

But Znaimer doesn't want to issue any more licences until after the New York production because if it takes off, the value of the property could double. In New York, he is in the process of renting an armoury at the corner of 66th Street and Park Avenue to house the unusual play but needs municipal permits before the final go-ahead.

Znaimer may follow up with a play based on the Yalta Conference where Churchill, Roosevelt, and Stalin divided postwar Europe. Meanwhile, his attention is fixed on extraterrestrial matters. His Tour of the Universe attraction, which simulates a spaceship journey to Jupiter in the year 2019, is operating at the foot of Toronto's CN Tower. "Unlike *Tamara*, which is very much an elitist experience because the intimacy of it drives up ticket prices, our functioning Space Port has much greater mass appeal," he explained. "At the core of the idea is a machine we invented that combines 70-mm motion picture technology with a full-fledged 747 flight simulator for the first time anywhere in the world.

"People are quite knocked out by it," he added, "but Canadians have a hard time relating to the notion they might actually be confronting something first that was actually invented here." The idea is also being franchised, with the first installation now being completed at Osaka. It is being financed by Seibu, one of Japan's largest corporations, which has also purchased rights to Tour of the Universe for the entire Pacific Rim. Just last week a team left to visit Australia to plan the first unit Down Under.

Although he could have an active career as an actor (he was featured as a smarmy hood in two feature movies, *Atlantic City* and *Best Revenge*), Znaimer isn't taking any roles these days because he doesn't like to be typecast. "I'm fed up with the archetype, though I got a kick out of it in the beginning," he said. "It's only in this part of the world that all the good guys are blond and all the bad guys are dark. I just don't want to play any more Chicano dope dealers."

What he does want is to keep innovating. "My personal taste has always been to seek out the different," he says. "That's not perversity, it's just that if lots of people are doing something already, nobody needs me to do more of it." With live theatre, a successful TV operation, a national music network, simulated trips to Jupiter, and several other projects in the works, Znaimer's busy universe is unfolding precisely the way he thinks it should. Everything's coming up Moses.

—1987

Peter Campbell

EVERY DAY JUST AFTER NOON, Dr. Peter Campbell, president and chief executive officer of Wood Gundy Corporation, leaves his Wall Street office, climbs into his armoured Cadillac, and asks Otis, the North Carolina-born combat-medic who doubles as his driver, to take him to Christ Cella. This ecclesiastically named restaurant on East 46th is a popular hangout for the big hitters who survived the market-inspired slaughter that has decimated the U.S. investment industry in the past year or so. Over his favourite drink (double Chivas on the rocks), Campbell recently told me why he expects his New York branch operation of Canada's Wood Gundy Limited to grow so fast that before the Eighties are over the parent firm will be earning only a minority of its profits in Canada. "We're on a roll," he says, over the rim of his glass. "We're exploding exponentially – and it's a super environment to do it in because the industry is disintegrating all around us."

Wood Gundy has run a New York office since 1916, but it was something of a marginal outpost until Campbell moved in. "When I came down here," Campbell explains, "I first got to know everybody, then I dispatched all the empty helmets – about a third of the existing staff. We are now doubling the size of our New York staff and will be doubling our business every year from now on."

Campbell's personnel recruiting efforts have become legendary on Wall Street, particularly because he has managed to attract some of the Street's most influential traders, and partly because of his unorthodox interviewing methods. He spends many an evening flitting between the private dining rooms of four New York restaurants, including a steak house in Brooklyn in a neighbourhood so tough that the doorman always stands inside and there is a massive trailer parked across the entrance to deflect machine-gun bullets that might be aimed at departing patrons. Campbell meets his recruits in each location for a long interview, then, moving on to his next call, leaves them to be vetted and briefed by associates.

The approach is more than a little unorthodox for an investment house that in the past has earned and deserved its reputation for stuffiness as much as integrity. Campbell is solidly entrenched within Wood Gundy as one of the few partners who hold equity in the firm. ''I'm a real trader,'' he says. ''I've got lots of guts and I'm blessed by being a good people picker. I am a Gundy man through and through, but on the executive floor I'm known as the company's hit man.''

When Campbell was being moved around various Wood Gundy divisions in Toronto, turning their bottom lines from red to black, he broke the industry's customary patterns so often that the Investment Dealers Association of Canada had to change its rules three times to accommodate his novel methods. At one point he was commuting between Saudi Arabia, Tokyo, and Zurich taking care of the sudden flood of Eurodollars, rolling with the OPEC-inspired revolution of the world's money markets.

Campbell's background is as unusual as his methods. A 1959 gold medallist in economics at the University of Toronto, he worked first as a code-breaker for the communications branch of the National Research Council in Ottawa–then Canada's equivalent of the National Security Agency. He learned Russian well enough to monitor the intership communications between barge captains on the Volga River and helped perpetrate some dirty tricks at the height of the Cold War, which he still won't discuss. Planning to become an academic economist, he went back to university, put in a solid apprenticeship at the Bank of Canada, and in 1961 joined Wood Gundy as a clerk in the bond cage. Except for a stint at the London School of Economics (where he earned a doctorate on the theory of money markets), he has been with the company ever since.

At the moment, Campbell is applying his heretical notions in a New York environment, where they don't seem nearly so outrageous. He works in his shirt-sleeves right on the trading floor, refusing to have either an office or a secretary, and is determined to become one of the Street's major players.

But the highlight of his routine is his daily lunch at Christ Cella. He was recently talking up a fellow moneyman he describes as "the Number One institutional trader in America" when he was called away to the phone. "The panic bell went off in my mind," he recalls, "because people don't phone me. Everything's delegated. If a guy can't handle his job, he shouldn't have it. So I'm nervous, but I go out to the kitchen to grab the phone. It's my wife, and it does turn out to be a minor crisis. I'm so startled that I drop my cigar into a soup pot. I fish it out after I hang up, wipe it off, and light up again. No one's seen me. I go back to my corner table and tell my target guy: 'The soup of the day had Campbell's cigar in it.'

"But the Numero Uno institutional trader in America doesn't bat an eye. 'Don't worry,' is all he says. 'None of us ordered soup.'"

—1984

Ian Sinclair

THERE'S NO OTHER JOB IN CANADA like it, and when its occupant departs, the country's business climate undergoes a sea change. Ian David Sinclair, who has stepped down as chairman and chief executive officer of Canadian Pacific Limited, was known to everyone who ever worked for him (you don't work *with* Sinclair) as "Big Julie." His figure and the span of his ambitions were truly Caesar-like, though his ruthlessness was softened by a sense of humour and grudging respect for tough opponents.

His influence extended far beyond the boundaries of CP's huge empire, to directorships at Seagram, Sun Life, the Royal Bank, Union Carbide, and half a dozen other major corporations. He was an elephant hunter, and those who negotiated deals with him lived to regret any thoughts of trying to best him. During the 1973 negotiations to buy the 25 per cent of Algoma Steel held by Mannesmann AG for sixty million dollars, he came face to face with Egon Overbeck, then considered Germany's toughest industrialist. Overbeck had served as a member of the German General Staff during the Nazi blitzkriegs and had been wounded in action seven times. After four hours of trying to twist Big Julie's arm, the Prussian caved in, confessing he had met his match.

The only thing that ever baffled Sinclair was the behaviour of Canada's politicians, and he hated to be reminded that the CPR was originally built on Ottawa subsidies. His pursuit of bottom-line profits for his very Canadian company was unrelenting, even when it meant building ships in Japan and operating them through a Bermuda-based subsidiary. What he accomplished during his long and fruitful stewardship was to turn CP Ltd. from a hidebound transportation company into a world-class, free-swinging conglomerate, moving its assets from $4 billion to $13 billion.

My own experience with the man was typical. He at first adamantly refused to be part of ''The Canadian Establishment'' television series. But once he'd agreed, he threw himself so enthusiastically into the project that he virtually took over the cameramen and invited the CBC unit into so many CP Ltd. board meetings that he eventually had to swear the crew in as ''insiders'' to meet the security regulations.

Ian Sinclair will continue to serve CP for a while yet, but the glory days of his stewardship will not come again. A dozen Big Julies would turn Canada into an ungovernable industrial oligarchy. But I'm glad we have one.

—1981

Jack Gallagher

NO MATTER WHAT OTHER LARGE DEBTS or small triumphs may be concerning them, members of Canada's investment community are obsessed by the still unresolved fate of Dome Petroleum. The bankrupt Calgary company was to have been the centrepiece of Canada's march to industrial maturity and energy self-sufficiency. Instead, it has become a symbol of mismanagement and failure on a grand scale – the *Titanic* of Canadian business.

In the debate about how and why it all happened, the voice of Jack Gallagher (who has been the architect of Dome's hothouse growth) has been notably absent. The Dome chairman has dug himself in on the top floor of the Dome Tower in downtown Calgary, inaccessible to commiserators and critics alike.

"It's well known around here," he told me, "that I have always been philosophically against growth by acquisition, partially because people usually get hurt but mainly because I enjoy working in a smaller company where you can directly motivate people and have a hands-on operation. I didn't oppose our pattern of growth during the past two years because I was close to retirement and felt that I shouldn't impose my philosophy on the younger people who would be taking over. This was obviously a mistake on my part."

In justifying the four-billion-dollar takeover of Hudson's Bay Oil and Gas (HBOG) in 1981 – the manoeuvre now threatening to sink Dome – Gallagher maintains that it was necessary to increase the company's Canadian-content rating under the National Energy Program.

"In our effort to help in the Canadianization process – and to increase our cash flow so that we could continue exploration and development in the frontier areas – Dome acquired 53 per cent of Hudson's Bay Oil and Gas from U.S.-based Conoco. We were then obliged by the Ontario Securities Commission to make a comparable offer to the remaining 47 per cent of HBOG shareholders in a rapidly declining market. HBOG's major and critical shareholder, the Hudson's Bay Company, would not accept our equivalent Dome common-stock offer, even though Dome stock was, at the time, selling at a 25-per-cent premium over HBOG shares. Nor would the Bay accept a Dome preferred-share plus common-stock warrant offer without a bank guarantee, which ultimately involved the pledging of oil and gas assets as security. In reorganizing our security package, our Canadian banking group demanded the conversion of the ten-year, $1.3-billion term loan used to buy the original 53 per cent of HBOG into a nine-month demand loan, due September 30, 1982. When this loan conversion was accepted, it looked as though we would be able to sell off our non-Canadian assets and some of the non-essential HBOG assets to satisfy this $1.3-billion loan. But, in the down market, this was not possible.''

"In the year it took to complete the HBOG merger,'' he went on, ''interest rates climbed and remained high; our production of light-gravity crude was heavily prorated due to the intrusion of foreign crude into Eastern Canada; gas reserves continued to be shut in, due to lack of market; and the price of minerals dropped to Depression levels – turning HBOG's large mineral investments into heavy losers. We ultimately had to trade on a preferred-share arrangement guaranteed by a bank, which is the same as a debt instrument. This was never our intention.''

The explanation will hardly satisfy Dome's creditors, but Gallagher and his supporters stress that the company's asset position continues strong, with estimates of net worth running at twelve billion dollars. The reason this will not cover the company's eight-billion-dollar debt load is that current market conditions have reduced liquidation values to about six billion dollars.

As I left, I asked him how he viewed the future. ''I'm always an optimist,'' he said. Then, with a macho accent, added the Spanish sign-off: ''Adios.'' It was not the farewell of a defeated man.

—1982

JACK GALLAGHER'S RECENT RESIGNATION as Dome's majordomo is one of those rare events in Canadian business history that fundamentally alter the way things are done and, to those who care about such matters, chill the soul. It was the price the chartered banks exacted for their continuing support of Dome.

In both his thirty-year rise and his sudden demise, he was the man against whom others gauged their career trajectories and the outer boundaries of their ambitions. Gallagher transformed Dome into Canada's most important energy consortium and managed to do it entirely with other people's money, not paying out a single dollar in taxes or dividends in the process.

He was never very interested in making money for himself or for his shareholders, preferring the less mundane pursuit of altering the world's geography. He did just that – even if it takes another quarter-century to prove that the Beaufort is another Persian Gulf, bursting with ninety billion barrels of crude, cold oil.

What made Gallagher stick out among the Nervous Nellies who populate most Canadian boardrooms was that he would take the gambles that make corporate responsibility seem banal. It's this quality that allowed him to winkle entire treasuries out of the feds, divine oil out of ice, and amass loans for Dome larger than the national debts of many of the world's countries. As Dome chairman he was unique because he made the system work for his company on a scale no one else had before or probably ever will again.

Gallagher understood that the real conflict in Canada is not between East and West, Left and Right, French and English but between the reactionaries and the rebels, between those who obey authority and those who don't. The reactionaries' view is that everyone and everything has its place. The rebels' starting point is that, as Norman Mailer once put it, "Man must serve as God's agent, seeking to shift the wealth of our universe in such a way that talent, creativity, and strength of the future will show us what a mighty renaissance is locked in the unconsciousness of the dumb."

That was the root of Gallagher's power. He was able, without ever actually lying, to enlist investors' imaginations, so that a board lot of one hundred Dome shares that could have been bought for $380 in 1951 was worth $120,000 three decades later – even though in the interval the company had not conclusively proven out a single major new oil or gas discovery.

It was Gallagher's smile that got all the attention. And it was true that on September 7, 1979, when the Dome chairman was asked on TV about the rumours of a major oil strike in the Beaufort Sea, his answering smile not only drove his own stock to a new high but moved the entire TSE Energy Index up an unprecedented 186 points. The Cheshire grin was so blinding that it created its own field of force, but what he said was equally important.

He could talk on several levels at the same time, philosophy or politics, this world or the next, dazzling his listeners. He used tax dollars to build a fleet that rivalled the tonnage of Canada's navy and knew how to play on the fears of federal energy ministers. Wasn't it true, after all, that the more subsidies and tax incentives were shovelled into producing oil and gas from the federal lands in the Mackenzie Delta, the less likely it was Peter Lougheed could dominate the country's energy future?

He never really enjoyed anything except work. Up at 6:30 most mornings, he would jog along Calgary's Elbow River, munch a toasted turkey salad sandwich at his desk for lunch, and grab a Dome jet to call on some whimpering banker or trusting politician. He belongs to the Calgary Golf and Country Club but has not once played through its eighteen holes. Except at the very beginning, he was not interested in running the day-to-day business of Dome, preferring to act as its minister of external affairs, holding court at Ottawa's Four Seasons Hotel, the Ranchmen's Club, or the Canadian Imperial Bank of Commerce boardroom. Like all great politicians, Gallagher understood that the ultimate accolade was to have governments consult *him*, and they did. Donald Macdonald, then federal energy minister, asked him for suggestions about who should head the new Petro-Canada agency, and Gallagher was regularly called on to bless (or kill) government energy-regulating proposals. The superdepletion allowances in Trudeau's 1977 budget (which allowed taxpayers to write off *twice* their investments in the Beaufort) was perhaps his most breathtaking achievement, but his influence wasn't limited to Liberals. Joe Clark's 1980 budget, had it been passed, would have allowed Dome to pay itself for its own drilling program and turn a profit even on dry holes.

It was an accident of timing that brought Gallagher to ground. He piled up eight billion dollars in debt just as interest rates went sky-high – and Dome's properties weren't ready to pay the bills.

The Canadian economy has lost its resident dreamer. How many other business types really believe those fancy Ferrari ads that claim, "WHAT CAN BE CONCEIVED, CAN BE CREATED. . . "?

—1983

❄   ❄   ❄

DESPITE HIS UNCEREMONIOUS DEPARTURE from Dome, Jack Gallagher is a busy man these days. He is helping with plans to build a university for Inuit and Indian students at Yellowknife (to be called University of the North); he is working on a methanol plant on Melville Island to utilize gas from the Arctic islands; he is on the board of a small oil exploration company; and he remains the largest individual shareholder in the Eau Claire real estate development in downtown Calgary.

But Gallagher's main concern is how the federal government should be restructured so that it becomes more representative of the whole country. "The current system," he says, "is essentially consumer-oriented, so that it encourages short-term decisions for political gains. If we continue to suppress the voice of the primary producer, our country will break apart."

Gallagher wants to change all that. He'd like to reduce the size of the House of Commons by a third, double the pay of MPs, and allow each government a two-year period before any no-confidence votes are counted. Each new majority administration would remain in power for a set four years, but no prime minister could serve more than eight.

Gallagher's main concern is to gain fairer representation for the West and other resource-oriented regions. He has long advocated a separate political party representing these sectors that could hold the balance of power in Parliament: "We could elect thirty or forty MPs, and if either the Liberals or Tories get back with a minority, that's the time you'd say, 'We want three ministries in your cabinet – energy, forestry and fisheries, and agriculture.' Then whoever is prime minister couldn't dump our guys if they parted their hair wrong, because he would know they have a party behind them and not just constituencies.''

Since even Gallagher admits this is an impossible dream, he advances the alternative of reforming the Senate. He believes half the upper house should be made up of provincial appointees with the balance elected, eight from each province. The term of all senators would be limited to six years. ''Such a new senate,'' he says, ''would have to approve all legislation that originated in the Commons but it could not defeat the government.''

The problem with Gallagher's political ideas is that no one at the moment is taking them seriously. Brian Mulroney has yet to acknowledge his letters, and John Turner wrote back that he didn't want to see the government restructured in any way that would slow it down. To which Gallagher replied, ''What you really want, John, is to perpetuate the semi-dictatorship that you have in a majority government. When you have Toronto with more seats than Alberta, this country can't work. The United States was originally controlled by the golden triangle (Washington, New York, Boston), and they would have retained that control if they hadn't had a Senate with equal representation from every state.''

Gallagher is on safer ground with his own version of a national energy program: a tax holiday until payout on exploration costs, and a commitment to world pricing of all products. He also wants regulations governing the industry set in place for the term of exploration permits so there can't be any retroactive changes in ground rules. He advocates Canadianizing the industry further by forcing foreign investors starting or buying companies to sell 50 per cent of their equity stock over a period of twenty years and making the stock purchase attractive by decreasing capital gains taxes at the rate of 10 per cent a year, so that at the end of a decade the profit on oil and gas shares would be tax free.

Gallagher still believes there is an elephant-sized pool of oil under the Beaufort Sea. ''There's a basin 350 miles wide and 150 miles north-south up there,'' he says. ''So far, Dome has drilled sixteen holes and has found oil or gas in nearly every one. This summer I'm positive we're going to hit one or two big ones. They drilled two hundred holes in the North Sea before they found any oil – now they've got six hundred and they're still finding more."

Trying to measure Gallagher's clout these days to judge what effect, if any, his political initiatives may have is difficult because the man has created his own version of reality. Dome's bankruptcy has hardly dinted his self-confidence. He blames it on accidents of timing and dismisses his critics as termites along the glory road of Canadian energy self-sufficiency.

"I stayed too long at Dome," he admits. "Three or four years ago I told them I wanted to step aside because I wanted to do some of the political things I'm talking about now. But three members of the Dome board who had been with me since its inception thirty years ago said, 'Jack, you quit, we quit.' So I stayed, but I know I'm not suited to be running a big company – that's why I left Standard Oil to start Dome in the first place. I love to build something and I love hands-on operations."

The Dome that Gallagher hoped to create is dead, but it remains engraved in his heart. Oddly, it is precisely because he is a visionary willing to gamble on his own dreams that his political campaign cannot be written off: Dome stock has been in a free-fall market, dropping to $2.50 from its 1981 high of more than $25. One shareholder who has been holding onto his stock all the way down is Gallagher. He now has more than five million shares. "Even at today's levels," he flashes his renowned ivories with that gleam that once moved millions, "I'm not exactly hurting."

The only way to save the company is to sell it. Or they could bring Jack Gallagher back to run it. "Actually," he says, "I had a group come after me to see if I would do just that. But I told them, jeez, I was too damn old." Too bad.

—1984

Jimmy Pattison

DURING THE EARLY 1980s, I spent a few days at Jimmy Pattison's retreat in Palm Springs. Considering the neighbourhood, it was a relatively modest villa backing on the twelfth hole of the Canyon Golf Club. What I remember best from that long weekend (which included sharing the platform with Henry Kissinger in addressing Jimmy's "partners in pride," the men and women who run his companies) was our departure. I had been lent a car to tour the mountains above the desert and thrown snowballs while still wearing light-weight cottons. After I reluctantly left both the pine forests and the palm groves, Pattison drove me to the airport where his private jet was standing by to whisk us back to Vancouver.

We gave our luggage to a waiting porter. As Jimmy and I were ambling toward the gates, he veered away and, to continue our conversation, I found myself walking beside him as we passed a long row of pay phones. In a ritual obviously evolved from long practice, Jimmy pulled open the change slot of every telephone. He scooped out whatever coins had been forgotten and never missed a beat as he continued toward his waiting jet.

I was speechless. Was this the ultimate capitalist – a man so money-minded he felt compelled to collect pay-phone leftovers on the way to his three-million-dollar jet?

I asked why he had done it. "Habit," he deadpanned. "My first job was as a bellhop at the old Georgia Hotel, and I made more money from forgotten telephone change than from tips. So even now, whenever I see a phone, I go for it."

That's Jimmy Pattison, sole owner of Canada's seventy-fourth-largest company, ahead of such well-known Canadian-based enterprises as Thomson Newspapers Limited, Southam Incorporated, and Falconbridge Limited. Another difference is that these are publicly held companies; Jimmy owns every share of all but one of the four dozen profit centres that make up his corporate holdings. Apart from his main activities – selling and making foods, manufacturing recreational vehicles, producing outdoor advertising, and distributing magazines – he owns such eccentric assets as the Louis Tussaud's Wax Museum in Copenhagen, the *Ripley's Believe It or Not!* cartoon strip, and a finance company in the Channel Islands.

As proprietor of a private company, Pattison keeps his earnings secret, but he has a *net* cash flow of at least ten million dollars a month and probably a lot more. His companies' total sales passed one billion dollars in 1984; his target is to hit two billion dollars within the next four years. That would put him in a league with the Eatons and Bronfmans – except that he has earned every penny himself, instead of inheriting a head start. His main assets are a constitution that thrives on eighty-five-hour weeks and a mind that retains the minutest details. ''I go to Switzerland Friday nights,'' he explains, as if he were describing a trip to the local bowling alley. ''Get on Lufthansa in Vancouver at 6:15 and arrive in Frankfurt Saturday afternoon. I fly to Geneva, have my meeting on Sunday and Monday morning, then catch the 4:20 out of Frankfurt. I'm back home for a late dinner and lose only one Vancouver working day.''

His secret? ''I have a basket behind my desk which lists, on a daily basis, the key indicators of each industry we're in. Every business has a soft spot, and if you want control of what's happening, you keep watching those indices. I never wait for the weekly financial statements; there's too long a lag. I just keep tabs on things like forward bookings on my radio station, for instance. In the car business, the key is not having any ninety-day used cars on your lot. That's the kind of thing I worry about. In the food business, it's volume that's critical, because when you have a high fixed overhead, you've got to keep sales high.''

These and the many other indicators of how his companies are doing are no theoretical framework for Jimmy's management style. He acts quickly on what those indicators tell him. Every Friday, for example, he gets a list of every used car that has been on any of his lots more than ninety days. "I get rid of them," he says, "because that's where you get in trouble with bad inventory."

What's unusual about Jimmy is that he is a man not only solidly in command of his financial worth but also acting as if he were in charge of his soul. He seems genuinely to believe there is some holy sanction involved in his success. "I represent what the free enterprise system allows people to accomplish," he once told me, "and I'm grateful to God that He allowed it to happen." Yes, he still occasionally attends the Glad Tidings Temple on Fraser Street and, yes, he still prays before going in to negotiate major business deals. But he no longer plays the trumpet at the Sunday morning services, preferring the harmonies and rhythms of one of his five electric organs. (He has one in his house at Palm Springs, one aboard his boat, and three at his home in British Properties.)

Religious inclinations aside, it is because he is so utterly devoid of sham or pretence that his touches of self-righteousness come through as personal strength rather than arrogance. He makes it easy for people to supply their own reasons for liking him and has surprisingly few enemies or even critics.

Because his companies are privately held, no accurate estimate of his personal earnings is possible. But despite his vast monthly income, Pattison takes out only about $150,000 a year as a spending allowance, reinvesting the balance in his more than four dozen profit centres. His senior managers benefit from complicated bonus schemes based on performance, but operations are not devoted to expansion for its own sake. "Quality growth is what matters," he maintains. "Profit is only a by-product of success." What makes his companies so intriguing is that they work on the Japanese "quality circle" principle, allowing employees at every level to participate in decisions on how to keep enhancing productivity.

But being Jimmy's employee is not always easy. Because work to him is the main reason for breathing, Jimmy tends to expect from his staff not only perfection but the same single-track dedication that he himself expends on his business affairs. Every article ever written about Pattison repeats how, when he was starting out as the owner of his first car dealership, he fired the salesman with the lowest turnover at the end of each month. The story is true, and I can vouch for another example of how nervous his high standards can make some underlings. When one of his people had a heart attack and ended up in hospital, where his pulse was closely monitored, a witness who was there when Jimmy walked in to pay a friendly visit swears that the pulse rate shown on the machine nearly doubled. The felled employee later explained he felt guilty that he was caught resting instead of helping the Pattison Group meet sales quotas.

Paradoxically, while Pattison is very much a part of Vancouver society, he does not fit into the ambling geniality of the West Coast. He instead personifies the supercharged tenacity of a big-game hunter who seldom abandons his quarry. Allan Fotheringham once described him as ''a freckled little buzz-saw – he dresses like Nathan Detroit and thinks like J. Paul Getty.''

It's not so much that Jimmy doesn't indulge in any spare-time activities, it's that he doesn't indulge in any spare time. He belongs to three golf clubs, for example, but has played the game precisely three times since leaving university. His pride and joy (to the extent of having white broadloom in the engine room) is the eighty-five-foot luxury cruiser *Nova Spring*, yet during the first twenty-one months he owned the boat, he slept aboard only four nights. The only two-week holiday he scheduled during the 1970s lasted no more than five days before he took off from the Spanish seaside resort toward Zurich to negotiate the underwriting for one of his bigger coups.

He is the West Coast's premier deal-maker. Most used-car salesmen are born with silver tongues. Jimmy's is platinum.

—1986

Edgar Kaiser

WHEN HE LANDED on February 22, 1988, at Vancouver International Airport, forty-seven hours, forty-three minutes, and twenty-six seconds after he had left the same point to fly around the world, Edgar Kaiser had jetted 23,414 miles and set nine new speed records for the size of aircraft (a British-built Aerospace 800) that he and his two co-pilots had been flying. As a result, he became the first owner-operator to set a round-the-world record since Howard Hughes did it in July 1938.

One purpose of the journey was to collect funds for Kaiser's favourite philanthropy, the Kaiser Substance Abuse Foundation, which he and his wife, Judy, had set up just over two years earlier to help prevent drug abuse by the Pacific province's youngsters. More than $160,000 in pledges have been received for the flight, but immediately after he returned Kaiser was more interested in its psychological implications. "The real issue is less raising money than raising people's consciousness," he told me. "If the kids we're trying to reach with our program can visualize a middle-aged top gun going around the world and all that neat stuff, they know what can be done by staying healthy and not getting on drugs. That's really what made the trip important."

Kaiser thrives on creative philanthropy. He has already put more than three million dollars into the foundation to "confront the collective denial" of alcoholism and misuse of drugs by British Columbia's adolescents. The focus is on prevention. "At the rehabilitation stage," Kaiser declared, "helping means rebuilding; it's bricks, mortar, and lost time for those in therapy. That's the high-cost way to deal with the problem. If you explain about drugs and alcohol abuse in the context of an established value system, particularly as part of the regular curriculum – that's the efficient way to go.''

The foundation's main project at the moment is to help develop and establish a drug education program in British Columbia's primary schools from kindergarten to Grade 7 by the fall of 1989. Said Ross Ramsay, the professional addiction expert hired to run the foundation: ''We believe prevention efforts should be focused on people, not on substances. The emphasis must be on people's empowerment and freedom, not on their disabilities and addictions.'' British Columbia should be fertile territory for the Kaiser mission: a 1982 survey showed that of the province's youngsters aged fourteen and under, 58 per cent had smoked, 57 per cent had drunk alcohol, 28 per cent had used cannabis, 21 per cent had inhaled glue, 7 per cent had tried cocaine, and 2 per cent had used heroin.

Kaiser is a rare bird, even among the high-flying acquisitors who roost on Canada's Pacific coast. The son and grandson of moneyed U.S. aristocrats (the Kaisers owned major steel, coal, and aluminum interests and built many of the U.S. Second World War Liberty ships), he took out his Canadian citizenship in 1980 and has since turned over at least two fortunes in various resource ventures. Edgar rarely involves himself in projects that do not link his affinity for physical adventure with his propensity for risk. He is one of those rare derring-do entrepreneurs who believe that a man reduces himself by backing away from any challenge – even if it is self-imposed. ''I realize that my round-the-world trip wouldn't have much appeal to someone like the chief executive officer of General Electric,'' he told me just after he landed, ''but it does appeal to the kids I am trying to reach as an adventure they can identify with.''

Kaiser works hard and plays hard. The round-the-world air race was only the latest of his exploits. He is a championship skier and sailor and an accomplished guitarist, and he recently piloted his own yacht, the *Calliope*, up the Amazon. (The vessel's communications equipment is so sophisticated that it has its own area code.)

On the business side of his ledger, Kaiser has been investing in such leading-edge enterprises as fish farms and the marketing of glacier ice – said to make drinks more exotic. The company in which he owns a key interest, Aquarius Sea Farms, will hit the market with 650 tons of cultivated salmon, shipped live and destined for luxury restaurants in Canada and the United States. With eleven farms, it is already the largest integrated fish producer in the country, but Kaiser's imagination does not stop there. He says he is convinced that careful development of the industry could turn the Pacific province into the world's best pleasure-fishing destination. "I can visualize the international chains putting huge hotels into Campbell River, for example," he said, referring to a mid-size fishing mecca on Vancouver Island's east coast, "with a full-scale jet strip to accommodate Americans and Japanese coming by the ton-loads to enjoy the sport."

Kaiser's core staff of twenty, including an adroit financial expert named John Thomas, has agreed to purchase up to 12 per cent of Ice Age Incorporated, a company pledged to exporting "the Perrier of glacial ice" from northern British Columbia, as well as one million shares of Allure Industries Corporation, which recycles hazardous wastes. The latest recruit is Terence Heenan, the former president of British Columbia Telephone Company, who has been hired to organize Kaiser's new merchant banking venture.

That takes a lot of guts, considering Edgar's last, abortive swing at banking as chairman of the Bank of British Columbia. When Kaiser took over, the institution was suffering from serious internal squabbles, with its chairman and president communicating only through memos, besides the fall-out of the recession that was draining its treasury by a net outflow of about ten million dollars a month. Independent experts believe that it was within three weeks of collapse because unlike most Canadian banks that are leveraged twenty or twenty-five to one, it had a loans/assets ratio two or three times as high.

Kaiser moved in like a tank, writing off most of the bad loans in one swoop by selling them to the Singer family in Calgary at a discounted rate – having obtained Ottawa's permission for such an unorthodox bail-out tactic. To get some equity flowing into the bank again in a hurry, he did not wait to go through the long and cumbersome process of selling a public issue. Instead, he got on the phone and in ten days had convinced moneyed friends to invest seventy-two million dollars (at six dollars each for treasury shares) and bought a million dollars' worth himself. That was eventually followed by an eighty-one-million-dollar public issue, with Kaiser acquiring another 200,000 shares. Within three months the bank was in the black, its more than fifteen thousand shareholders were a happy lot, and many Pacific coast customers responded with a vote of confidence by leaving their funds on deposit with the bank. The path from that temporary euphoria led straight down, and much of it was the result of plain bad luck. "For everything in life," confessed Kaiser, "you need a little bit of luck, and we just didn't get it. Nobody could have projected the bankruptcies of the Canadian Commercial and Northland banks and especially the way they were handled. That really hit us. That and the internal debate that began on the future of the smaller banks, which eventually turned off our interbank funding. No one could have predicted the bottom falling out of oil prices, which affected so many of our customers, the decline in the value of the Canadian dollar, and the subsequent rise in interest-rate spreads. It was all these factors compounding at once that really hurt us."

The final blow, according to Kaiser, came when he was desperately looking for some solid endorsement from the Western provinces by having them commit token funds to his bank, and everyone agreed it was a great idea; but not one of them actually did it. "If British Columbia had declared, 'Okay, this is a local bank, we're buying 5 per cent of the equity' – that would have been it. All the negative speculation would have stopped," said Kaiser.

"Also, we needed the confidence of Bay Street and particularly the Big Five banks, and because I knew I would not be accepted as a member of the club, we hired some of the best bankers available: Dale Parker of the Montreal as our president and George Hare of the Scotia as our vice-chairman. With two of their own here, I expected more support, but it was never forthcoming."

The harassment of the Big Five was never very subtle. A fifty-thousand-dollar letter of credit drawn on the Bank of British Columbia was conspicuously not honoured, and when inspectors brought in by the Big Five gave the B.C. bank a clean bill of fiscal health after the Canadian Commercial Bank fiasco, not one of them made the fact known publicly. "It was not any decline in our retail base but the difficulties we had in interbanking funding that caused our liquidity problem," said Kaiser. That and some large loans that turned sour, particularly the $100 million divided between Peter Paul Saunders's faltering Versatile Corporation and Pangea Petroleum in Calgary.

Those loans, combined with an exaggerated report on CBC TV about the bank's problems, made the situation untenable, and Kaiser started to look for buyers.

The low point in those negotiations came during a session with federal deputy minister of finance Stanley Hartt, who, according to a witness at the meeting, turned to Kaiser and taunted him with the remark, "You're a rich American, why don't you just put more money in the bank?"

At the end of our talk, I asked Kaiser, "Wouldn't it have been better for Ottawa to take that $200 million it gave to the Bank of Hongkong and give it to the Bank of British Columbia, which would have been enough to save it?"

"There are those," replied Kaiser, with not a trace of humour in his voice, "who say that."

—1988

Harrison McCain

REGIONAL REACTION TO FREE TRADE with the United States is fairly predictable: the West wants it; Ontario doesn't. But what's the word from the Maritimes, specifically from the region's most successful international entrepreneur, Harrison McCain?

"Enhanced trade and guaranteed access – that's what we want," he thunders. "My basic complaint is that some economists claim free trade between Canada and the United States should be based on some magic fifty-fifty formula. That certainly wouldn't work for Canadian agriculture – or manufacturing, for that matter. Even if you forget about the conventional-wisdom issues, like the economies of scale, the Americans have enormous climatic advantages and cheaper transportation costs. So when they claim that fifty-fifty is a fair deal, it damn well is not."

McCain, who exports to twenty-six countries and manufactures in seven, wants Ottawa to negotiate free trade in specific sectors so that Canadian farmers, fishermen, and manufacturers would not only gain access to the larger arena but be guaranteed a share of the expanded market as well. This would amount to negotiating a series of auto pacts involving various industrial groupings and commodities.

Not unnaturally, McCain is concerned about agriculture in general and spuds in particular. "Agriculture in this country, but not theirs, is run by marketing boards," he points out. That helps make the price of Minnesota cheese, for example, just a fraction of what it is in Ontario. Under free trade our farmers couldn't stand the competition, and any government that accepted the closing up of important parts of Canadian agriculture would not stay in power very long.

Engrossed with potatoes, McCain believes the Americans would swamp Western Canada with cheaper brands because many farms in Washington State, for instance, enjoy two and a half times the productivity of Alberta or Manitoba fields. Much of the land is more fertile, it is serviced by sophisticated irrigation systems, and the area has a longer growing season.

"Peter Lougheed displayed a very cavalier approach about free trade," accuses McCain. "He promised more jobs for Ontario as a result of growth in Alberta and conveniently overlooked the flow of manufactured goods that would flood into Ontario. I'm an internationalist by nature, but this carte-blanche approach is not fair. Anyone following it would be making a tragic mistake." McCain is particularly concerned that so much industrial capacity in the northern United States is underemployed because manufacturing expansion has largely been transferred to the American Sunbelt. Under a free trade arrangement U.S. manufacturers would redeploy their production into these underused facilities, allowing them to compete even more fiercely in the Canadian market.

McCain does not hide his disappointment in Brian Mulroney: "He's probably a pretty good fellow, but whenever he speaks all I hear is a great deal of verbosity. Why the hell doesn't he just spit out what he intends to say? Trudeau went too far the other way, but I admired that. You have to take your chances – spit it out, and get it over with."

The Fries King believes that the true wealth of any country is the educational level of its citizenry. "My idea of an educated man," he says, "is one who is not worried about problems; he just says, 'Where are the books?' " He is baffled that despite the high quality of Canadian schools and universities and the fact that many graduates have drifted into business there are "so damn few doers."

McCain certainly qualifies as a "doer" himself. Along with his three brothers and two sisters, in 1953 he inherited a modest seed-potato business that has since become one of Canada's most successful international businesses.

This summer, without any public announcement, McCain Foods Limited – still privately owned by the family – passed the one-billion-dollar sales mark. The company now employs seven thousand people in twenty-eight factories on three continents and is rapidly diversifying out of its original french fries lines. In 1981 McCain purchased a large Toronto-based orange juice company from Daniel K. Ludwig, the New York recluse believed to be the world's richest man. He has also bought three cheese plants in rural Ontario with which he intends to challenge the American cheese giant, Kraft Incorporated. He believes that his company's strength is based on brand loyalty. "McCain is established and has good brand acceptance in Canada, Australia, Germany, and England," he says. "Brand loyalty is not widely understood outside the food business. It doesn't show on the balance sheet, but it is the company's most valuable asset."

Harrison spends at least 150 nights a year on the road, and his private jet must be the only aircraft in the world that files a flight plan from Florenceville, N.B., to Amsterdam. McCain was recently sitting in a commercial jet beside an executive of International Telephone & Telegraph, detailing the scope of his operations. The big wheel from ITT asked how many layers of executives the New Brunswicker employed at his international headquarters. Harrison offered to bet a bottle of champagne if he could guess.

Figuring that McCain was too self-confident to share much decision-making and so probably ran a lean shop, the ITT man estimated that a staff of forty might be just enough to run the billion-dollar empire. "I work at it part time, so does my brother," McCain shot back, "and that's our total international staff."

What this country needs – instead of free trade with the United States – is a platoon of Harrison McCains.

—1985

125

PART THREE

Power Politics

Farewell to The Chief

THE INDELICACY OF A POLITICIAN'S lingering on when he is no longer needed eventually becomes a kind of crazy proof of his importance. The Diefenbaker years are long gone in Canadian history. Yet their hero survives, defying the odds, pleading for salvation.

The first volume of his memoirs lifts a burden from John Diefenbaker's critics. It is no longer necessary to satirize his rages and caricature his crusades. He does the job too well himself. Here is The Chief, come down from Prince Albert to avenge himself on his vilifiers and set history straight. Like some giant magpie with quivering beak and glittery, glittery eyes, he produces from his nest of ancient grievances a jumble of remembered faces and old hatreds. ("Prime Minister King did not like me. I presume it was because I took a particular interest in him." Or again, in writing of Jimmy Gardiner, Mackenzie King's Prairie lieutenant: "In time I became the object of his destruction. No candidate running against me ever found himself lacking any necessary assistance.")

This important book chronicles in exquisite detail Diefenbaker's every failure. He was defeated in five elections, running for every available office including the mayoralty of Prince Albert in 1933. Each setback drove him on. Filled with visions of self-destiny, he became a street singer in the corridors of power. It was only while campaigning in the rural West that Diefenbaker's dreams touched reality. There he could give tongue to his monumental sense of affront, damning the adjudicators of the great power blocs, those midnight philosophers peering down from their Toronto penthouses who dismissed him as some sort of unfathomable electoral accident – a political troubadour who had to be silenced.

Diefenbaker's politics are defined by this volume not as the advancement of any set of identifiable policies but as a series of pageants meant to hurl defiance at these forces of darkness who sought his downfall. Always the outsider, he thrived on rejection. After being defeated at the 1948 Tory leadership convention by George Drew, he notes: "On the night of Drew's victory, I went up to his suite in the Chateau Laurier. They were celebrating. I was an intruder. I went to congratulate him. I walked into that gathering and it was as if an animal not customarily admitted to homes had suddenly entered the place."

All that loneliness, all that contempt simmering in the smithy of his soul made him a lousy prime minister. He never enjoyed exercising power half so much as pursuing it and, once ensconced in office, turned himself into a political kamikaze without a parachute.

Through Diefenbaker's long career and longer lifetime, it has always been possible to admire the man's instincts without respecting his performance, to be in awe of the spirit that took him so much farther than most politicians who started with a great deal more. Even if he finally reduced his unprecedented parliamentary majority of 1958 to a rump, he brought to Canadian politics a rare sense of courage and compassion.

His memoirs are written with all the unrestrained candour of old men and small boys who know the secrets of the dark. John Diefenbaker has found a worthy subject for his autobiography.

—1978

❄   ❄   ❄

It's an hour before closing time and the Princess Café, a fluorescent-lit Chinese and Canadian food emporium on Prince Albert's Central Avenue, is nearly empty. A truck driver with a crewcut and knotty, walnut skin is talking to a kid in a Hawaiian shirt. In one corner sit three Indians with closed faces, not saying anything, just sipping giant

Cokes, and in their silence you feel as though the fumes of their loneliness were leaking out of them.

The kid is talking politics. "I'm for Dief. He don't care about agreeing with nobody. He's his own man."

The truck driver leans into his coffee. "Yeah," he says. "Show John the grain, and he'll go against it."

IT IS TUESDAY NIGHT of the week before polling day, and his tiny retinue of handlers is nervous. It is the last rally of John Diefenbaker's last campaign. Will the old man fill the hall, even with Peter Lougheed being flown in for the occasion from Edmonton? Can he hold his audience's attention? Will he use the meeting for one final, bitter assault on everyone in sight? Can he be trusted?

By eight o'clock nearly four hundred supporters have filled the chairs and suddenly, marching in behind a piper and the Alberta premier, comes The Chief. He looks like a slightly comatose veteran of the Boer War, but he can still change the temperature of any hall he enters, even this plastic ballroom of the Sheraton Marlborough Hotel with its red ceiling and crematorium cheerfulness.

This is Diefenbaker as icon. Canadian history on the hoof.

Lougheed is all tact and heart in his introduction, careful not to upstage the ancient warrior's political swan song. There is a kind of forlorn elegance about the ex-prime minister, slumped on the platform, waiting his turn, trembling with age. But once he's up, the blood rushes into his limbs. His voice is strong, his manner confident, and, contrary to the fears of his stagers, he performs with style and grace.

"They say I'm too old," he bellows, mimicking his Liberal and NDP opponents. "I'll take those birds for a three-mile race any time . . . providing they first agree to an examination [*pause*] from the neck up!" (Asked later in private how he's really feeling, Diefenbaker's eyes twinkle as he confides: "Like a twenty-minute egg [*pause*], but the doctors scared the hell out of me. They said I was as sound as a dollar.")

He stands, right hand on hip, left forefinger pointing, the clipped participles and long, open vowel sounds lending his speech biblical cadence. His notes keep falling off the lectern, but it makes not the slightest difference. His train of thought seldom survives more than a sentence. (''Where is Canada going? My friends, I never had a family. The one thing denied me.'') The galloping non sequiturs and fractured metaphors are aimed mostly at Pierre Trudeau.

He blames Canada's horrendous inflation rate directly on the Liberal leader's extravagances in refurbishing his official summer residence at Harrington Lake. (''When I was prime minister, we spent twenty-five dollars a year. Olive made the curtains.'') He goes on to accuse Trudeau of approving secret loans to Idi Amin, showing little respect for the Commons (''Parliament is but a memory''), and being arrogant (''if Trudeau goes back, Canada ends'').

The exaggerations grow tiresome, but his timing remains perfect. ''There is nothing,'' Diefenbaker drops his voice to confess, ''nothing more lonely than being a former prime minister. Being the only one . . .'' The long pause reduces the room to hushed reverence. Then comes the punchline: ''But after next Tuesday night, I'll have company!'' The good, windblown faces in the audience crack up, and one finely coiffed Baptist matron in front of me laughs so hard her hairpins pop out.

The electricity flows through his listeners. Other parts of Canada might be a political graveyard or minefield for him, but here they still love the old Chief. This is Diefenbaker Country, and will be long after he's gone.

His performance grows boring only when he insists on reeling off an endless litany of his past manifestations of courage, almost back to the time he didn't flinch when he was getting a smallpox vaccination in grade school. The speech unrolls for fifty minutes, like some wild, finger-painted fresco. The climax comes when Diefenbaker recites the moving coda from his Bill of Rights.

There isn't a dry eye in the house.

AT EIGHTY-THREE, DIEFENBAKER retains two ambitions: to plant Prince Albert's Diamond Jubilee flag at the North Pole and to outlast Sir Wilfrid Laurier's forty-five-year record as a sitting MP.

In private, he is quietly preparing the pageant of his passing. He has set $100,000 aside for a home for disadvantaged children in Prince Albert to be named after Olive, but his main preoccupation is with the details of his burial. After a state funeral in Ottawa, John Diefenbak-

132

er's remains will be carried across the country to Saskatoon aboard a special, slow-moving train ("just like Churchill's"). Unyielding beyond the end, he has drafted one very specific provision for the ceremony: his casket is to be draped with the Red Ensign that he fought so hard to preserve as the flag of the country he loves.

—1979

❋　❋　❋

IT WAS EASY ENOUGH to make fun of him and caricature his crusades. But it was the stride and stance of the man – his sheer guts: the brew of his laughter and the dint of his compassion were the qualities that made John Diefenbaker, dead at eighty-four, a politician apart. Like P.G. Wodehouse's fictional butler, Jeeves, he entered any room "as a procession of one."

Although Diefenbaker seldom stopped talking about himself, his essence remained a mysterious mixture of vanity and charm, vulnerability and brass, outrage and mischief. He single-handedly transformed Canadian politics into the country's leading spectator sport.

The dilemma of most Canadian politicians is how to stress the marginal differences between themselves and their rivals so that they can conceal their basic similarities. Diefenbaker's problem was exactly the opposite: how to place enough restraints on his combative nature so that he would sound more like his electable and less individualistic contemporaries. Even in his declining years, he remained a political giant ambling on his knees in a land of midgets.

Most leaders find themselves in conflict with their times either because they remain reactionaries who try to resurrect the past or because they attempt to become visionaries and find their aim exceeds their grasp. Diefenbaker suffered the rare distinction of being both. His intellect was frozen in another time; his heart was an open city.

He was born only four years after Sir John A. Macdonald's death; his life spanned Canada's modern history. He could draw on memories of times when Red River carts still creaked along the Carlton Trail and buffalo bones littered the prairies. During a 1962 campaign stop at Melville, Saskatchewan, I happened to be standing behind him as he asked a group of oldtimers in what year they had come West. When the eldest replied, "April of 1903," a delighted Diefenbaker shot back, "We came in August!"

No Canadian politician ever rose so steadily through a succession of defeats. He was soundly beaten in five election campaigns before finally squeaking into the House of Commons as a member of the Conservative Opposition in 1940.

He won many converts on his endless circuit of speech-making across the country, but inside the Conservative party hierarchy he was dismissed as "the Bolshevist from the West." At the same time, the Liberals harassed him by redistributing his seat out of existence and even descended to the petty ploy of converting the house next to his Prince Albert home into an interim residence for unwed Indian mothers. But Diefenbaker knew how to wait, and he had a nose for power. In 1956 he fooled the pundits by capturing the Tory leadership and the following year managed to win a minority mandate.

Elections savage a man's pride and poise, but Diefenbaker loved to campaign. In 1958, he decided to transform himself into an incarnation of the Canada he knew. The asylums are full of people who imagine themselves to be Napoleon – or Jesus Christ – but Diefenbaker persisted in his identification, becoming a personification of the national will for whom all things were possible. Trumpeting his "Vision" of Northern development, he went on a charismatic rampage that made his audiences quiver. They cheered every time he paused for breath. When he stood bareheaded in the rain addressing a small outdoor crowd at Penticton, B.C., I watched some of his listeners deliberately closing their umbrellas. In Fredericton, a crush of swooning women held their children up to touch him. When Ed Morris, then a Conservative candidate in Halifax, was introducing the PC leader, he began by saying: "My friends, what shall we say of this great man?" A voice from the back rows caroled out: "Dear John . . . Dear John." Morris bowed his head. "Yes," he intoned. "We may as well say, Dear John . . . ." Two thousand men and women stood up to roar their approval. (Not everybody got his signals right. At a ceremony in West Vancouver's Park Royal, an Indian chief called Mathias Joe presented a walking stick to the PM with the tribute: "John Diefenbacon, you're the thunderbird of our country.")

On election night Diefenbaker won 208 seats, wiping out the Liberals in six provinces. It was the largest mandate ever given a Canadian prime minister. Even if his French couldn't get him past a Berlitz receptionist, Quebec accorded him 62 per cent of its votes – just one point behind true-blue Ontario.

In the golden months that followed, Diefenbaker acted less like a politician than a force of nature. During a Commons question period on July 2, 1958, when he was asked by Hazen Argue (then of the CCF) what his government intended to do about drought on the prairies, Diefenbaker matter-of-factly replied, "Yesterday and also the day before when I was in Brandon, several localities received rain for the first time." A couple of Liberal back-benchers giggled nervously. But to most members of Parliament it seemed only mildly ludicrous that this all-powerful leader could order water down from the sky.

He took office just short of sixty-two, too late to erase the habits of all those lonely years as a struggling defence attorney in the tomorrow country of northern Saskatchewan. His magnificent victory at the polls condemned him to a permanent sense of anticlimax; he interpreted the people's acclaim as adequate proof of his greatness and became intoxicated with the trappings rather than the substance of his office. In a sense, it was not power but the absence of power that had corrupted him. He had spent thirty-seven years in the political wilderness, denied what he felt to be his rightful place. All that apartness, all that contempt, simmered up to dominate his every act.

His government initiated many enlightened measures, but as PM he remained preoccupied with settling old scores. He never absolved anyone from the slightest rebuff. On April 4, 1967, when the Liberals announced that they had named former Conservative House Speaker Roland Michener to be Canada's twentieth governor general, Diefenbaker alone failed to applaud the appointment – because Michener had ruled him out of order during a procedural wrangle eight years earlier.

Before he became prime minister, Diefenbaker had heard his party vilified so often for being too cautious that, once in power, he indulged freely in populist radicalism, which was his natural instinct. His conviction – born in Saskatchewan during the droughts of the Thirties – that the economically underprivileged can help themselves only through collective political action found its expression in his concept of social justice, based on the commendable notion that every Canadian has the right to expect equality of opportunity. During six years in office his administration spent almost as much money as all governments between Confederation and 1946 combined (including the cost of two world wars) in a wild jumble of programs designed to help develop the North and assist farmers, fishermen, and other low-income groups.

Afloat on a sea of generous impulses, Diefenbaker seldom understood the details of his own policies. In the 1965 campaign, for example, his party strategists worked out an elaborate scheme for allowing some urban house owners to deduct municipal assessments from federal income tax. Diefenbaker tried vainly to explain what it was all about until he gave up in Winnipeg by lamely conceding he thought his plan "might be limited to home-occupied houses."

Instead of advancing any set of identifiable principles, his brand of politics turned out to be little more than a drawn-out sequence of morality plays staged to combat imagined forces threatening his downfall. Whether his audience filled a tiny Legion hall in northern Saskatchewan or an auditorium at one of the thirty-five universities that granted him honorary degrees, he used every public occasion to hurl defiance at the nameless adjudicators of Canadian society's great power blocs. He thus caught himself in his own trap of demanding to be loved for the enemies he had made.

He was at his best among his own people on the prairies and campaigned on every conceivable occasion, whether there happened to be an election in the offing or not.

IT WAS DIEFENBAKER'S EYES that were his saving grace, acting as jovial monitors of his innermost emotions, mocking the pomposity of his own performances. But at his nightly rallies he would turn on his audiences like some medieval necromancer dispensing rhetorical fire. With an energy born of gloating, he would dance out his joy at the wickedness of his political opponents. When he accused the Liberals of "shedding tears of falsehood," his audiences knew what he meant, and when he confessed that his errors as prime minister were "mistakes of the heart," they rushed to forgive him. He was the champion of every boy who ever had a pimple, the candidate of every woman sustained by romantic visions of deliverance from humdrum realities.

His language was a splendid artifice, the words fanfaring his message in the cadence of Southern camp meetings, where the language of exhortation, graceless by choice, takes the place of logical discourse. "Join with me," he would plead, "join with me to catch the vision of men and women who rise above these things that ordinarily hold you to the soil. Join with me to bring about the achievement of that Canada, one Canada, the achievement of Canada's destiny!"

Like most self-made men, he worshipped his creator. During the Brantford, Ontario, rally that wound up his 1963 campaign, he clarified once and for all just exactly how he obtained his best advice: "I ask myself, 'Is a thing right?' And if it is, I do it."

To identify not only his audience but also himself with the aspirations of the "average Canadian," Diefenbaker tried to ally his own past with every part of the country. That never sounded more preposterous than in a Halifax speech when he established his family contact with the Atlantic port by earnestly proclaiming: "Had it not been for the trade winds between here and Newfoundland, my great-great-grandmother would have been born in Halifax."

But all that thunder had little to do with the art of governing the country, and gradually it became clear that Diefenbaker viewed legislation more as a posture than a process; his government never demonstrated any clear purpose except to retain power. His administration's final collapse in 1963 (with seventeen ministers leaving through various exits during its last ten months) was like the ruin of some great papier-mâché temple built for a Hollywood spectacular when the rains come down and wash the whole Technicolor mess into the sea. By the time Diefenbaker had lost his last election as leader in 1965, his once-great Conservative party had been hived into a coalition of the discontented and the dispossessed, with only one Tory MP surviving in the fifty constituencies of Canada's three largest cities.

Politics is a process of elimination. But John Diefenbaker refused to be eliminated.

In the last decade of his life he moved off into a private world, becoming a figment of his own imagination, the starved topography of his face illuminating the nation's TV screens as he gloomed about whatever was happening at the time. But occasionally the humour still bubbled up, as in the joke he would tell his Prince Albert cronies about Pierre Trudeau's swimming pool: "He's a great swimmer; a great athlete. But just after construction finished he got stuck on some of the underwater furniture. Standing alongside, looking down at him, was a chap with a sign of LIFEGUARD on his hat. Trudeau finally got out and said, 'Aren't you the lifeguard here? Why didn't you help me?'

"He replied, 'I can't swim.'

"Trudeau then asked him: 'How the griggins did you get the appointment?'

"He said, 'I want you to understand I'm bilingual!' ''

Diefenbaker's partisan fevers never subsided. In the fall of 1971, he was suddenly taken ill during a visit to Wales, and Trudeau extended the courtesy of sending a government jet to bring him home. The ex-prime minister was loaded aboard on a stretcher, but during the journey the attending doctor filled him with six pints of blood and enough iron pills so that by the time the plane landed in Ottawa he was able to stride down the ramp. He immediately called a press conference to attack the Liberals' overspending habits – especially their pernicious use of government planes for private trips.

Through John Diefenbaker's long career and longer lifetime it was always possible to admire the man's instincts without respecting his performance. His was the most primitive of partisanships, but he shattered textbookfuls of Canadian political traditions: the idea that the Conservative party was an instrument of Toronto's Bay Street; the long-accepted convention that political leaders in this country should talk grey and act neutral; the very notion that prime ministers must lick the velvet hand of the Canadian Establishment.

When a great man dies, some promise of a country's life is buried with him. That sentiment was most dramatically caught in the terse obituary haughtily declaimed over French national television in 1970 by Prime Minister Georges Pompidou: "General de Gaulle is dead. France is a widow."

Canada may not be widowed, but we are no less bereaved. John George Diefenbaker's passing begs to be taken more as a symbol than an event. We mourn his death as we might grieve for the loss of our own youth, for a way we were and can never be again.

WHEN I FIRST HEARD OF JOHN DIEFENBAKER'S wish that his body be carried by train across the country he loved, I had two strong reactions. The first was to recall a phrase from the official program of Sir Winston Churchill's funeral, designating how his body should travel on a funeral barge along the Thames "with the pomp of waters unwithstood." Somehow, that description fitted perfectly The Chief's own final journey as his unrepentant remains were borne from Ottawa to Saskatoon.

My second reaction was to relive the five elections I had covered from aboard the Diefenbaker train, tumbling through the night of time in a press car filled with the noise of tapping typewriters and tinkling glasses. I particularly remember the 1965 campaign, when we all knew he couldn't win, but Diefenbaker kept searching for some totem to further his fortunes. When a supporter in Richmond Hill, Ontario, gave The Chief a canary, he spent hours coaxing the bird to sing, convinced that this was the omen he had been waiting for. The bird just sat there staring back at him. But a week before polling day, when Diefenbaker's back was turned, a railway steward took pity on him and did a passable canary imitation. The Chief got very excited, and the incident noticeably boosted his energies for the final push.

John Diefenbaker was at his best moving through the knots of Prairie farmers who turned out everywhere to greet him, looking into men's eyes and women's feelings, absorbing their sense of shared loneliness, the fear of living at the margin of things. Out there among his own people, The Chief became the breathing reminder of a simpler age when God was alive and one man's courage could still change history.

At Stettler, Alberta, two raggedy kids were holding up a huge hand-painted cardboard sign with the letters "DEIF FOR CHEIF." At Swift Current, Saskatchewan, twenty blue-gowned ladies on the back of a truck broke into "Land of Hope and Glory" and sang "Mademoiselle from Armentières" for an encore.

At Taber, Alberta, Diefenbaker told an audience of hushed school-children: "I only wish that I could come back when you're my age to see the kind of Canada that you'll see. So dream your dreams; keep them and pursue them."

When we stopped briefly at Morse, Saskatchewan, a local band of musicians was out on the platform, serenading Diefenbaker with their ragged version of "The Thunderer." None of us could file our stories because the telegrapher was playing the drums.

Later that day an old man sat by the tracks and, as The Chief's train rattled by, held up a homemade sign in the twilight that read: "JOHN, YOU'LL NEVER DIE."

He was right.

—1979

Mike Pearson's Quest

H E WAS A GOOD MAN in a wicked time.
Lester Bowles Pearson, who died in Ottawa, was a rare human being among the diplomat-politicians whose decisions shape our lives. Although he spent a long career having to react to the exigencies of the moment, he never allowed his basic instinct for decency to be subverted.

He is gone, but we are still living under a world order that he, more than any other Canadian, helped to create. No matter how ramshackle, Pearson's initiatives have at least avoided another major conflict for more than a quarter of a century.

Pearson's lifelong quest for peace abroad and unity at home produced neither, but he did as much as any man could to bring us closer to these ideals and became a model against which we can assess our collective future. The quality that stood out in everything Pearson did never changed. Whether he was engaged in hushed bargaining with world statesmen or addressing a rowdy meeting of bush workers in the Algoma East constituency he loved, he never for an instant pretended to know the answers to the intractable and ambiguous problems of his time.

He was simply a man bent on trying to get the questions straight. It is this honesty of approach that will be missed most by those who knew him, however slightly. That and the warmth of his wit. It was no accident that the most memorable aspect of the Pearson style was a wry, self-deprecating sense of humour that flourished under stress. A politician, like a clergyman, is wise not to jest too freely about his vocation, but Pearson could make his puns work for him, both as a way of puncturing his opponents' rages and as a means of maintaining his own equilibrium.

During a question-and-answer period at a Canadian University Liberal Federation convention held in Ottawa on February 2, 1967, he told a story to illustrate the point. It was about the Indian fighter who crawled into a frontier fort with three arrows in his back and was asked whether it hurt. "Only when I laugh," he replied.

"My job," Pearson added, "only hurts when I don't laugh."

Even when he already knew he had the cancer that would eventually kill him, his humour somehow remained unaffected. On October 17, 1972, when Pierre Trudeau staged a mammoth election rally at Maple Leaf Gardens, he asked Pearson to boost his sagging fortunes by making a brief guest appearance. The same day, Trudeau had announced one of his so-called election goodies for Toronto – a thirty-million-dollar waterfront park. In the first draft of his speech, which he later decided not to use, Pearson planned to come on stage and say: "Good evening, ladies and gentlemen. I'm your election goodie for tonight."

Despite his lightheartedness, Pearson's apparent detachment resulted not from the fact that he cared too little but because he cared too much and found it was only through jokes that he could compose himself for a world filled with disorder and anguish. He was probably the first man to serve as prime minister of Canada whose public and private personalities were one and the same. The reason he appeared to stir so little passion in the four general elections he fought as leader was that there was about him an air of reserve, a basic shyness that prevented him from invading other people's privacy or compromising his own dignity. During one campaign tour of Toronto, at a time when unemployment was the main issue, his cavalcade happened to halt in front of a lineup of jobless men outside a Salvation Army hostel. "Come on in, Mike, the soup's fine," one of them yelled.

But Pearson refused to get out of the car, even though his advisers begged him to have his picture taken with the group. "No," he said. "I won't exploit their misery for political purposes."

He acted always within the consciousness of his own limitations and the voters' awareness of them. One of his senior aides remembers taking the draft of a speech to his residence where, to his horror, the

Pearsons' poodle started to play with it. When he tried to rescue the manuscript, Pearson waved him away with the comment, "Oh, let him have it; he'll have more fun with it than I will."

A study of Lester Pearson's life reveals less the making of one individual than the evolution of a procession of men – the soldier, the historian, the bureaucrat, the diplomat, the politician – all favourites of fortune. His abnormally normal existence – which saw him rise from the obscurity of a manse in the Ontario heartland and his first job as a sausage stuffer in Hamilton to the Nobel Peace Prize and the prime minister's office – was elevated into something of a charmed life by a combination of his own sheer likableness and circumstances conspiring to push him ahead at every turning point.

Canada is still a nation close to the land, and Pearson's roots always remained in the small towns where he grew up. There was little introspection and no gloom in him. ("Always be kind and understanding to the people you pass on the way up," he wrote in the first volume of his memoirs published last year.) It was this quality that made him such an appealing (and successful) diplomat. During the nine years he spent as Canada's secretary of state for external affairs, he took the striped pants and frown out of our foreign policy and replaced them with a tilted, polka-dot bow tie and a small-town-Ontario grin on a face as comforting as a bowl of apple butter.

In the loosely organized postwar world, Pearson's unflappability and flair for constructive conciliation earned him nearly every honour the diplomatic community could bestow, including the council chairmanship of the North Atlantic Treaty Organization (1951–52) and the presidency of the United Nations Assembly (1952–53). Walter Lippmann wrote that Pearson "incarnates the hope of building a true community of the Atlantic peoples." Gunnar Jahn, chairman of the Nobel Prize committee, declared that at the time of the Suez crisis, Pearson had "saved the world."

Pearson emerged as the *beau ideal* of international statecraft. During that brief flowering of diplomacy between the innocent past when ambassadors still wore handkerchiefs up their sleeves and the darker present when presidents tape their conversations, LBP set an exuberant style all his own. Light on both feet and ready to move in any useful direction, he came to be regarded as an immensely capable talisman whose powers of positive negotiation kept the Cold War cold. He became the "honest broker," an eternal seeker of the middle ground, testing all of the infinite contingencies that might lead to a way out. He was not always successful, but his interventions somehow seemed to spark a progression of crises that precipitated their own solutions, like thunderclouds that send down the rain to clear a sultry day.

Always the rational man in an irrational world, forever trying to make the best out of a bad situation, Pearson epitomized the concepts of middle-powermanship, then the cornerstone of Canada's foreign policy. This approach allowed Canada to exercise an influence quite out of proportion to the country's real stature. At the same time, it found ready response at home because there was something in the national character of Canadians that clung to sweet reasonableness as the only possible posture in the face of the country's geographical, social, and economic problems.

Both as a diplomat and as a politician, Pearson heeded the private advice Mackenzie King had given him, on a train going to New York, in the late Thirties. "You may one day have some responsibility," King had told the youthful External officer. "I would just give you one bit of advice. Remember that in the course of human history far more has been accomplished for the welfare and progress of mankind in preventing bad actions than in doing good ones."

When he became prime minister, in the spring of 1963, Pearson never lost sight of the fact that the great movements of history hinge not on day-to-day triumphs or setbacks but on the conversion of ill-defined problems into great moral issues, and he tried to cast Canada's problem of French-English relations into such a context. His persuasive powers were not always adequate to match his performance with his intentions. But his gift of being able to soften collisions and smooth tempers and his unwillingness to draw drastic conclusions from the temporary tactics of his opponents became considerable assets in the struggle for national unity.

His stewardship as Canada's fourteenth prime minister was a mixture of triumphs and failures, though he did bring his party into power after the great Diefenbaker sweep of 1958, which had left the Liberals with forty-nine seats, the smallest parliamentary contingent since Confederation. His rivalry with John Diefenbaker grew during the ten years the two men faced each other across the Commons until it even extended to their leisure hours. They were both avid fishermen, but neither had much luck at Harrington Lake, the official summer residence of Canadian prime ministers. When Pearson moved in, he kept hearing rumours that the Prince Albert politician had caught a four-and-a-half-pound trout. Unable to match that record, Pearson insisted on tracking the story down to a local farmer and was delighted to discover that while Diefenbaker had indeed hooked such a fish, he had not managed to get it into his boat.

The Pearson years are probably best remembered as a time of some very inelegant fumbling in Ottawa's corridors of power. Part of this was due directly to Pearson's methods of governing. He was at his best in times of great stress when his diplomatic training let him under-react to the torrent of events threatening to engulf him. "We'll jump off that bridge when we come to it," he would airily say to nervous aides, as they fretted about the next catastrophe that could befall the government.

During the five turbulent years he presided over the Canadian government, there was constant speculation about Pearson's ideology. But the motives that chiefly guided him were disarmingly simple. They were as uncomplicated as the need to avoid a third world war and the necessity to preserve Canadian unity.

These sentiments were probably most warmly expressed in a personal note Pearson sent his daughter, Patricia, in 1954, when his grandson Paul was born. "A warm welcome to my little grandson," he wrote, "who by now no doubt has already expressed vocally his opinion of the world into which he has been ushered. We will have to work harder to make it a better one than it is now."

Mike Pearson loved going home to his northern rural riding of Algoma East and enjoyed reminiscing about his campaigns. There was the story of the farmer who made what must stand as the shortest political introduction on record: "I have been asked to introduce Mr. Pearson, who has been asked to speak to us. I have. He will." And a glimpse of the little boy with an I LIKE MIKE sign hung around his neck, a little uncertain about his instructions, who kept yelling, "I like Milk." A fond remembrance of the old lady who greeted him with the benediction: "God bless you, John Diefenbaker."

His fellow politicians are telling us that Mike Pearson will be missed. But they do not tell us why. One very good reason is that he was the quintessential Canadian, always speaking out honestly and with little self-interest about the realities of power in the contemporary world. He saw history not as an orderly succession of events but as an accumulation of tumbling paradoxes in the midst of which anything might happen. He regarded politics as having the formidable mission of trying to cope with the resultant chaos and saw himself as a creative improviser possessed of the capacity to put disappointments aside, place them in a new perspective, and move on. To shrug your shoulders and smile sometimes remained the only sane response to the preposterous incongruities of human existence.

The essence of Lester Pearson was caught in something Cesar Chavez, the California labour organizer, once said: "When we are honest with ourselves, we must admit that our lives are all that really belong to us. So it is how we use our lives that determines what kind of men we are."

It seems a fitting epitaph.

—1973

Joe Clark's Interregnum

HE STEALS INTO MY OFFICE like a wild fawn caught eating broccoli. His limbs arrange themselves into various tableaux of discomfort, the hazel eyes remain wary, and his composure betrays the studied confidence of the eternal "Big Tory on Campus." Joe Clark has come a-calling.

He is an easy man to caricature, yet it has become difficult not to take him seriously. Here is the constitutionally designated head of the country's alternative government, the man who may be one Goldfarb survey away from Pierre Trudeau's throne. Until recently, there was about him the uncertain aura of a politician being swept away in a sea of contradictions; now he is at last beginning to appear in charge of his own destiny.

Clark has managed to survive the cruellest tag ever to haunt a Canadian politician: the JOE WHO? headline coined by an anonymous *Toronto Star* deskman, as baffled as the rest of the country on the morning after his triumph over the Conservative party. Thirty-one months into his job, "Joe Who?" remains an open question. During his stewardship, at least twenty Tory MPs have deserted Clark's cause – many of them for the kind of patronage plums the Government party usually reserves for its own electoral casualties.

But he has become a man in motion, and for those who take the trouble to listen, his words make sense. Canada's current dilemma is not so much whether the Man from Yellowhead is adequate to his calling as whether anyone is equipped to govern a country that appears to be becoming ungovernable.

There is in traffic law a seldom-used doctrine holding that, other evidence to the contrary, the driver who has the "last clear chance" of avoiding an accident must be held responsible. With Quebec's impending referendum, an economy performing the fiscal miracle of both higher unemployment and double-digit inflation, and a dollar whose value threatens to equal that of late Czarist bonds, the man who wins the next election could well be exercising our "last clear chance" as a nation. Whether Joe Clark can master this awesome responsibility has yet to be established.

What bothered me most, after the couple of hours I spent with him recently, was that there is no existential dimension to his quest for political office, little gut yearning, and no visible sweat. There seems to be much in life still inaccessible to him, a litany of hard-earned truths he has failed to grasp. Joe Clark has yet to spend his apprenticeship in the anterooms of some personal hell – a handy training ground for any man who dares covet this nation's highest political office.

—1978

AS HE BECOMES Canada's sixteenth prime minister, Joe Clark can be accused of neither clairvoyance nor premature senility. He fought a clever campaign and demonstrated a refreshing disdain for the traditional sources of power in this country. He has successfully challenged the myth that only Liberals are endowed with the divine right to govern this large, troubled land. The cynics pouring out their premature scorn for the Conservatives are reminiscent of the doomsayers who maintained the Egyptians would never be able to operate the Suez Canal.

Governments are forged in the fires of practice, not in the intellectual vacuums of campaign rhetoric. And if Joe Clark's election seemed more of a letdown than an epiphany, it may be the fault of his style more than his intentions. Unlike his cruelly articulate opponent, Clark suffers from the gravest of political sins: his thoughts tend to come out raw and awkward, failing to communicate his inner convictions. It is as if his words were being formed by a cookie-cutter.

The two dozen major campaign pledges that accompany him into office are such a jumble of contradictions that Clark's stewardship could become a nightmare if he attempts to translate all of them into law. The central core of Joe Clark's problem is exactly the opposite of that of the politician on whom he has ideologically modelled himself: Jimmy Carter. The U.S. president was savaged by both his enemies and his former allies for running as a populist yet behaving in office as a conservative. Clark, who campaigned as a conservative, must govern as a populist.

Under the new distribution boundaries, the nature of the parliament and country placed in his charge has changed considerably from Pierre Trudeau's time. It was no electoral accident that on May 22 the prime ministerial seat was transferred from Mount Royal to Yellowhead. For the first time since Confederation, the Prairie Provinces and British Columbia occupy more seats in the Commons than does Quebec. The burgeoning political forces of the New West will demand as much attention as the deep-rooted aspirations of Quebec. At the same time, this is the most urban of parliaments, with 160 of the 282 newly designed seats representing Canada's sixteen largest cities and the traditional rural constituencies having shrunk to a mere four dozen.

Getting used to Joe Clark's absence of style will not be easy for a country run during more than a decade according to the soigné dictates of a prime minister who could concede political defeat with the grace and pride of Pierre Trudeau. Perhaps we should find comfort in a recent confession by Abba Eban, the former foreign minister of Israel: "My experience tells me that men and nations do behave wisely, once they have exhausted all other alternatives."

Even if he sometimes behaves like a reject from "The Gong Show," Joe Clark's the only prime minister we've got.

—1979

BEYOND THE PRESTIGE his office confers upon him, a prime minister depends for his effectiveness on the aura of authority that people deduce from his actions. Such perceptions are created as much by his imaginative policy initiatives as by his public demeanour, his style of rhetoric, selection of advisers, and approach to power.

Before Joe Clark was elected prime minister, the major concern about him seemed to be whether he would have the necessary heft – what the Romans called *gravitas*, the weightiness of character so essential in a man of public affairs. Because of his unspectacular but solid performances at the Tokyo economic summit and the Lusaka Commonwealth Conference, those doubts have been at least partially resolved. But the Man from Yellowhead has yet to place his personal stamp on the office he holds. So far, most of his ministers have done little more than perpetuate the policies of the Trudeau administration that only three months before they had been busy condemning.

Election declamations and campaign promises are not set in amber. But Canadians didn't necessarily elect a Conservative government merely to get rid of Pierre Trudeau. Joe Clark's win was a mandate for change. He himself recognizes this notion, even if he has yet to act upon it. At a ministerial meeting in Jasper, Clark admonished his cabinet, "Forget about your departments; we're here as people pledged to undertake certain changes."

That sentiment deserves to become the Clark administration's most urgent priority. Meanwhile, it has already become sadly evident that Clark committed a major political gaffe in dividing his cabinet into senior and junior ministers, with most of the authority exercised by the dozen insiders. The idea of an inner and outer cabinet was considered by all prime ministers preceding Clark and was rejected for the simple reason that it would have created more problems than advantages. Every prime minister develops his favourites, but it causes much less trouble to gather them in weekly informal lunches at 24 Sussex Drive than deliberately to create unequal rings of influence within the cabinet chamber.

Joe Clark has made a decent beginning. But he has yet to manifest the criterion by which history will judge him: the transcendence of a leader over the circumstances of his time.

—1979

150

THERE WAS A KIND of oldtime radio rhythm to Joe Clark's crucial speech at the Conservative convention in Winnipeg last week as he kept insisting that he is everything his scrapbooks claim him to be.

His cheeks made brave attempts to become jowls as he chewed his thoughts, calling on the tricks of a lifetime in politics to rescue him. The appeal didn't rouse the doubters because the speech – and the man making it – failed to comprehend what Canadian politics is all about. It is not, as Clark kept repeating, about such bunkum as "beating the Liberals" or "fulfilling Canada's destiny," whatever that is.

Political leadership in these frigid latitudes ultimately requires magic. It has to do with a party leader's capacity for filling his followers with enchantment, a sense of mission that goes beyond partisan name-calling: the leader's ability to turn himself into the embodiment of the nation he hopes to govern.

This, Joe Clark could never do.

He has, after all, been campaigning since the 1981 leadership review, stumping the country, making countless "do not reject this man" speeches about himself. Yet he has managed to raise his approval rating by a stunning half per cent.

All politicians are haunted, not by their enemies but by their former selves. It is seven years now since Joe Clark was chosen to lead the Conservatives into power. He did it, ending a sixteen-year streak of Liberal rule, only to be humbled back into Opposition by a combination of miscalculation and just plain stupidity. The memory of his brief fling in office is not that of a maker of decisions or dispenser of favours to power-starved Tories but of a frightened creature retreating from his own policy clinkers, such as moving the Canadian Embassy to Jerusalem and dismantling Petro-Canada.

Last week's convention demonstrated that Clark has come dangerously close to wearing out his welcome. Just as few TV comedians now have a viewing expectancy of more than a couple of seasons (though they could go on for twenty years on the vaudeville circuit), a politician must succeed or be replaced.

Clark's failure to impress the Conservative party was caused by some self-inflicted wounds. He suffered from poor intelligence from Quebec, listening to the discredited hacks left over from the Union Nationale era while ignoring the outriders of the new political army Brian Mulroney was mobilizing east of the Ottawa River. At the same time, Clark discarded too many of his former alliances. Of the five key organizers who had masterminded his original bid for the leadership in 1976, for example, only two (Harvie Andre and Jim Hawkes, who became MPs) were in Winnipeg. The others (the campaign's national co-chairman, Montreal lawyer Pierre Bouchard; Dave King, an Alberta Tory who is now Peter Lougheed's minister of education; and Ralph Hedlin, a Saskatchewan-born energy expert) weren't even invited.

Watching the Tory party in conclave was a sobering experience, even if the delegates themselves drank enough booze to pickle a pharaoh. They were all there: the bushy-tailed Mulroney people, with smiles on their faces and murder in their hearts; the defrocked zealots from the Age of Diefenbaker, worn out by years of political outrage; the prime-time guys who had jetted in from Toronto, scrutinizing Clark through slit eyes like pawnbrokers trying to calculate the downside risk of sticking by him; the charmers from British Columbia; and the heavy breathers from rural Saskatchewan and Alberta, sipping Styrofoam coffee out of Styrofoam cups, cursing a world they never made.

What these and other delegates had in common – what unites the Conservatives into a political movement – is that no true-blue Tory recognizes any statute of limitations in the party's internal feuds. Conservatives' hatreds for one another don't fade like sorrow or fizzle like anger. They just keep growing. It's not a new phenomenon. Between 1887 and 1948, for instance, the Liberals stayed loyal to two leaders: Sir Wilfrid Laurier and Mackenzie King. The Tories, on the other hand, managed to inflict on themselves no fewer than twelve new chieftains who kept them out of power during most of those same sixty-one years.

The Tory spectacle had the sad aura about it of a bunch of confused kids mucking about in quicksand, determined to preserve Canada as a one-party Liberal state. (The television technicians, looking like moon men under their electronic apparatus, allowed us a quick glimpse of Robert Stanfield. It was a reminder that the Tories not only eat their young but swallow their old.)

Then there was the Clark speech itself. Just before the PC convention started, the CBC ran an ad for Pampers – the new-style synthetic diapers – that ended with the animated, porous pad telling the baby it was covering: "You deserve all the dryness I can give you." Clark's mixture of homilies that followed had the inspiration of a soggy diaper.

His passage up to the platform remained the highlight of his appearance. He made his way through the cheering throng (nearly all of them wearing Clark badges, but at least a third of them about to vote against him) doing the right thing: grabbing delegates with that possessive pat on the shoulder and tight grip on the forearm that make the spear carriers of the political world think they're one of the chosen.

That's always been Joe Clark's problem. He has memorized all the correct gestures, he has championed many of the right causes, and he can organize anything down to a chicken coop. What he can't do, what he can never learn – because it's either born in you or it's not – is how to transmit electricity to a crowd.

The revival of the national Progressive Conservative party is essential to Canada's future. Even Joe Clark's ardent supporters must now realize that his political effectiveness has been used up, that there is nothing in his cause worth the sacrifice of keeping it alive. No great political party should be forced to accept the loss of yet another election as the price of solving its leadership problem.

What Canada lacks at the moment is a government with moral authority. We have at the helm of our political parties an odd couple of used-up hoofers with no prospect of rescuing themselves. Now the process of succession has begun, and, with the Tories launched into a leadership contest, the Liberals cannot afford to be far behind.

Joe Clark may have guts to burn, but as a national leader he has nowhere to go but out. The only thing that saved him from an even worse humiliation in Winnipeg was that most of the other contenders for the Tory crown were relative strangers to the party's rank and file. Even so, for Joe Clark, familiarity did not breed consent.

—1983

The Member from Winston's

THEY GATHER EACH DAY just after high noon in the burgundy plush of Winston's Restaurant on Toronto's Adelaide Street, the high-rollers who conduct, or like to think they order, Canada's economic and political universe. They come here to compare corporate exploits, share fiscal confidences, and make the deals that will eventually spread their money and talent, their arrogance and sense of predestiny across the country and the continent. During two-hour lunches they savour the pleasures of flexing their clout before slightly awed visitors from lesser circles of power – those guys with not quite enough chin and too much cuff whose eyes dart about the room, like pilot fish collecting sharks.

Only one presence rivets all of their attention, one spot they approach like suppliants at Lourdes. Right there in Winston's southwest corner, at Table 23, most days sits John Turner, the answer to all their prayers.

In political exile since he stormed out of the Trudeau government on September 10, 1975, Turner is practising law with McMillan, Binch and sitting on ten boards of corporations with aggregate assets of twelve billion dollars. His sudden departure may have soured some Liberal colleagues (who believe the only honourable way to leave the Commons is to accept a senatorship) but for a growing number of Canadians – and not just the patrons of Winston's – Turner is coming to represent the last hope of giving this country forceful political leadership. The decade he spent in cabinet opposing higher federal expenditures has suddenly made his brand of politics popular again.

154

Bored with abstractions, Turner views Liberalism not as an ideology but as a state of impatience with the order of things. He still talks like some McLuhanesque political disk jockey and continues to find his own presence a bit overwhelming. But underneath that flash and footwork, the hard core of the man has grown and matured, found some accommodation between his image and his real self.

John Turner commands an impressive national constituency of power-brokers in every province, based on his Club of 195 – the delegates who stuck by him in the last ballot at the 1968 leadership convention. He seldom spends a day without riffling through his personal index file, making sure he's not out of touch with somebody who counts. He has, for example, contacted Claude Ryan exactly twenty times (at six-month intervals) during the past ten years. Above all, Turner is one of the very few political figures in this country still possessing a measure of credibility, perhaps the only Liberal extant who wouldn't be suspected of lying, even when he was contradicting himself.

Winston's Restaurant isn't exactly comparable to the sanctuary of Colombey-les-Deux-Eglises, where Charles de Gaulle retired for three years before France's elite called him back to command a troubled republic – but it'll do.

—1978

❋   ❋   ❋

AS HE HUNGERS for the Liberal crown, John Turner brings with him into the campaign the advantage of being the only candidate true to the Liberal party's tradition in renewing its leadership. This has little to do with alternation between French- and English-speaking contenders, about which Turner cannot say much, because he wanted to break that chain when he ran to succeed Lester Pearson in 1968.

What makes Turner such an apparent shoo-in is that, alone among the serious candidates, he is firmly within the Liberal party's well-entrenched custom of passing the leadership on to outsiders. This was true in 1919, when William Fielding, a veteran insider, was bypassed for William Lyon Mackenzie King, who had been minister and deputy minister of labour and union-busting adviser to the Rockefellers. It was true when King anointed Louis St. Laurent, a Quebec City lawyer and a relative newcomer to Liberal ranks. The same pattern repeated itself when St. Laurent ignored the claims of Paul Martin and others to promote Lester Pearson, who had spent most of his life as a professional diplomat. Pearson in turn did his best to manoeuvre events so that Pierre Trudeau, whose previous party involvement had been with the NDP, would be his natural heir.

The miracle of John Turner, who served a full decade in Liberal cabinets, is that through the judicious application of silence during the past eight and a half years, he has turned himself into just such an appropriate outsider. Alone of the party's potential future leaders, he can (and will, with a vengeance) disown the Trudeau record, insisting that he had nothing to do with its many excesses and imperfections.

One example of how Turner tried to dissociate himself, even as a member of the Trudeau cabinet, occurred during the 1972 campaign when he refused to repeat the party's cuckoo slogan, ''The Land is Strong.'' Turner told some students at the University of Winnipeg, ''I used it only once and that was to see if I could get it out without breaking up.''

Current circumstances may make Turner ideal for the leadership, but whether or not he can overcome his poor standing in the Gallup poll is very much an open question. Certainly he has some impressive advantages. He returns to politics at a time when not spending more money is no longer condemned as an unacceptable right-wing position, though his ideology was never as reactionary as his enemies have painted it. A Pearson-style pragmatist, he is much more interested in workable ideas than in grandiose abstractions.

Turner believes that social welfare measures in this country have exhausted their effectiveness and that emphasis should now shift to incentives that will attack and cure the economy's structural faults. The chief source of Turner's policy advice is John Payne, a Montreal-based savant who once worked for Pearson and has since acted as an external conscience for Liberal ideas. Payne, who not only has a good mind but understands the sweaty little arts of politics, has already drafted national policies on transportation, industry, environment, agriculture, resources, and communications.

It will be interesting to watch where Turner comes down on the issue of Canadian nationalism. As a Bay Street lawyer he has compared FIRA and the NEP to something just short of having the plague. But during his previous run (at a rally on March 16, 1968, at Richmond Hill, Ontario) he flatly declared, "I am a Canadian nationalist." At the time, he supported the objectives of the Watkins report (which helped establish FIRA), attacked the extraterritoriality of American laws, and suggested that an Ottawa ministry be set up on foreign ownership and investment. "I know," he said, "that there are those who deplore nationalism. But they are wrong. I believe Liberals in the next decade must give leadership in the continual pursuit of national independence."

In psyching himself up to take over the Liberal party, Turner faces the dilemma of not only having to reconnect himself into the circuits of a political machine he abandoned nearly a decade ago but also of facing in Brian Mulroney a far more astute and powerful Conservative leader than Trudeau ever faced. The mathematics remain biased against a Liberal victory under any auspices, and if he takes the final plunge Turner could be facing a term or two in Opposition. But the Liberals like winners, and that image is Turner's strength.

Turner's biggest problem will be to prove that he is acceptable to all wings of the party, not merely as a man who the reactionaries will claim can stem the "socialist" and/or "French" tides in national affairs. To achieve such a sense of reform, Turner will have to attract to the party what Trudeau once called "new guys with new ideas" – and make them stick.

"Leadership is more than magnetism or sex appeal. The Kennedy model of simple clarion calls would not work in this country," Turner once confided to me in the privacy of his parliamentary office. Then he moved on to a touch of mysticism. "Joining a political party," he said, "is like joining a church. It means a *degree* of commitment. You owe it to your leader to play according to certain rules. But you don't have to become an intellectual slave."

That dogma could take the Member from Winston's far along the Canadian political trail. But first he will have to loosen up his campaign style. In his previous run for the leadership, John Turner was charged with kinetic energy. But he was about as spontaneous as a computer.

—1984

EVERY CONTENDER in the Liberal leadership race had his retinue of handlers and boosters, the John Turner people being the most distinctive among them. They were cheerleaders of both sexes, with bronzed faces, sculptured cheekbones, a restless grace in their limbs, and that slurring of consonants in their voices that marks what passes for an upper class in this country.

The winner himself projected strength (the Caribbean-blue eyes issuing the feral command, "Love me, damn it"), yet as a politician he remained blurry about the edges, as nervous as a beaver in heat.

The Turner campaign was a triumph of networking. He has continued to stay in touch with everybody who counts – keeping the lines open, constantly expanding his constituency. Now that he has grabbed power, Turner will fight the forthcoming election on economic, not social, issues, trying to create the impression that he is returning the Liberal party to its rightful roots, hinting that the Trudeau years were really an aberration dominated by guys who had never met a payroll. His main address to the convention touched all the tranquillity bases – that he may be an ally of big business but his heart belongs to the small family farm, that he is not an insensitive right-winger about to Reaganize Canada. It was a vintage performance, and Turner even managed a touch of poetry when he described the challenge of governing this country with the comment, "We must reach for the stars in a land that has no horizons."

The speeches of all but one of the candidates found an echo among the delegates. The exception was Eugene Whelan, who sauntered into the hall out of step with his own 182-piece marching band, delivered a dumb speech that alternated between Harry Truman and Kaiser Wilhelm, loped back to his tiny huddle of supporters, and promptly fell asleep. An exhausted John Munro, looking as if someone had been practising taxidermy on him, followed with a raspy appeal in which he promised the delegates everything except a guarantee against varicose veins. Mark MacGuigan challenged the notion that successful politicians have to be charismatic, then proceeded to prove his point by scoring a solid zero on the charisma meter. John Roberts made the best speech of all, ensuring his place in the Liberals' ideological Hall of Fame if not inside a Turner cabinet. Don Johnston, the most attractive candidate, kept looking puzzled, like a diver exploring the wreck of his own ship, trying to place distance between himself and his hurt.

Jean Chrétien's performance was vintage *Mr. Smith Goes to Washington*, but his policy impulses revealed a mind groping towards orthodoxy.

A fascinating sidelight of all the rhetoric was the way it helped define the root differences between conservatism and liberalism. In the same hall a year ago Tory candidates had spouted their hopes and dreams, almost entirely in terms of ideas. Not so the Liberals. They see Canadian democracy almost entirely in terms of its institutions and processes.

No speaker came close to the bravura farewell performance of Pierre Trudeau. Standing in front of eight thousand people without a note in hand, he delivered from memory a perfectly structured, elegantly crafted valedictory. Written by his principal secretary, Tom Axworthy, it was full of grace and lightning, evoking the wonder of Canada ("a country to defy eternity") and a long litany of his stewardship's miracles.

Listening to his version of the record that he carved in Canadian history over the past sixteen years, it was hard not to be impressed. But it was also easy to see what had gone wrong. All prime ministers, even superior ones like Trudeau, have two distinct reputations: their popularity with the voting public and the professional prestige they carry with Ottawa's senior bureaucrats. Because he came into the national limelight so suddenly back in 1968, Trudeau made little impact on the federal mandarins before taking office. The electoral triumph that followed made him feel smug enough about his standing with the public that he became determined to spend most of his time in office consolidating his *professional* reputation. This, in turn, was partly to offset his *public* reputation as a political theoretician unaware of people's everyday problems.

John Turner is the opposite. His *professional* reputation in Ottawa is secure, even though it dates back a decade. His time in finance when Simon Reisman was his deputy minister was probably the best partnership ever between a politician and a senior Ottawa mandarin. That's why when he goes to the people to get a mandate, Turner will be concerned solely with his *public* reputation, trying to persuade Canadians that he can do the job better than Brian Mulroney.

—1984

159

MOST FEDERAL CAMPAIGNS in this country are fought along so many regional splits and on such diverse local issues that voting day feels like a coincidental coming together of 282 by-elections. Clusters of new MPs assume the pomposity of office without disturbing the essential rhythm of the governmental process.

But not this time.

Two decades of Liberal rule proved to be enough. Brian Mulroney won the election, but the Liberals defeated themselves.

The cosmology of John Turner's appeal seldom moved beyond the plea that his party should be returned because he wanted to retain power. He seemed uncomfortable from the start, and as election day approached, Turner's flash appearances took on the taste of panic. Machine-gunning his way through some ghost writer's laborious jottings, the Liberal leader gave little evidence of projecting any coherent view of the future or of being in touch with the gut concerns of his audiences.

Brian Mulroney has earned the right to occupy the centre of the political stage. But John Turner faces much more immediate tests of his character and leadership. He must prove to a humbled but still powerful political movement that he has the heart, the will, and the stamina to remain as Liberal leader and is willing to pull the party back into contention. This will initially involve assuming full responsibility for the Liberal defeat, an early assertion of his leadership against the inevitable calls for Jean Chrétien to succeed him, and an immediate start on rebuilding the tattered remains of the once invincible party's political machine.

His timetable is tight. A Liberal caucus is being convened in the second week of September. This post-mortem on the election will bring together not only the new Liberal MPs but also all those who didn't make it back under Turner's leadership. Unlike the Tories, who genuinely surprise themselves whenever they happen to win an election, the Liberals consider holding office a God-given right, requiring Turner to do a lot of fast explaining. The party has called a Reform Convention for October 1985, and even though a leadership review is not on the agenda, little else is likely to be discussed.

The Liberal party is planning to hold its next formal party meeting in 1986, when an accountability session and leadership review will head the official order of business. One of the more cruel anomalies of Turner's current situation is that because of the reduced House of Commons contingent, senators will play a much more significant role within the Liberal caucus. They will prevent Turner from dismantling any of the policy initiatives that originated during the Trudeau years. By filling the Senate with his ideological soul mates, Trudeau has, in effect, perpetuated his government retroactively in the Upper House.

Besides defending himself against this internal threat to what is his main source of authority, Turner has as his most pressing assignment the rebuilding of bridges to Quebec. By repudiating Pierre Trudeau outside Quebec during the campaign and appearing soft on Bill 101 within French Canada, Turner sent a message to the formerly impregnable Liberal stronghold that he had no intention of perpetuating the bicultural efforts of his predecessors. All this was happening while Mulroney was waging a brave defence of French-language rights in Manitoba – in effect donning the Trudeau mantle and earning French Canada's votes in return.

Despite this grave strategic error, Turner's advisers are shell-shocked by the speed of Quebec's desertion from the Liberal cause. This was due partly to Quebec's wanting to have its native son in power – and Mulroney qualified almost as well as Trudeau – but there was more to it than that. Ever since Confederation, Quebec has been the most skilful province in knowing how to play the politics of self-interest – as opposed to the West, which tends to vote on the basis of emotions. That explains why western voters are so volatile and why British Columbia and the Prairie Provinces so seldom attain the political clout their economic strength deserves.

Apart from negotiating a separate peace with Quebec, Turner must try to return Canadian Liberalism to its genuine roots as the party that reflects middle-class aspirations, fulfils ethnic expectations, and initiates fresh political ideas. The Liberal party has been flying on automatic for a long time, its policy matrix having been set at the Kingston policy conference of 1960. The Kingston innovations – universal medicare, minimum wages, old-age pensions, among others – were all redistributive measures predicated on a federal government with a large and growing surplus looking for ways to provide its citizens with social dividends. That is no longer the case. The Canadian government is bankrupt.

Ironically, some of the ideas for revitalizing the Liberal party may come out of the final report of the Macdonald commissioners, who have been wandering the country for the past year, looking for an excuse to justify their fancy salaries. (When the Trudeau cabinet first discussed forming that royal commission, one of its boosters remarked, ''These guys could provide us with the policies we can govern by.'' To which a more realistic colleague replied, ''Or the kind of policies we'll need to help us out of opposition.'')

The Liberal party lost the election because, after two decades of holding power, it had grown corrupt and lost the will and competence to govern. John Turner's most pressing assignment is to prove this is a curable condition.

—1984

The Boyo from Baie Comeau

ECAUSE OF HIS PUSH-BUTTON SMILE and the ham-actor reso-
nance of his voice, Brian Mulroney, who declared himself a
contender for the Tory leadership this week, has seldom been
considered a serious political thinker.

Those who have vaguely followed his career – from electrician's
son in Baie Comeau to gold-spurred member of the Montreal Establishment – have casually dismissed his ideological stance as Mount
Royal Club chic. Because he moves so easily through Canada's chan-
deliered chambers of corporate power, style has been mistaken for
substance.

But behind the ambassadorial coiffure there still lurks the small-
town boy with humble instincts. Neither rebel nor reactionary, he is
less opportunistic than pragmatic and probably comes as close as
anyone to personifying his party's label: a *Progressive* Conservative.

Mulroney's personal philosophy has come out of the cauldron of
the three most influential experiences of his life: growing up in the
God-awful economic climate of Quebec's North Shore, attending Saint
Francis Xavier University in Antigonish, N.S., and being a member
of the royal commission on labour troubles in Quebec's construction
industry in the early Seventies. Mulroney's youth was dominated by
his father's lifelong need to hold down two jobs to make ends meet.
The family managed only one holiday each year: a trip to Quebec City
in the Mulroneys' 1938 Pontiac. "We would leave at four in the
morning – my parents, the six children, the dog, fourteen sandwiches,
and a six-pack," he recalls, "to begin a mad race over unpaved roads

to catch the ferry at Bersimis, followed by a heroic gallop to catch the ferry at Baie Ste Catherine – the children crying, the dog barking, my father grinding his teeth, and my mother in the back seat saying the beads for the third time.''

When he signed up as a pre-law student at Saint Francis Xavier, he came under the influence of the co-operative teachings of Moses Coady, who implanted the notion that an active social conscience is life's highest goal. Mulroney remembers particularly a Coady lecture in which the cleric described the ideal graduates: ''We want them to look into the sun and the depths of the sea. We want them to explore the hearts of flowers and of fellow men. We want them to be eager to discover and develop their capacities for creation. . . .''

Whatever romanticism was left in Mulroney's soul evaporated during the 164 days he spent as a Quebec royal commissioner. Along with Robert Cliche, a former Liberal lawyer who had turned into a New Democrat, and Guy Chevrette, a farmer's son from Joliette, he was charged with cleaning up the rot in the province's construction industry. Altogether, 279 witnesses testified, revealing the corruption caused by unbridled unionism and capitalism. The commission's 132 recommendations brought peace to the industry, and Mulroney learned many of the valuable lessons about labour-management relations he later applied as president of the Iron Ore Company of Canada. After he turned the company around, one of his first decisions was quietly to double the pensions being paid to widows of employees. When he closed down the company's Schefferville operations earlier this year, he allocated ten million dollars to alleviate the shock to the community, even though declining markets meant that there were only 167 full-time employees left to be laid off.

The sum of these experiences has made Mulroney a confirmed advocate of self-sufficiency and a sworn enemy of the unearned hand-out. ''There are no fancy-pants heroes any more with elegant theories and magic wands,'' he contends, ''just overworked and harassed businessmen, labour leaders, and ordinary Canadians who get their hands dirty every day dealing with the pedestrian problems of providing jobs, meeting payrolls, and producing products – only to come home at night to learn on TV that some brave new social artist has invented another government plan that will add to costs, increase paperwork, and lessen competitiveness.''

He is opposed to "the Swedenizing of Canada," proposing instead "a dimension of tenderness: the vital responsibility of government to demonstrate compassion for the needy and assistance for the disadvantaged." He wants to reactivate the economy by raising productivity, eliminating the interest-deductibility provisions on corporate takeovers, and allowing municipalities to issue tax-free bonds. Mulroney is not a knee-jerk Liberal-baiter and in fact has dined more frequently at 24 Sussex Drive with Pierre Trudeau than with Joe Clark. But he attacks the Liberals for fostering dissension and unrest. "There was a time," he says, "when many Canadians looked on Pierre Trudeau's penchant for confrontation as a kind of political theatre. We may still find that four hours of Napoleon versus Europe makes a good movie, but we know now that fourteen years of Trudeau versus everyone else makes lousy government."

Provided that Mulroney can attract some gutsy political advisers instead of the Westmount preppies who ran his last campaign, he could become leader. Even prime minister.

The most intriguing issue raised by the Mulroney candidacy is what effect it will have on John Turner's chances for the Liberal leadership. The two men are friends, ideologically and personally, so that any electoral contest between them could become the most elegant campaign ever fought in this country.

May the best profile win.

—1983

❉   ❉   ❉

IT WAS, IN ITS PECULIAR WAY, a battle of opposites: the veteran politician who had never met a payroll and the corporate bottom-liner who had never been elected.

Brian Mulroney won for two reasons: because he has the charm of the blarney – and because he's not Joe Clark.

The long, hot convention was as much a defeat for the Man from Yellowhead as a victory for the smoothie from Westmount. Joe Clark is difficult to define. Hampered by limbs that move as if they were encrusted with salt, he is undaunted and tough. He is a charter member of the Chinese Water Torture School of Politics, exhausting his opponents by slowly wearing down public support for their positions. He will never set the world on fire, except by accident. But what he does have, and what has allowed him to go so far, is a bulletproof psyche. His real tragedy was not so much in losing the leadership review at the Ottawa Civic Centre as in what he failed to do with the mandate he won in the spring of 1979 and, as if he were an unwanted child, lost nine months later.

He was so stunned at having achieved power that he never recovered from his collegiate way of doing things. Outwardly incapable of being insulted, he paraded across the country as a kid who had grown into prime-ministerial boots. But behind the scenes he turned out to be a closet paranoiac with no imagined insult small enough to claim his forgiveness.

During his various leadership contests, which seemed to occupy most of his adult life, Clark constantly affirmed his own importance by listing his puny accomplishments. He counted on his campaign team's organizational skills to deliver the convention, but it wasn't enough. His ultimate rejection by the party cost him not just the leadership but his dream. Overnight he has become a footnote to history.

John Crosbie, who would have won had Clark's pride not kept him from forming an alliance with the Newfie giant, ran a fine race. But the combination of being unilingual and a right-wing continentalist made him too tempting a target.

Smiling through the sweaty proceedings was David Crombie, a good man in the wrong place at the wrong time, his followers huddling around the campfires of decency that refused to illuminate the Tory landscape. He sold the smallest piece of himself during the gruelling afternoon, and the mischief of laughter was never far from his soul.

The somnambulant Michael Wilson candidacy had about it the brooding diffidence of a man waiting for something that had already happened. His campaign literature proved his desperation: a photograph of ''Mike,'' racquet at the ready, with a caption claiming: ''Wilson is an accomplished athlete and one of the few on Parliament Hill who beats Finance Minister Lalonde at squash.'' All through Wilson's therapeutic speech, the delegates assumed their sermon-enduring positions as their moods altered between mild boredom and mild despair.

Peter Pocklington emerged with his dignity intact, aspiring to opportunism but holding beliefs too strong ever to make it.

Then there were the fringe candidates, led by John Gamble, all chest and no neck, blowing through his moustache, the madness of a hermit in his eyes.

And the winner.

Brian Mulroney has set in motion the changing of Canada's political guard. His upset victory will eventually alter the balance of power among the federal parties. He is an unusual mixture of old- and new-style conservatism. Raised at John Diefenbaker's knee, he exudes a similar field of force, though he has yet to hone his oratorial talents. But he glommed onto the secret of Canadian politics: that most people vote against, not for, policies, so that the less of your position you expose, the less reason there will be for voters to oppose it.

He is no ideologue or intellectual, but he does have compassion and, most important of all, understands how this country works.

—1983

❄   ❄   ❄

THE FEDERAL TORIES have chosen in Brian Mulroney a reactionary reformer determined to spread a large umbrella over the ideological centre of Canadian politics, then pull the majority of the electorate under it with him.

What makes Mulroney so different from any other Tory daring enough to take on his party's leadership in the past is that he has grown up as a Conservative in Quebec. That influence is important because Quebec is the only province in the country without a provincial Conservative party of its own, so that its adherents have no spiritual home except the larger field of the *national* organization. Mulroney can only think nationally; his political past will turn out to be a dominant influence in his formulation of a policy future for his party and, eventually, for the country at large.

The pundits are falling all over themselves trying to ascribe some recognizable philosophy to the new Tory leader. None of these efforts means very much because Mulroney is nothing less than the reincarnation of Mackenzie King, the man who turned pragmatism into a state religion.

What Mulroney believes is that each political party in Canada, his own included, exists not as an apparatus for implementing coherent sets of ideas but as an instrument for the accommodation of individual, regional, and national differences. Like Mackenzie King, who used the tactic successfully in his six election victories as leader, Mulroney will aim the appeal of his party during the first national campaign at a wide variety of special-interest groups – then act as a broker among them in the actual governing process.

It's no accident that both King and Mulroney spent their formative years as labour negotiators. The two share a cast of mind deeply rooted in Canadian political tradition: the impulse to dampen fanaticism of any kind. Theirs is an almost gravitational pull toward compromise, conciliation, tolerance, and the tendency to subscribe to the Orwellian-sounding dogma of strength through diversity. In the place of ritual and hierarchy that has tainted Canadian politics for a generation, Mulroney's approach is to try and avoid letting himself become the protagonist in any situation. His world is not black and white but shaded in a wash of ever-changing pastels.

Although both men would be appalled at the comparison, Mulroney's position on the vital issue of using public enterprise to achieve public policy objectives is roughly comparable to that of Jack Austin, the Liberal senator in charge of the Canada Development Investment Corporation who saved the Liberals in British Columbia from becoming an underground cult. In pioneering the Trudeau government's reconciliation with the private sector, Austin's criterion for judging the extent of government involvement in any new economic venture is something he calls "the social discount factor." It's the equivalent of the "commercial discount factor" used by businessmen to measure the value of their investments in the commercial marketplace – a way of calculating, among other factors, the real return after the effects of inflation. "When it comes to investment by governments," says Austin, "decisions should be based on a 'social discount factor' which implies a lower rate of return because of a longer time frame. But there must be other, accompanying benefits, such as returns to the community at large, rather than an individual investment group.''

Brian Mulroney and Mackenzie King would have recognized this sort of word game and heartily approved. It is precisely such verbal gymnastics that allowed the strange bachelor from Kitchener and the boyo from Baie Comeau to move through many worlds, without belonging to any but their own.

—1983

❄   ❄   ❄

DRIFTING AROUND THE PRIVATE RECEPTIONS before the meeting of the Economic Club of New York last week, a reporter would have found it hard to name any Canadian power-brokers who had stayed home. They turned out to pay visible homage to the prime minister's official American debut. Dressed in their best regalia, the Canadians were sending Brian Mulroney a clear signal that they approved of his message.

More remarkable was the heft of the representatives from the U.S. investment community who came to this, the 306th dinner in the seventy-seven years the Economic Club has been holding such shindigs. It must be the most influential audience outside a joint session of Congress, representing a distillation of the decision-makers who redistribute U.S. investments among the world's time zones.

These are the Wall Street big hitters, men with large corner offices who never dial their own telephones and would happily finance another assault on the Alps by Hannibal if he could only keep his books straight. Many of their wives were there, attracted by the reputation of Mila and Brian as North America's newest and most glamorous power couple. They looked like the kind of women who raise Lhasa Apsos, wear aviator glasses for walks in the country, live for great parties, and never eat the top lid of their sandwiches. "Listen, Malaura," I overheard one of these creatures breathlessly briefing another, "this is really a big deal. That guy with the hair is the President of Canada!''

What Mulroney understood about the guests who thronged the huge hotel ballroom was that, even more than craving fat bottom lines (and thin female ones), his listeners wanted to be loved. At a time when any politician in the Third World and most of Europe can get elected by depicting Ronald Reagan as a senile Dr. Strangelove, these men and women chomping their filet mignons resented their isolation and ached for strangers to underwrite their righteousness.

Mulroney's message, delivered in his best Kirk Douglas whisper, was direct: send us your megabucks and we will be your friends. "To all who seek a definition of peaceful association between nations, I say look no farther. It is unlikely you shall find a better illustration than the simple story of friendship and prosperity that has marked the evolution of our two countries over the years."

Mulroney understands these power paladins in a way that Pierre Trudeau and René Lévesque, who addressed this same group, never did. These merchant adventurers are not frightened off by investment risks and were never bothered by Trudeau's anti-Americanism or Lévesque's noises about separation. What they cannot tolerate is any politician who changes "the rules of the game" under which funds were originally committed.

That was why the loudest ovation of the evening greeted Mulroney's declaration: "There shall be one game – building Canada – and one set of rules. These shall not be changed after the game has started to the detriment of any of the players."

Mulroney said little that was new, but his words carried a disproportionate impact because the chief executive officers of the Fortune 500 in the audience never bother with statements of policy issued by foreign governments, or even the "situationers" prepared by their own PR flacks. They like to get the news directly from the source, the big guy who's running the country. That was why Mulroney made such a production of his retreat from his predecessor's Canadianization measures. He stuck yet another sword into the Foreign Investment Review Agency, surely history's most toothless dragon, declaring that it was really dead, done for, kaput.

Mulroney once again demonstrated his ability to place himself squarely in the centre of an audience's emotions, so that he seemed to be speaking on a one-to-one basis with each of the fifteen hundred diners. He played them as masterfully as Johnny Carson. When he interrupted himself to ruminate on the undefended border between the United States and Canada, he ad-libbed: "There hasn't been a shot fired in anger between our two countries since 1812. That wasn't much of a war. We captured Detroit, took one look around, and gave it back." Even the bookend-Mounties guarding the dais managed to stay awake throughout his address, looking as proud as the Royal Canadian Air Farce's Sergeant Renfrew *after* he regains consciousness.

Most Canadians don't realize that Mulroney is genuinely at home with the Wall Street barons who turned out for him. From 1980 to 1983 he was a director of the Hanna Mining Company of Cleveland, the Iron Ore Company's corporate parent, which has since slipped under the control of Conrad Black. But before that Hanna was the centre of a giant spoked wheel, uniting investments from five great family fortunes: the Mellons of Pittsburgh, the Hannas and the Humphreys of Cleveland, the Bechtels of San Francisco, and the Graces of New York. While he never became one of them, Mulroney established the connections and the credibility he is now exploiting to attract new investment funds into Canada.

As the evening ended and the crowd dispersed, the faces of the Economic Club members were relaxed in a post-coital glow of satisfaction: Canada is A-OK. The guy with the hair who's running America's attic is user-friendly.

It had been a tough crowd to charm, and as they climbed back into their limos, the Wall Streeters were already reverting to type.

"Hey, Virgil," somebody yelled across the street, "what's the world's fastest animal?"

"Beats me."

"A chicken in Ethiopia!"

—1984

René's Reign

POLITICS IS ULTIMATELY NOT A SCIENCE decided by the elegant droppings of computers but an exercise in sorcery filled with illusions and enchantments, challenges that men or women will invent to test themselves against. René Lévesque knew this. Robert Bourassa did not. The former premier came at the voters with the oblivious air of one of those frigid creatures who permanently inhabit a glass souvenir bought at Niagara Falls. (You shake it and the artificial snowflakes swirl about – but there is no way to tell the little man gazing out through his protective shell that the seasons have changed.)

Bourassa thought he could embrace power in the name of federalism; instead, he disgraced democracy in the name of Confederation. By the end of his inept campaign, the Liberal leader was acting like the head of a retreating army that has lived off the land for so long that its soldiers (and generals) have long since forgotten the original patriotic impulse for their war. Baffled by signs of his impending defeat, he soiled the air with his threats and his fears. Liberal ministers roamed the province demonstrating all the instincts of dogs, except for loyalty.

In contrast, René Lévesque's campaign had about it the élan of those Second World War films glorifying the French resistance movement – all throwaway heroics and noble enunciations. As the campaign progressed, the Parti Québécois leader kept hunching over as if he were standing permanently under a low, leaky roof on a rainy day. It was at the televised press conferences that his skill as a professional performer really came out. He mastered the art of the pause. Asked a question, he would hesitate, not, it seemed, to protect himself from careless answers but to intrude into his own privacy the way a child does to come up with a full and true reply. His blue eyes darting like hyper minnows from one camera to another, his mouth forming that tight loop of sincerity that TV can best appreciate, Lévesque kept hinting that some of his best friends were WASPs, that somehow we would all survive and prosper together.

Lévesque just could be right. But no accommodation will be possible with the New Quebec until and unless English Canada begins to understand this pivotal politician whose moods and methods, whose ideology and sense of priorities will produce a new country, hopefully with Quebec still within its borders. (At the same time, Lévesque and his ministers will have to realize that typical WASPs no longer wear pastel clothes, have pale, pale skins, and eat porridge, muffins, and tea for breakfast, basking in the spiritual invincibility that is their reward for generations spent trying to uplift the natives of the countries they've conquered.)

Even if Lévesque's amazing sweep was less a vote for separation than a celebration of the true root and flow of democracy, the party he leads was created for only one purpose: to turn Quebec into an independent republic. In the interval, Lévesque must walk the same tightrope as all other Quebec premiers. Any overt evidence of punitive attitudes from English Canada could turn the forthcoming referendum into a separation mandate. The terms of that plebiscite will be set as much outside Quebec as within it.

The key to the province's future may be Lévesque's decision about maintaining a common currency should separation occur. Keeping the same dollar would imply common tariffs, co-ordination of monetary policies, equal exchange rates, and other steps which just might retain enough links so that Lévesque would come away with an arrangement he could choose to term ''independence'' while Pierre Trudeau might be left with something he could still label ''national unity.''

In a way, Quebec has always set the cultural tone of this country. Now it commands our political mood as well. The essence of politics has always been power, not law, and Quebec intends to advance her case by straining against the reality, not the legality, of the current situation. This will require, at the very least, a brand-new Canadian constitution. ''Too many people,'' Daniel Johnson, the former Union

Nationale premier of Quebec, once told me, "treat the British North America Act like a sacred cow, even though it has been violated many times in closed hotel rooms at federal-provincial conferences."

Whether French Canadians continue to like us is less important than what value we place on each other, how useful both parties can be within a continuing Canadian alliance. As Lévesque and his disciples coo the siren song of self-determination, the political leaders of English Canada will find themselves faced with new challenges to their sense of moderation. Having no familiar framework within which to fit Quebec's inexorable impulse toward social change, they will be tempted to interpret each of Lévesque's moves to limit federal powers as the hot breath of revolution.

What makes Quebec different, what allowed Lévesque to win, was that his sense of country had long ago moved beyond policy or even ideology. At this critical juncture of Canadian history he finds himself buoyed up by the existential superiority that Albert Camus once described in a letter to a friend: "This is what separated us from you; you were satisfied to serve the power of your nation while we dreamed of giving ours her truth."

—1976

LIKE A DEBUTANTE who has strayed into an abattoir, Canada finds herself face to face with some harsh new realities. During most of our brief existence as a nation we were all but exempt from the terrors of modern history, a lucky people inhabiting a wonderful hunk of geography. For 110 years the superstructure of Canadian society, which has always depended on some form of French-English understanding, remained relatively undisturbed. Nearly every Rotary Club speaker worth his rubber chicken, after apologizing for not knowing French, would insist that some of his best friends were from "La Belle Provahnce," while most Quebeckers figured that as WASPs go, at least we weren't as brash as the Americans. French-speaking Canadians retained the folk memory of their clergy preaching during the long

174

silence after the Conquest that "the best way to remain French is to stay British."

But as 1977 begins and we are being forced to ponder the true implications of René Lévesque's victory last November 15, Canada's future will be decided by an interminably dreary sequence of federal-provincial conferences. Apart from the real possibility that we can survive simply by *talking* ourselves into the twenty-first century, some English Canadians may find the very idea that we should be sitting down to debate our continued existence an intolerable prospect. To those of us who love this country, any discussion among reasonable men on whether or not Canada is worth preserving may seem a little like challenging Euclid to prove that a straight line is the shortest distance between two points. But the issue won't disappear and the debate has already been joined.

As we begin to grapple with René Lévesque's terminal threat to our continuity as a nation, it seems to me that only one direction offers any hope of success: the rallying of Canadians from all provinces (including Quebec, where 60 per cent of the voters cast ballots against the Parti Québécois) into a nonpartisan movement dedicated to the idea of preserving Confederation, even if in radically altered form. This new-style nationalism would promote in a thoughtful manner the many practical advantages of Canada's continued existence by illuminating and magnifying the view we hold of ourselves and the society in which we live.

Ironically, the man who by definition ought to be leading any national effort to counter Quebec's powerfully entrenched Parti Québécois finds himself a prisoner of his past record as a constitutional expert. Pierre Trudeau has been waving the constitution (like some leper's bell) at anyone who'll listen, apparently never realizing that law can be used only as the binding force of an existing consensus, not as the *means* of changing the attitudes of individual citizens. While it would be senseless for Ottawa to treat Quebec with boundless generosity – like some dying millionaire inundating his favourite ballerina with lavish presents – it seems equally silly to keep insisting that the status quo remains a viable ideology. Caught between militant demands and moderate possibilities, Trudeau has retreated into petulance, acting out of political vibrations far removed from reality, instead of those primary impulses and voltages that first brought him into prominence. In the process he has alienated so many of his one-time followers that instead of wanting to support him most members of his natural constituencies only desire to exact political revenge so terrible that it has no name.

In the circumstances, Confederation's supporters will have to work through their own, extra-parliamentary channels to mobilize and redirect the strong patriotic feelings that already exist across this country. Once English Canada achieves that state of grace of believing in itself, it should be much less difficult to convince enlightened Quebeckers that their best chance of surviving as a proud, autonomous society is through a firm alliance with the larger powers of the Canadian nation. There is no other way to ensure that a highly individualistic culture of not quite six million people can stay afloat in a continental sea of nearly three hundred million strangers.

—1977

❄   ❄   ❄

THE REAL ESTATE BROKER, a sullen, exasperated man with a bartender's face, had finished showing a house on Wood Avenue in lower Westmount recently when his prospective client, an American engineer just transferred to Montreal, said, "This place doesn't really suit me. But I like the street. What else have you got?"

The salesman spread out his hands in a gesture of mock ecstasy, cracked a hard smile, and replied, "Hell, every house on this street is available. The only reason there aren't more signs out is people are afraid that would drag prices down even further. So take your pick."

The exodus has started. Non-French Montreal is up for sale.

No matter who has held power at Quebec City in the past, the Anglos have always managed to negotiate a separate peace. They traded off their political support for economic dispensations of various kinds and magnitudes, safe in the knowledge that they were needed, if not loved. But with René Lévesque categorically rejecting future ties with Canada on alternate Wednesdays, some of the province's mobile upper middle class has started to make plans for moving out.

176

Guy Joron, one of the PQ's militant ministers, calls the exodus "nothing less than a form of surrender. Already, a vacuum has set in at the decision-making level in the economy, as if part of the battlefield is conceded to us before we have even tried to occupy it."

Signs of the Anglos' sombre mood of acquiescence are everywhere, the currency of their lives being spent with a fright and abandon that belie the "muddling through" tradition of their upbringing. Even the majority who are at least temporarily staying on are registering some mortgages in Toronto, sending their stock certificates to Vermont, and nervously leafing through Palm Beach telephone books.

Most of the large accumulations of private wealth have been moving out for some time. The Molsons have long since transferred their headquarters to Toronto; the Websters are investing heavily outside Quebec; even the Simard family (French Canada's richest clan) has moved most of its assets into the tax havens of the Bahamas and the oil refineries of Corpus Christi in Texas (through a holding company called Simcor).

Texaco Canada, IAC, and most of the city's other large employers, including the Bank of Montreal and the Royal, have moved key head-office operations away from Montreal in the past five years. Two of the largest headquarters remaining in place are Canadian Pacific and Bell Canada. Their chief executive officers, Ian Sinclair and Jean de Grandpré, come to work every morning. But in each case the main symbolic asset that remains in the province is their desks. Less than 10 per cent of CP's five-billion-dollar empire is still within Quebec's borders. Bell has moved many of its important operations to Toronto and its Quebec business is down drastically because so few new telephones are being connected.

Some of the really forward-looking companies are bypassing Toronto by making provisions to operate out of Calgary. Royal Trust, originally chartered in Quebec, for example, recently incorporated its Canadian operation under an Alberta address. Harold Milavsky, president of Trizec, the huge real estate company that owns Place Ville Marie, Montreal's largest office building, works from Calgary.

Few of the factories that remain in the province are being expanded. "We just won't commit any more investment dollars until we know what the rules of the game are going to be," says a Toronto-based director of several large conglomerates with Quebec operations.

"Right now, we're even cutting down our maintenance costs, hardly changing burnt-out light bulbs. It's not just the PQ's new directives on language and culture that worry us, but Quebec's possible revision of its tax system, its potential new relations with GATT, currency regulations, and the whole gamut of decisions that together make up the economic climate in which we'll have to operate."

The real source of businessmen's sense of panic is not so much the PQ's pledge to split away from Canada as it is the nature of the party's economic aims, which, they fear, would turn Quebec into a kind of subarctic Caribbean island – its industries hobbled by enforced "local" partnerships, with decisions having to be made not according to the free play of market forces but the quixotic dictates of Quebec nationalism. At the same time, they claim Lévesque has elevated the vague, centuries-old notion of a French nation on the North American continent from the wispy status of a people's spiritual sustenance to the primordial sanction of blood (race). The one way for the PQ premier to escape his government's fiscal problems is to divert attention from Quebec's economic difficulties by launching a struggle based on racial purity.

Lévesque and his separatists are getting most of the blame for the decline in Montreal's economic importance. But election of the Parti Québécois merely accelerated a process that dates back more than forty years, when the Toronto money men took over financing of the country's burgeoning mining industry through their Wall Street connections, while the old-family Montreal investment houses continued to deal in blue-chip equities with the bluebloods of Boston and London. St. James Street, which was a symbol of their power, is now all but deserted, and the old Montreal Stock Exchange has been turned into a theatre.

Unfortunately, private investment is drying up just when Lévesque has been unable to prime the provincial economy because his own treasury is facing a growing deficit. It's this state of the province's impending fiscal crisis that provides the departing Anglos with a touch of gallows humour. A story going the rounds in Westmount these days concerns Finance Minister Jacques Parizeau bursting into Premier Lévesque's office to report some good news and some bad news. "I'll give you the good news first," he says. "Even though they have assets in Quebec worth one hundred million dollars, Johns-Manville have

178

decided to sell the province their asbestos holdings for only one million dollars.''

"That's great!'' Lévesque replies, ''just the kind of boost we need. Now, what's the bad news?''

"They insist we pay them a thousand dollars in cash as a deposit.''

—1977

❆   ❆   ❆

THEY WERE THE REALLY BIG FISH in the Wall Street aquarium, but when René Lévesque came to address them within the solemn enclave of the Economic Club of New York, something went wrong. A mutual fund guru sitting across the table from me kept leaning over to his partner and muttering, ''Hell, this is a declaration of civil war, Harry. These guys want to do Gettysburg and George III all in one go.''

"Oh, I don't know, Barney,'' his partner, a bright-eyed man with a broken nose and America's last crewcut, replied. ''I've crunched these Quebec numbers backwards and forwards through our computer, and it still looks better than Gabon.''

Maybe it was that damned tuxedo Lévesque had leased for the occasion. Imprisoned within its unfamiliar confines, he spoke with none of the speed and sky he usually radiates. I've seen Lévesque in action on the Quebec hustings, when his body seemed to be held together by elastics and the world was his ashtray, able to charm and enthral even the most hostile of audiences. On such occasions, he made his listeners feel that Quebec independence was the most profound moral option of our time.

But not tonight. He goes on, in that GI-Joe English he learned while serving with the U.S. infantry as a correspondent during the Second World War, describing the inevitability of Quebec separation, trying to wring some kind of reaction out of his phony comparisons with the American Revolution, returning constantly to his theme that Canada was conceived in sin and that those Canadians who refused to accept his thesis (because of not having been born in Quebec, scepticism, or just plain WASP cussedness) were dead wrong.

179

The performance doesn't jell. The mask slips. Instead of appearing to be one of the great political prophets of his time, René Lévesque stands revealed as a fanatic in a rented tux. In planning his appeal, the Parti Québécois leader forgot the cardinal rule of dealing with American money men: they always insist on knowing the rules of the game. Now, Lévesque was telling them not only that he intended to alter the rules but that he was changing the game itself.

There is little ideology involved in measuring credit ratings. Even the worst risks of all, such as Czarist promissory notes or New York City debentures, seem to find buyers. Quebec will probably be able to raise all of the funds it needs, but the all-important interest rate – the cost of that money – will be higher than it was before Lévesque made his speech. The province already has long-term debt obligations of more than three billion dollars outstanding and the James Bay power development itself will eventually require sixteen billion dollars in funds. So far, the difference between Ontario and Quebec issues has been about seventy-five basis points (one basis point is equivalent to 1/100th of 1 per cent), but no Quebec bonds have been sold. (The last Montreal issue of $214 million went for a considerably higher rate than some Venezuelan debentures floated the same week.) Canada's offshore borrowings total about eight billion dollars, and the Parti Québécois victory is driving up the cost and difficulties of all such transactions.

The Economic Club speech probably seems more of a turning point in the hardening of Lévesque's position than it need have been because it provoked the very first real hostility he has encountered. But for the Quebec premier to accuse "English-Canadian businessmen out to spread their antediluvian ideas about Quebec south of the border" of having somehow sabotaged his performance is silly. He managed that trick all by himself.

Even though the overall reaction was clearly unfavourable, in retrospect it's not easy to tell exactly how comprehending Lévesque's audience really was. As I left the ballroom of the New York Hilton, I overheard two American bankers exchanging views on the evening's proceedings.

"I damned near fell asleep in there, Virgil. What did he say?"

"I'm not sure, Oswald. Something about a quiet revolution that didn't go far enough."

"Well, we're not going to put money out to finance any revolutions, that's for sure. . . Say, did you ever read my 'Let's Repeal the Twentieth Century' speech? Must send you a copy."

"You just do that."

—1977

       ❈   ❈   ❈

CLAUDE MORIN'S SECRETARY, a splendid creature with hair framing her face like a prayer shawl and breasts that promised the consistency of a well-made soufflé, showed me through the door of his ministerial office with the introduction: "Monsieur Morin . . . c'est PAUL Newman."

We both dissolved into laughter, reflecting our common Hollywood heritage, and I found it hard to think of this dapper intellectual as a threat to my country. Yet as minister of intergovernmental affairs, Morin is in charge of taking Quebec out of Confederation, and it would take the overthrow of this man's considerable conscience to soften the PQ's determination. We talked for most of an hour, but he hurled no sweet harpoons of redemption my way.

On the contrary, it seemed to me that Canada's break-up, if it comes, will be based on a cruel hoax and that this shrewd and charming politician will be its chief architect. It was, after all, the same Claude Morin who devised the strategy by which his party tricked its way into power in the first place – by promising to place its social platform ahead of the drive to independence, which has since become the PQ's sole preoccupation. (Finance Minister Jacques Parizeau buried the PQ's social policy pretensions in his first budget, when he declared that no major reforms would be undertaken, because "the road to independence must be paved with sound financing.")

In our conversation, Morin indicated that he intends to utilize similar sleight of hand to win the separation referendum. By claiming that the plebiscite will really involve an option in favour not of separation but of the chance to enjoy a virtually undisturbed economic association with English Canada *plus* the glories of independence, he feels assured of victory. It's a great tactic, but it's also a piece of dishonest nonsense. Economic association is politically impractical and fiscally impossible. The policy has already been rejected by every important political leader outside Quebec – a consideration that bothers Morin not at all, since he regards any criticism of his objective as "bargaining."

Except for his resolve on the association issue, Morin's discourse, like that of René Lévesque, is a prevalence of ambiguities – grand opera in which words serve merely as pretexts to be engulfed in tones, textures, and declamations. But the music rings true. The two-hundred-year numbness of being a conquered people is suddenly being washed away, and the long-slumbering child within each Québécois is being invited to come out and be filled with love and wonder. "Our move toward political self-determination is absolutely unstoppable," Morin proclaims, "because it's cultural and sociological – a civilization thing. Our feelings aren't worked out, but they're always there, the idea of 'Why can't we have a country?' When we hear Gilles Vigneault and Félix Leclerc, they are part of us. They *are* us."

Eschewing the corruption of the Bourassa days or the clenched regimes of the Union Nationale, the Lévesque government has brought together a cadre of impressive activist-savants, dedicated to Gunnar Myrdal's proposition that it is easier to cause big changes rapidly than small changes gradually. Their sense of command is most visible at the daily sittings of Quebec's National Assembly. There they casually bat down the pathetic jabs of Liberal front-benchers who, the day I was there, looked from the visitors' gallery like an untidy troupe of mechanical dolls that no one has bothered to check lately for run-down batteries. There was a kind of moist desperation in Opposition Leader Gérard Lévesque's question: "Is there a way to disagree with this government without being thought of as bad Quebeckers?"

The reply was conciliatory, but it's true that the Parti Québécois has appropriated for itself an air of Jesuitical disdain for non-believers. They dismiss Pierre Trudeau's declamations on behalf of national unity as attacks on the natural order of the universe. At the same time, most Quebeckers' main surviving contact with the federal government is through the workings of the post office – a prospect that should fill every federalist with unalloyed panic.

We've been asking for nearly two decades just what it was Quebec wanted. Now we know and most of us feel confused and frightened. Quebec independence is no simple sentiment that can be eliminated by the outcome of one election or referendum. Instead, it seems to me that politicians on both sides of the issue should concentrate more on the causes and less on the effects of separatism.

The seminal issue for French Canadians is cultural survival, and their best chance is through a firm alliance with the larger powers of the Canadian nation. To believe anything else is to ignore the very genesis of Canada: that we are and always will remain greater than the sum of our parts.

—1978

❋   ❋   ❋

HALFWAY THROUGH HIS MANDATE, Réne Lévesque has finally answered the question that has been haunting Canadian politics for most of the past two decades. The solution to what Quebec *really* wants, it turns out, is a unique relationship with the rest of Canada to be known as "sovereignty-association." Even in a country where one of the major parties insists on calling itself both Progressive and Conservative, this spacy concept ranks high in the lexicon of political absurdities.

Lévesque's declaration places him on a platitudinous plateau few Canadian politicians have dared scale. He stands squarely in support of simultaneous virginity and motherhood. Since Quebec already enjoys the benefits of a full customs and monetary union with the other provinces, Lévesque's policy amounts to a brilliant deception.

He has not spelled out exactly how much sovereignty and how much association the Parti Québécois will be demanding during the referendum campaign. But it's clear that the "sovereignty-association" approach is little more than a trick, a softening of the way toward his ultimate aim of independence.

Compared to the tainted regime of Robert Bourassa, the Parti Québécois has run a wide-open administration of provocative partisans who know in their hearts that they're right. But Lévesque and his ministers have betrayed the most basic premise of their 1976 campaign: that they would provide good government and leave their independence aspirations in abeyance. Instead, from the morning after election day, nearly every one of the government's actions and policies has been determined by how it might best make the province politically independent. The government's chief and perhaps fatal error has been to enact the militant language and culture policies of Camille Laurin. By proving that protection of Quebec's heritage can be accommodated within confederation, Lévesque has jettisoned the most powerful single banner of his chauvinistic crusade. Without the atmosphere of cultural insecurity, Quebec nationalism has lost much of its sting.

None of this means that the Parti Québécois referendum will necessarily be defeated. Lévesque has succeeded in persuading many of the province's voters that preservation of the French-English status quo has become the most radical position of all. By hacking away at Ottawa's presence in Quebec, he is gradually reducing federal involvement in the daily lives of most French Canadians and taking away most of the compelling reasons for remaining faithful to the tenets of confederation.

The best description of the Canadian dilemma was Montreal comedian Yvon Deschamps's recent wisecrack: "I don't know why the English think of us as inconsistent. All we want is an independent Quebec within a strong and united Canada."

—1978

❆　❆　❆

IT'S SOMEHOW TYPICAL that the leader of the movement whose aim it is to destroy Canada should be not a hollow-eyed young revolutionary with clenched fist but a middle-aged charmer with the hand gestures of a Las Vegas comic. René Lévesque was in the other day promoting his autobiography, *My Québec*, which he dismissed as "a lazy man's book" because it's little more than the transcript of his interview with Jean-Robert Leselbaun, an editor of Paris's *Le Nouvel Economiste*. It's certainly not great literature, but as a straightforward statement of political aims, this is an essential document.

At a press conference, Lévesque punctuated his natural Gallic exuberance with such quintessentially WASP mollifiers as "to be fair about it . . ." and "with due respect . . ." But his message was crystal-clear: the sovereignty-association being pushed by his Parti Québécois is nothing more than a smokescreen for the breakup of Canada as a political and social unit. Beneath that gallantry, moxie, and charm lives a ramrod fanatic who believes that Quebec's only acceptable future is to become a republic with himself as president.

On the human level, *My Québec* chronicles an odyssey of profound disillusionment from being called a "pea-souper" in New Carlisle, the anglophone village in the Gaspé where young René simmered up, to his current bitterness, best caught in his paraphrase of the Winston Churchill metaphor: "Canada and Quebec cannot continue to live like two scorpions in the same bottle."

The volume documents both his strong affection for Quebec and the conviction that the province has been relegated to colonial status by most other Canadians. "The more I got to know Canada, the more I cut myself off from it," Lévesque recalls of his mood in the early Sixties. "I felt like an Indian leaving his reserve each time I left Quebec." The book's most curious section is his discussion of the upcoming Quebec referendum during which, he confesses, "We must put as much luck as possible on our side." His argument abandons logic as he places the onus on the other nine provinces for accepting Quebec's eventual – and, in his view, inevitable – independence. Seldom has a politician dismissed more than a century of democratic evolution with as much contempt as Lévesque when he proclaims that the referendum "will be the first chance that history has given to Quebeckers to decide, themselves, on their collective future."

Unlike most politicians, René Lévesque is not afraid to announce the reality of his intentions. Asked how he felt about being lumped together with Peter Lougheed and Allan Blakeney in a jab by Pierre Trudeau naming the trio as the villains of Confederation, the Quebec premier took quick umbrage at being included in any such tally. "They're not separatists," he said. "I *am*."

—1979

185

A VERY LONG TIME AGO, when French-English relations were still an appropriate subject for jokes in this country, Eric Nicol, the Vancouver humorist, wisecracked that Confederation reminded him of a mail-order brassiere – "intended to contain and uplift, it has instead drawn attention to the cleavage."

Now, barely a month before the referendum vote, that cleavage is threatening our existence as a nation. With astounding legerdemain René Lévesque seems to be convincing an increasing number of Quebeckers that sovereignty-association is not a partisan issue designed to aggrandize the limits of the PQ's powers as a provincial government. He has somehow managed to move the idea of a separate Quebec into that misty realm that transcends not only politics but also ideology.

He has accomplished this by the simple device of pretending that the referendum is nothing more than the call for a stronger constitutional bargaining position. But, as Pierre Bourgault, one of Quebec's original separatist leaders, has pointed out, "In the last provincial election, some people voted for René Lévesque not because they agreed with him but because they wanted to get rid of Robert Bourassa. Well, you can't have one without the other. If you voted for Lévesque you must expect him to govern according to his program."

That program, which Lévesque has openly espoused in his writings and pre-referendum pronouncements, calls for the tearing up of Canada by the establishment of an independent Quebec. It would command its own army and occupy a separate seat at the UN. Quebec City's legislative assembly would exercise the usual powers over taxes and laws possessed by national parliaments. This all sounds very glorious, but in terms of the average Quebecker's future it would come down to a lower standard of living and sharply reduced civil liberties.

The rules of the referendum battle have conveniently limited direct participation in the debate to Quebec's own citizens. But it is Canada's existence as much as Quebec's future that will be decided on May 20. That most Canadians have opted out of any personal involvement reminds me of a dialogue in one of Arthur Koestler's early novels in which a citizen innocent of wrongdoing is being interrogated by a secret service official.

"I accuse this man," the prosecutor says wearily, "of complicity in murder and crime of the present, past, and future."

"I never killed a fly," replies the astonished defendant.

"Ah, but the flies you didn't kill brought pestilence to the whole province."

—1980

✳   ✳   ✳

THE MOST PUZZLING ASPECT of René Lévesque's referendum rhetoric is that he insists on spelling out the details of how his newly separated nation would operate – right down to the size of its icebreaker fleet, its policy on NATO, and the tune of its national anthem. Yet he has failed to articulate a single good reason for trying so hard to make Quebec independent.

Politicians routinely dispense false hope to the faithful, but seldom more so than in this campaign. Lévesque has always played with fire, finding his way along the chain of sparks he ignites with his assaults on the status quo. But by advocating the substance of separatism without any accompanying rationale that would justify Canada's break-up, he is misleading his own followers. His simplistic, emotionally charged crusade is an attempt to take his province on a journey back through time less reminiscent of Conrad's *Heart of Darkness* than of Coppola's *Apocalypse Now*.

Liberal leader Claude Ryan is launched on a very different course. He believes that the confinements of French Canada's place within Confederation can best be broken by a sequence of constitutional reforms that would transform this country without destroying it. His campaign, ineptly managed as it may be, is rooted in the fundamentally sound proposition that any appeal to sectarian interests on the basis of racial purity is bound to be self-defeating. His is a tough proposition to sell in the face of the arguments of the Parti Québécois that a referendum defeat will only earn English Canada's disdain, closing the door to significant change.

In this context it's essential for English Canadians to get across to Quebec's voters the clear message that they will interpret their "no" ballots as more than a rejection of separatism. Lévesque's defeat would be welcomed by those of us who live outside Quebec, not because it would set back his delusions of nationhood but because it would signal Quebeckers' reaffirmation of faith that Canada's two major communities respect and want to accommodate each other's differences.

Claude Ryan's contention that a new deal is possible without resorting to secession remains credible only if English Canada is prepared to interpret a "no" victory as this kind of restatement of mutual trust. The issue is not – as the constitutional purists in Ottawa seem to believe – the dubious legal validity of the sovereignty-association option. The more urgent reality is that the country and its economy cannot function without the confidence of both partners that their continued union is serving the best interests of each.

—1980

❊　❊　❊

EACH OF THE MAIN COMBATANTS in Quebec's referendum war is arguing that his option offers the greatest long-term security against tyranny, economic decline, and cultural assimilation.

This cynical appeal to vestiges of French Canada's lingering sense of insecurity strikes me as fatuous and unrealistic. René Lévesque has threatened that political leaders in the rest of Canada will be forced to negotiate "on their knees" if there is a strong "yes" vote on May 20. In fact, nine provincial premiers and the prime minister have already rejected the concept of sovereignty-association, and if Quebec actually separates, its relationship with Canada would be the same as that between any two nations. No more and no less.

In his government's white paper the PQ leader defined the degree of sovereignty to which he aspires by stating that "the only laws that will apply on Quebec territory will be those adopted by the National Assembly, and the only taxes that will be levied will be those decreed by Quebec law." At the same time, he wants to maintain economically advantageous associations with what's left of Canada through a customs union and a common currency.

It's an impossible dream. By unequivocally committing himself to full control over taxation, social and investment policies, public borrowing, and all the many governmental edicts that inflate or deflate the value of national currencies, Lévesque has doomed the possibility of keeping Quebec and Canada on the same dollar.

Probably the most telling criticism of the sovereignty-association concept has come from Eugene Forsey, Canada's most knowledgeable constitutional expert: "Sovereignty-association is a horse that won't even start, let alone run. If Mr. Lévesque came to Ottawa to negotiate sovereignty-association, a government of Canada, of whatever party, would simply have to tell him the thing can't be done. . . . You can no more negotiate sovereignty-association than you can negotiate sour sugar, dry water, boiling ice, or stationary motion."

—1980

❉   ❉   ❉

IN THE PARADE OF REPARTEE, cris de coeur, and mudslinging that has marked Quebec's referendum campaign, only one stone-truth has emerged: that no matter what its results, Canada cannot stay the same. Continuing to debate the shadings of interpretation in the 147 clauses of the British North America Act in smoke-filled hotel rooms will no longer satisfy even the most ardent of Quebec's federalists.

The current constitutional arrangement is only one of six that have governed French-English relations in this country, the others being those of 1763, 1774, 1791, 1840, and 1867. There is no reason we can't agree to a new administrative format that would allow Quebec to create and control the kind of economic and social institutions that would truly reflect French Canada's soul. That's what Daniel Johnson, the province's shrewdest postwar premier, meant when he mused: "Where the French-Canadian nation finds its freedom, there too will be its homeland."

René Lévesque has taken that approach to its illogical extreme by tying his followers' political fortunes to a hybrid and unworkable concept that has no modern precedent except for the madcap constitution of the Austro-Hungarian Empire. (The PQ's sovereignty-asso-ciation option echoes the addle-headed battle cry of the top-hatted nineteenth-century politicians who recognized no contradiction in describing Canada as "a self-governing colony.")

The case for keeping Canada together has probably been put best by Ontario Premier Bill Davis. "There are some who believe that we're little more than a race of cost accountants and lawyers with no passionate commitment to anything other than the balance sheet and good business," he told a Toronto audience recently. "Those who believe that delude themselves. Our strong faith in Canada should not be interpreted as smug satisfaction with the existing state of affairs. We're deeply committed to the traditions of this country, to its history, to the promise it provides our young people, for the kind of lifestyle its freedom and institutions guarantee. We are not prepared to see those basic tenets of our nationhood ripped apart or negotiated away. It's just that simple."

What's essential about the outcome of the May 20 referendum is that neither side misinterpret the results. A decisive "yes" victory would inexorably begin the process of Canada's dissolution. Should Claude Ryan's "no" option receive a majority mandate, the real battle for a Canadian future would begin. Either way, if our politicians don't succeed in implementing a new constitution by the end of this decade, they will have no country left to govern.

—1980

❄   ❄   ❄

SURELY THE MOST UNFORGETTABLE MOMENT of a memorable night was the ghostly dignity of a tearful René Lévesque, his face soft and delicate as in an Oriental painting, blessing his cheering supporters as he stood before them confessing defeat. The requiem for a heavy-weight, this was the concession of a man confident his ideas will survive any sojourn in the purgatory of postponed dreams.

A defeat it was for the hybrid sovereignty-association option of the Parti Québécois. But for those who live outside Quebec, the result was less a victory than a reprieve. The onus has now shifted to English

Canada: we must achieve an equivalently convincing state of grace of believing in ourselves and a common future.

Probably the most important factor in the referendum campaign was that it could be held at all. How many countries are there left in the world that would calmly allow a democratic vote on their own disintegration? Perhaps it was this subliminal benevolence that swung the undecided balance into the federalist camp.

For more than two decades, French and English Canadians have been dealing with each other in a series of confrontations of unequal intervals and unpredictable intensity, seeking but never finding the ultimate compromise. The argument of the intelligent separatists has inevitably followed the same logical exposition: that while communities can be integrated, individuals can only be assimilated, so that until Quebec becomes independent (or the next thing to it) English Canada's efforts at bilingualism and biculturalism, no matter how well-meaning, are doomed to failure. The federal response has always been that Ottawa would gladly grant individual equality (within the federal civil service, for example) but that to treat Quebec as a separate entity was not negotiable. Now we must seek a middle way that will satisfy both the collective and the individual yearnings of French-speaking Canadians.

Those Quebeckers who voted "*non*" gambled that their best chance of surviving as a proud, autonomous people was through a firm alliance with the larger reality of the Canadian nation.

Not to betray that act of faith will require nothing less than literally reinventing Canada – creation of a new nationality that will convincingly serve both of the country's founding societies.

—1980

The Man in the Iron Mask

IT WAS A GLORIOUS APRIL MORNING in that once-upon-a-time spring of 1968, and the Pierre Elliott Trudeau who greeted me as I stepped into his as-yet-unfurnished office had just been sworn in as Canada's fifteenth prime minister. During his term in Justice, Trudeau had passed on several cabinet leaks about plans for his department. As I set up my tape recorder, I said, "Hey, I'm really glad you won the leadership. Now you'll be able to leak news to me from *all* the ministries. . . ."

"Listen," Trudeau shot back, his face suddenly hard as an iron mask, "the first cabinet leak you get, I'll have the RCMP tap your phone."

Trudeau was legally correct to squash my feeble attempt to poke fun at the Privy Council oath that binds cabinet members to secrecy. But his reaction to what was obviously a tension-relieving joke was so extreme that our exchange has always stayed with me. It was a DEW-line signal of how fast and how completely power would change the man who, literally hours before, had been on the convention floor, doing the boogaloo, shrugging away his victory, and kissing the girls under the shimmer of television klieg lights.

Pierre Elliott Trudeau's candour, his intellectual curiosity, his nose-thumbing at the staid traditions of this country's highest political office qualified him as our first existential political hero: the man with the red rose in his buttonhole, the guy who rescued us – finally – from the age of Mackenzie King.

He saved Confederation by facing down the Front de Libération

192

du Québec in 1970 and winning the referendum on French Canada's future a decade later. He made us all aware that politics at its best consists not of backroom deals but of sharing the passions of our age. His reign overlapped the terms of five American presidents and five British prime ministers; he served more time in office than the combined total of nine leaders of the Conservative party since 1919. He won four elections, kept the Liberals in power for all but nine months of the past sixteen years, and accomplished precisely what he set out to do: bring home Canada's constitution and create a "new Canada" within which talented Quebeckers could take their rightful place.

Trudeau brought out the best and the worst in us, providing a catharsis from the national ennui under his predecessors. He exposed our collective prejudices, regional jealousies, and general stuffiness, so that when his term expired, mixed with the public jubilation was the feeling that somehow we had let *him* down, that his challenge to all of us to be a little less grey, to play it a little less safe, had gone unanswered.

This dichotomy of feeling is caught in a quote from the French essayist Jean de La Bruyère, commenting on the demise of a literary rival: "It is rumoured that Piso is dead. It is a great loss. He was a good man and deserved a longer life. He was talented, reliable, resolute and courageous, faithful and generous. Provided, of course, that he is really dead."

Though they would endure a week of blackflies before admitting it, most Canadians, at the time of Trudeau's resignation, pined a while for the delicious feeling we had when we dared elect (not as a temporary fluke, but to rule most of a generation) such a fabulous smart ass. No other country could boast of a head of government who could dance the Arab *moozmaad* in Sheik Yamani's desert tent; practise his pirouette behind the Queen's back at Buckingham Palace; yell "*Mangez la merde!*" at striking mail-truck drivers; skin-dive, high-dive, and ride a unicycle; earn a brown belt in judo; date some of the world's most desirable women, marry a sexy twenty-two-year-old Margaret Sinclair, and have two of his three sons, Justin and Sacha (Michel is the third son), born on the same day as Jesus Christ. Even his marriage break-up would command world attention, as Margaret "liberated" herself in the company of the Rolling Stones, the Studio 54 crowd, and Manhattan's jaded jetset.

But even more than by his words or actions, Trudeau was defined by his gestures – the man's body language is worthy of a doctoral thesis in linguistics. He was always the dancing man, sliding down banisters, dodging (or slugging) pickets, hopping on or off platforms (some say *fences*). And then there was the chilly topography of his face, his intelligent, devilish countenance, unlined by what Balzac called "private defeats," offset by eyes the depth and colour of the sea. As Global-TV's Doug Small phrased it, Trudeau's is "an aboriginal face." Marshall McLuhan had said "tribal."

In a television age when most stars feel lucky if they last the season, Trudeau's hold on the Canadian imagination was only magnified by time. He became the resident Canadian wizard, doing his grainy thing.

LOOKING BACK ON THIS REMARKABLE prime minister and his times, it seems clear that we burdened him with expectations no mortal could meet. There *had* to be a gap between his intentions and his deeds, between his promise and his performance. But that didn't explain why he became the most despised prime minister in our history.

No realist thought Trudeau would in fact become a philosopher-king. All of our successful prime ministers quickly became adept at pragmatic improvisation. What we did have the right to expect in him was a leader who would not only tolerate but encourage discussion and dissent. Trudeau in power remained a supremely detached Jesuit with a splinter of ice in his heart. If it was true that John Diefenbaker too often "thought with his heart," it was equally true that Pierre Trudeau too frequently "felt with his mind," leaving the impression that he didn't give a damn.

Throughout the Trudeau years, Canadian voters waited in vain for that magic moment when Pierre would wake to realize that mind was not enough to revive his divided and economically downcast country. But compassion remained a quality that did not cast much of a shadow on his interior landscape. Trudeau in office was a Zen adept who could detach himself from whatever was happening around him, judging or not judging as he wished.

Despite a resoluteness of purpose unmatched by that of any other Canadian political leader, Trudeau operated out of a very deep fallacy: he tended to stifle dissent. During his time in power, Trudeau's inner court lived and worked in an environment as cloistered as a high-walled Gobi Desert treasure city before Marco Polo came by. What they forgot was that in a democracy, the minority's dissent is just as important as the majority's assent; that thoughts and feelings, however untidy, must be gathered from many sources and can never be irrelevant to the exercise of power. Before he became prime minister, Trudeau had travelled the country on the slogan that he was looking for "new guys with new ideas." Once in power, he behaved as though he wanted "new guys with the same ideas" – the same as his own.

As the Trudeau years rolled on and the voices of disorder began bellowing their demands even louder, his advisers felt threatened and began to play everything safe, placing the avoidance of disaster ahead of legislative adventures; their operational code became "Always the Lesser Evil."

Trudeau's retreat into petulance was reminiscent of nothing so much as a description of Francis Bacon by Lytton Strachey, who wrote that "Bacon's intelligence was external. He could understand almost everything except his own heart."

I recall the time I was discussing the prime minister with Gordon Fairweather (later named the first chairman of Canada's Human Rights Commission but then an Opposition MP from New Brunswick), who commanded enormous respect and affection in Official Ottawa. When the Trudeaus had given birth to one of their December 25 babies, Fairweather was delighted. In a burst of bonhomie, he went down to his local post office on Boxing Day to send a congratulatory wire. In the post office the telegrapher, a true-blue Tory, said she didn't want to transmit the message. She tried to get Fairweather to give up on it. He wouldn't, and found the whole episode quite funny, a vignette of his riding's style.

When the House session opened in January, he went up to Trudeau at the usual Speaker's cocktail party and tried to tell him what had happened, thinking Trudeau might find it amusing. Trudeau simply stared back at him, bored, and said – as though he thought Fairweather was fishing for a thank-you for the telegram – "Oh, I never saw it. There were so many hundreds of them we decided not to be bothered."

Fairweather later commented that he felt not so much hurt as punctured – as though he had been punched in the chest, hard.

—1974/1984

THERE WAS A HUSH in the ballroom of the Château Laurier Hotel when Pierre and Margaret Trudeau arrived just before midnight on July 8 to acknowledge their triumph. Little flares of fake lightning flashed around the couple's heads as the press photographers closed in for that one great shot they're always hunting. But near the back of the hall, behind the raised platforms on which the TV cameras stood like ancient artillery pieces mounted for a long siege, a member of the PM's staff said to no one in particular, "I can almost smell the familiar scent of Liberal arrogance wafting into the room." A Press Gallery veteran replied, "Yeah, when he gets to the microphone, I wouldn't be surprised if Trudeau announced that now he has his majority he's invoking the War Measures Act for the next four years so he won't have to bother his Perfect Self with all the little piddling details."

But in the next fifteen minutes, while Trudeau did his humble turn in front of the cameras, the wiseacres were proven at least temporarily wrong; nothing in the prime minister's political life became him more than his acceptance of this astonishing victory. Still, the cynics were expressing, in an extreme way, a vague fear that must have been in the minds of many Canadians as their hands wavered over their ballots earlier on that long summer day: how large a vote of confidence would it take to turn Pierre the Jolly Populist of 1974 back into Pierre the Pious Autocrat of 1972?

Nobody will know the answer for months, maybe years. But my hunch is that Trudeau won't retreat again into his ivory cocoon. If there is one thing this election demonstrated, it was his flexibility, the ability to bend his honed intellect to new circumstances and to take the advice of the enlightened pragmatists (Keith Davey, Jim Coutts, Jerry Grafstein, and Eddie Rubin among them) who rushed to his aid.

This same kind of flexibility of attitude should be applied at once to the problem of inflation. It has to be tackled, not in terms of how we're doing on the OECD scale of fiscal performances, but in terms of the terrible hardships runaway prices inflict on people's lives. Trudeau stumped the country telling the throngs that Tory solutions were wrongheaded and simpleminded, that his own approach was too complex to be described out there on the wharves and the pavements, but that it would involve his own brand of political courage.

It can be said (and it was, often, in the days just after his victory) that the great outpouring of support for Trudeau was as much a vote of non-confidence in his opponent, Robert Stanfield, as it was a vote of confidence in the PM. But why or how the Liberals won is far less relevant than the fact that Trudeau has been granted that rarest of political benefactions: a second chance. What he needs to demonstrate now is that he knows how to lead: not just that he can preside over a government, but that he can genuinely respond to a nation's needs.

—1974

✳ ✳ ✳

POLITICS IN CANADA has always been the art of making the necessary possible. This process depends for its success on a prime minister's ability to mix a genuine gift to inspire with brilliant negotiating skills and a creative urge to heal. Instead, Pierre Trudeau has tainted the political process with personal impertinence, a feeling that he cares more for what he *is* than for whom he represents.

A decade ago, when he was first catapulted into political prominence, Trudeau appeared to be what Professor Paul Fox, the political scientist, called "a consensual man"–there was something in him for everybody. We followed with happy spirit to see where his ideas might lead. His governing principle of not imposing views on others but allowing people to find their own way to his beliefs seemed ideal for the Sixties.

But gradually he became less interested in social change than in continuity, more committed to the legal niceties of constitutional reform than to any adventurous attempts to fashion a new brand of nationhood.

Feeling threatened by the angry voices of disorder bellowing their demands outside the safe confines of their inner circle, the prime minister and his aides closed ranks. Trudeau cut himself off from reality, mistaking the chatter of his court for the voice of the people. The initiatives of governing were increasingly assumed by bureaucratic functionaries who believed that social problems could be resolved through efficient management and whose notion of hunger was being exposed to bad service in one of Ottawa's many declining French restaurants. They went on their way treating Outer Canada (that part of the country beyond the ten blocks surrounding Parliament Hill) as a scattering of unruly colonial outposts, acting as if they were afraid that a group of more daring citizens might dump a load of tea into Victoria Harbour. Deaf to the urgencies of the moment, they have brought us as a nation to the verge of the Eighties bereft of imagination or much faith in a collective future.

The results of the fifteen by-elections have allowed the Liberal government to suffer defeat without losing office. But at the very least, the polls should have demonstrated to Pierre Trudeau that he can no longer keep creating his private vision of reality by imposing cool logic on the irrationality of events. There are moments in every public career – and this is one of them – when intellect is no longer enough, when a true sense of compassion and the genuine will to lead must claim a politician's full priorities. If Pierre Trudeau can no longer respond adequately to the crisis in leadership that is our most pressing national issue, he should resign.

—1978

❋   ❋   ❋

OUR DREAMS WERE HIGH in that hopeful springtime of 1968 when Pierre Trudeau had just taken power and among his first promises was "basic reform of the Senate" – a pledge to extend the commendable politically neutral record he'd earned as minister of justice in filling federal judgeships.

Then he made his first Senate appointment: Louis (Bob) Giguère, a Liberal hack from Montreal later charged with conspiracy and influence-peddling in connection with the Sky Shops at Dorval Airport.

It is that gap between promise and performance that has always puzzled me about this most unconventional of the curious men who have had the audacity to try running this country since 1867.

Politics is a hard trade that normally requires half a lifetime's apprenticeship. But like some sorcerer's apprentice, Trudeau suddenly flashed on the scene to capture our political souls through a magic we do not yet fully comprehend. Ten years later, his hold over our imaginations has scarcely diminished.

Pierre Trudeau's offhand arrogance produced the string of mad epiphanies that have marked his reign: "Where's Biafra?" "Why should I sell your wheat?" If he had planned it, he could hardly have managed to alienate each of his many constituencies so thoroughly: Canadian farmers are in revolt; Bay Street is apoplectic; the unions are pledged to his destruction; a million unemployed spit his name in cold fury. Yet he enters any meeting hall or appears on a television screen and the electricity still flows. He seems possessed of that rarest of political qualities, the one that Joe Clark and Ed Broadbent can only dream about: he walks into a room and the room is different. His presence seems somehow to affect not our minds or hearts so much as our nervous systems. (I remember once standing beside a Liberal matron at a party function. Just before Trudeau was due to be ushered through the door, she stiffened and turned to her huge block of a sideburned husband with the whimper: "What if I faint when he comes in?" The husband cut her in two with a look of total disgust, his eyes rolling heavenward, searching for relief. But when Trudeau finally loped by and happened to shake the man's hand, he quietly started to cry.)

Ten years into his job, Trudeau appears astonishingly vigorous, fully in command of his worth. His skin is permanently tinted with the incandescent glow that a million TV spotlights eventually impart to the flesh. Remote, austere, hermetically self-contained, the blue-ice inner core of the man remains inviolate. Intellectually threatened or distracted by some lesser mortal's dim assault, his face hardens, the eyes turn to azure marbles floating in lead. But most of the time his countenance is much more benign; the shrugs, hand gestures, flashes of intuition and wit tending to make him as difficult to read and yet as evocative as a Picasso charcoal abstract. He is a star.

Trudeau's conquest of the Liberal party and the calculated destruction of his real and perceived political rivals have been so complete that most people have forgotten how close he came to being beaten by the late Robert Winters, who lost the 1968 Liberal leadership convention on a fourth-ballot count that gave Trudeau only 51.1 per cent of the delegates. But his evolution into a "party man" has since been so successfully guided by Senator Keith Davey that even during the summer of 1976, when Liberal fortunes sank to a record low of 29 per cent on the Gallup poll, there was hardly a dissident murmur.

What the party professionals remember is the Trudeau of the 1968 election, when he touched and exploited all the right response centres in the Canadian psyche. I recall especially the hordes of teeny-boppers, long manes of hair streaming like banners in the wind, clutching their machine-autographed pictures of Trudeau like amulets to their breasts. Countless bemused toddlers were being held up on the shoulders of their parents and admonished to "remember him" as the excitement surged across the country. The press cameras clicked like a hundred hungry insects every time Trudeau would alight from his prime ministerial jet (conjuring up images of one of the minor Caesars of the late Roman empire) to make his triumphant way from one shopping plaza to the next.

What emerged out of all this Trudeaumania was a very different and unexpected phenomenon that became known as Trudeaucracy – conduct of the nation's affairs with Orwellian overtones that tended to reduce the role of government to the refining and implementation of bureaucratic directives. Those of us who took Trudeau at his word when he stormed the political barricades thought we were getting a leader who would not only tolerate but even encourage dissent. What we got instead was a cool cat whose byword might be a quote from Lord Acton, Trudeau's favourite political writer, who once confessed: "I don't hate humanity. I just don't know them personally."

Even though he is perceived as more of a patriarch than a democrat, Trudeau's popularity is nowhere lower than among the members of Canada's business Establishment. They view his every action with brooding suspicion. More seriously, they're moving so much money and investment intentions out of the country that unless Trudeau quickly finds some way of calming their fears, we could have a real economic crisis on our hands. This is hard to understand, because tax breaks, particularly to Western oil producers, have blossomed during the Trudeau years. By 1983 corporations (their assessments reduced by a long roster of special allowances and exemptions) accounted for only 13 per cent of federal tax revenues, compared with 28 per cent fifteen years before.

Trudeau has never been able to understand why big businessmen (whom he tends to lump as "the bankers") are so hung up on his mildly derogatory musings about the free enterprise system and not at all impressed by his administration's manoeuvres to enlist the private sector in job-creation schemes and capital spending allowances. His imposition of wage controls in October 1975 was an enlightened attempt to beat down the fires of inflation, as was the Six-and-Five program seven years later. Both initiatives were successful. But no matter what Trudeau does or says, the hate campaign goes on unabated.

A typical anti-Trudeau joke concerns six men on a small plane that has only five parachutes. The little jet gets into trouble, bursts into flames, and starts plummeting to earth. The pilot jumps clear, after pointing out that he has taken one of the parachutes so he can tell the plane's manufacturers what went wrong, and advises the passengers to fight it out among themselves to see which of them will get the other four. Trudeau claims priority and leaps out, explaining that, as the brains of Canada, he can't afford to be sacrificed. Two other passengers exit, giving their reasons, and finally there are only an elderly professor and a student left. The venerable academic goes into a lengthy dissertation about how he has already lived most of his life and that the youngster should save himself first. "No, it's okay," says the triumphant kid. "We can both go. There are *still* two parachutes. When 'the brains of Canada' bailed out, he used my knapsack."

The rationale for such Trudeauphobia is less the feeling that Ottawa has strengthened its interventionist grip on the economy than the after-effects of specific legislative acts: the retroactive directive preventing the sale of Denison Mines to a Canadian subsidiary of the U.S.-owned Continental Oil Company and the establishment of Petrocan, the Foreign Investment Review Agency, and the National Energy Program.

The main trouble with Liberal economic policies under Trudeau has been that they have alternated between following John Maynard Keynes (who taught that governments should intervene in the economy only as a means of smoothing out business cycles) and John Kenneth Galbraith (who advocated much more fundamental structural reforms), but ended up following neither with much conviction or effect.

Another story currently making the Establishment rounds helps illustrate the kind of pettiness with which Trudeau's royal court is being charged. It seems that recently Tom Enders (a Canadian Establishment folk hero who happens to be U.S. ambassador to Canada) decided to give a small private dinner to which he invited the prime minister as well as John Turner, the Establishment's Very Own Pretender to the Liberal throne. A few days before the party, an aide in the Prime Minister's Office telephoned to inquire whether Turner had accepted. The ambassador, who has been good friends with Turner for years, even before he was posted to Canada, confirmed the fact. The prime ministerial assistant clucked in disappointment and allowed this was a pity because in that case, the PM would not be there.

Enders replied that he hoped the aide would carry a message to his master: "Please tell him that my friendships are not negotiable."

Canadian prime ministers have always attempted to create a concurrent cabinet majority by sharing their powers with a senior colleague from the other basic culture. Trudeau is the exception. Not only does he lack an English political lieutenant but an incredible parade of twenty-seven ministers – most of them English – have resigned from his cabinet in the past ten years. His musical-chair shuffles have made farce of several important portfolios. There have been seven ministers of consumer and corporate affairs, for instance, six postmasters general, five ministers of national defence.

An administration that was to have been as delicately programmed as a third-generation computer has somehow turned itself into a troupe of careless pranksters who would have been the pride of the social director on the *Titanic*.

Kissing away most of that hope and all that expectation, Canada is ending the first decade of Trudeau's rule with the taste of ashes, wondering why this obviously great man has yet to fulfil his promise.

—1978/1984

❄   ❄   ❄

EVER SINCE PIERRE TRUDEAU was returned to office ten months ago, his government has exercised its mandate in mysterious ways. Through his constitutional hufflings and energy policy punches, the prime minister has attained a peculiar perch seldom achieved by any of his predecessors: he has managed to alienate every region of the country at the same time. Just about the only unifying activity left in Canada by year's end is sticking poison pins into Trudeau dolls.

The mood of disillusionment with Trudeau is particularly strong in Western Canada. A story that's currently cracking them up across lunch at the Calgary Petroleum Club concerns James Coutts, the prime minister's major-domo, who decides to test Alberta's political mood. He dresses up in an appropriate Western outfit so that he's not recognized, goes to the toughest bar in town, and yells out, "Trudeau is a horse's ass!" A gung-ho cowboy sitting nearby punches him in the face, sending the delicate Coutts reeling across the floor. As soon as he recovers, Coutts shakes his head in disbelief, muttering, "I didn't realize this was Trudeau country."

"It's not," the cowboy replies. "This is horse country."

THE EXPLANATION FOR THE QUANTUM LEAP in Trudeau's political tendencies is deceptively simple. Having decided to quit politics in the fall of 1979 and devote his declining years to collecting Margaret foldouts, Trudeau received a disillusioning surprise. As he leafed through his political obituaries, reading the various summings-up of his prime ministerial career, he realized that history would remember him for very little. His chief monument, it seemed, would be his brave attempt to turn French-language instructions about how to pour milk onto cornflakes into a motherhood issue.

Once Messrs Coutts, Davey, and MacEachen had restored Trudeau to his rightful place beside the heated swimming pool at 24 Sussex, Himself decided it was time to launch some grandiose flights of statesmanship so that he wouldn't end up in a footnote, described as the guy who beat Joe Clark.

The result has been a drastic shifting of political priorities in Ottawa, which has seen old ideas (patriating the constitution) presented as mind-blowers and new concepts (the Canadianization of the oil industry) disguised in the traditional raiment of worthy policies long overdue. Both these objectives are eminently worthwhile. But new legislative initiatives, especially such fundamental reforms as are now being debated, require the creation of a nationwide floating consensus – the gradual bringing together of people's natural tendency to oppose change with the realization that what they're being asked to approve is an idea whose time has come.

What we have had instead is a year that shattered the detached tranquillity of Canadian life. In his headlong rush to make history, Pierre Trudeau threatens to unwind the history we have so far made.

—1981

* * *

TERMINALLY COOL, Pierre Trudeau took leave of his office with a rare touch of civility. More than any of his predecessors, he had made unpopular decisions and challenged the voters to like him or lump him. They did both. By the winter of 1984, Canada's political terrain had become either a graveyard (the West) or a minefield (the rest of the country), and the electorate was lying in wait to humble him.

Trudeau had overdrawn his psychic bank account. He decided to quit because he couldn't think of a good reason to stay. The constitution was home; bilingualism was permanently in place; his peace initiative was stalled; the economy seemed beyond salvation. There was no fun in the nation's business any more; half the provincial premiers were acting like reactionary duds and the Tory Opposition had a respectable leader who didn't provide much good sport.

Another disturbing element for this most introspective of prime ministers had been the cabinet shuffle in the summer of 1983. William Rompkey, a Newfoundland Liberal who had bountifully established his bumbling incompetence, was replaced as minister of mines by a former high school principal from Burin–St.George's named Roger Simmons. Not only did a subsequent trial find Simmons guilty of tax evasion but his testimony also revealed that he'd neglected to have his driving licence renewed for so long that he was allowed to use his car only on a week-by-week basis; that his life insurance was cancelled because he forgot to pay the premiums; and that he seemed to have overlooked the fact that he had teeth, because when he finally got to a dentist he had ten cavities and three rotting molars. To replace this simple Simmons, Trudeau re-appointed Bill Rompkey, but the experience left him shaken and muttering about bottoms of barrels.

Trudeau kept his blue mood private, except for one curious occasion in mid-October 1983, when he interrupted a political speech he was giving at Strathroy to deliver a soliloquy on his thoughts as he was being driven through the Ontario heartland, a soliloquy that spoke of his bewilderment at the country he administered but never truly understood: "There was acre upon acre of farmland, and all we could see – though I pressed my forehead against the cold window – all we could see were little lights here and there. And I was wondering: what kind of people lived in those houses? And what kind of people lived, loved, and worked in this part of Canada?"

At about this time, the public opinion polls, which had swung in a tidal wave of approval for the choice of Brian Mulroney as leader of the Progressive Conservative party six months before, were failing to show any significant return to the Liberals. Not even the publicity surrounding Trudeau's peace initiative had budged his ratings very much. In Toronto, Mashel Teitelbaum, the artist who had circulated the original petition urging Trudeau to take up the Liberal leadership, was now sponsoring a very different appeal. "Since you seem to be totally out of touch with the everyday struggles of your constituents," he urged his former hero, "we, as your humble subjects, beseech you for the sake of the future of this country to do the honorable thing – and step down."

The Ottawa press corps was fretting to use all those pre-written resignation think-pieces and in-depth TV reports. On the evening of February 28, Trudeau phoned Martin Goldfarb, the Liberal party's guru on public opinion. The good news was that Liberal fortunes had at last started to climb, with the party as popular as it had been in the 1980 election; the bad news was that even though Trudeau was never more highly respected, most voters felt strongly that it was time for him to go.

The prime minister walked out into Ottawa's worst blizzard in four years, thought over his options, and decided to resign. "I went out to see if there were any signs of my destiny in the sky," he said the next morning, "but there weren't – there was nothing but snowflakes."

The initial reaction was unexpectedly muted. The *Toronto Sun*'s

Peter Worthington expressed the views of other Trudeau-haters when he declared that he wanted ''to drive a wooden stake through Trudeau's heart'' to make sure he was really finished. Most commentators, however, agreed with Trudeau's blood enemy, René Lévesque, who remarked, ''He sure made things more interesting – not necessarily more appealing, but certainly more interesting.''

The proposition Professor Kenneth McNaught, a University of Toronto historian, had put forth when Trudeau first joined the Liberal party (''His commitment is an act of supreme symbolic importance, and his political fate will likely be the political fate of Canada . . .'') had yet to be proved or disproved. When I asked McNaught to reflect on his forecast, he replied, ''I'm not surprised to see how accurately I predicted things. The great issues in Canada are the federal-provincial structure, language, and religion, and these were the areas for which Trudeau went into politics and had his greatest success. He can legitimately say, 'I've done what had to be done.' Without his victory in 1968, Canada would not have been recognizable today.''

That was true enough. Pierre Trudeau, the most inspiring and most reviled prime minister this country has ever elected, had saved Canada. And the reason most Canadians were so ambivalent about the man was that they remained ambivalent about their country. We were glad to have him as a visitor in our time – and a lot gladder he was moving on.

Trudeau had already issued his own epitaph more than ten years earlier. In a television interview on January 1, 1969, he said, ''I'm quite prepared to die politically, when the people think I should. You know, politicians should be like Trappists who go around in monasteries, and the only words they can say to each other are: 'Brother, we must die one day.' I think this is true of politicians. Brother, someday we may be beaten. If I am, what will I do? The world is so full of a number of things, I'm sure we could all be as happy as kings.''

During the intervening decade and a half, Pierre Elliott Trudeau, the constitutional-lawyer-turned-prime-minister, had broadened his universe and made the world his stage. No matter which theatre he chooses to occupy next, he will continue to uphold his ultimate civil liberty: the right to be himself.

HE HAD APPEARED ORIGINALLY from nowhere, an urbane Buddhist monk in mufti, and hypnotized us.

That first election campaign of Pierre Trudeau's was a combination of coronation and Beatles tour. Clutches of teenagers shrieked whenever he deigned to kiss one of their swarming number. I recall in particular one landing in Dartmouth, N.S. We in his 1968 media entourage trudged down the plane's steps on May 29 into a cold, drizzly night. That was wall-to-wall Tory country, but along the route from the airport, as if on a prearranged signal, people came out on their porches to wave at the procession. Many had backed their cars into driveways so that they could flash their headlights in silent salute to the great man.

It was not long afterward that a different reality began to set in. Trudeau defined the office of prime minister in his own image. Distracted by lesser mortals' dim assaults, his face would harden, his eyes tighten from having squinted into too many flashbulbs.

It was true that all of us bestowed on Trudeau too much hope for any leader to fulfil, but ultimately it was not what Trudeau did that left us so disillusioned. It was what he might have done.

As prime minister, Trudeau projected a shimmering intellect. He was by long odds the most resolute political leader this country has ever seen. But in his tendency to stifle dissent, even in his own ranks, there was a tragic fallacy. Tolerating dissent is the essential means by which Canadian society has always come to terms with change. Trudeau and his flunkies believed that they could impose logic on events; that they could govern the country through legalisms and reshape what was happening to fit those legalisms. But the events themselves – history, in other words – were not logical and never could be. They were born out of harsh realities and even harsher emotions, which could not be cut to fit any leader's wishes or good intentions.

Still, his bravura style made us noticed. London's *Daily Sketch* chose him as "the world's seventh-sexiest man"; he brought home our constitution; his regime outlasted virtually every other contemporary world leader's; and he crusaded valiantly for peace. He passed much worthy legislation. To a whole generation he became our first genuine political hero.

He never changed – but we did.

What brought Trudeau to heel was that he couldn't extend his reach to the whole of the country he was governing. The twelve million Canadians who live west of Toronto's Humber River never felt at ease in his world.

Canada's fifteenth prime minister leaves office still in command of his personal worth and not very different from the mysterious stranger he was when we first welcomed him. The difference between the Canada that greeted Pierre Trudeau and the Canada that overwhelmed him sixteen years later is poignantly marked by the contrast between the warm adulation that created him and the cold fury that now bids him adieu.

—1984

Bill Bennett Leaves Town

THE LEGACY OF BILL BENNETT'S eleven years in power is difficult to assess, because he leaves office with virtually none of his great goals – a balanced provincial budget, large-scale export of hydro power to California, establishment of his vaunted "free enterprise zones" – anywhere near fruition. His main accomplishments have all been physical: ribbons of newly paved highway, the $850-million Skytrain across downtown Vancouver, the Annacis Island Bridge across the Fraser River, and Peace River's northeast coal development.

Although he spent more than a decade representing a province of laid-back extroverts, Bennett wasn't one himself. At once paralysed by stage fright in public and painfully shy in private, he spent most of his time living as a recluse in Victoria's Harbour Towers Hotel. Except for his daily trips to the legislature and a morning tennis game, he seldom ventured into the capital city's society. He seemed to feel at home only in his home town of Kelowna.

Even at the height of Bennett's power there was a feeling of impermanence about his administration, not really sure of what it should or should not be doing. Despite the fifteen thousand or more jobs created by Expo, the B.C. economy remains in a state of barely apprehended cataclysm. The unemployment rate, even in the relatively prosperous southern and western portions of the province, is running at nearly 13 per cent, almost four points above the national average. A dozen of the province's main mines remain closed, fishing seems in permanent decline, the woods industries are struggling to modernize, and the much-heralded high-tech revolution is still in its mom-and-pop stage.

What has halted business expansion in British Columbia during the Bennett years, more than any other factor, has been the growing polarization of provincial politics. That gulf of misunderstanding, which occasionally bursts out into corporate-union civil wars, was based not so much on the contradictory ideologies of the Socreds and the New Democrats as on the fact that both parties – and the slices of society they represent – have really been operating on the basis of their own hidden agendas.

The NDP-supported labour movement has been led in large part by Scotsmen who acted as if they had arrived yesterday from Clydeside shipyards still fighting the British class wars. They often seemed less interested in the welfare of their rank and file than in overturning the established order. On the other side, the men who run most of the resource operations and provide hard-core support for Social Credit come straight out of the American union-busting tradition, more anxious to destroy the enemies of free enterprise than to accept better conditions for their workers. There are exceptions to those attitudes, but they have been prevalent enough to keep the province politically – and psychologically – divided into warring camps.

The Bennett departure raises the prospect of the disappearance of Social Credit as a political label. The movement, based on the monetary voodoo preached by an unstable Englishman named Major C.H. Douglas, first caught on in Alberta during the Depression. Douglas's two main disciples, William Aberhart and Ernest Manning, held on to the oil province's premiership for more than three decades. But Peter Lougheed's 1971 victory quickly reduced the Alberta Socreds to a powerless rump. Eventually the federal wing of the party, too, vanished without a trace.

In British Columbia, Social Credit has been less an ideology than a Bennett vehicle for assuming power, having been adopted by the premier's father in 1952 as a way of bringing the anti-socialist forces under one banner. That has been the Social Credit platform ever since, with Bennett making an occasional gesture to the few aging supporters who still take Douglas's rantings seriously.

With such a tenuous hold on the minds of its followers, chances are that the Social Credit aberration may vanish for good. The Bennetts

210

– father and son – have ruled the party and the province (except for the 1972-75 interruption by NDPer Dave Barrett) for more than three decades. The premiership became a family affair. Now the family has stepped out of politics, and all the bets are off.

If the Social Credit party does indeed disappear, British Columbia would at last join the mainstream of Canadian politics – and that could alter the equations by which we are governed.

—1986

The Kamikaze Premier

J UST FOUR FRANTIC DAYS before British Columbians gave free rein to their gambling instincts by entrusting their future to Bill Vander Zalm, I went to one of the premier's final rallies of the campaign. Held at the Macaulay Elementary School gymnasium in Esquimalt, a sleepy suburb of Victoria, it turned out to be one of only three brief appearances that the Social Credit leader made in the provincial capital. But the political voodoo that made his remarkable victory possible was on open display.

The audience was made up mostly of decent, middle-aged, middle-class citizens confused and troubled by a world they never made. There were a few yuppie bungaloids looking for a cause to follow; the odd leftover Sixties hippie, hair tied back Willie Nelson-style; a quartet of loud loggers with room-temperature IQs; a few stray dogs and mutual fund salesmen – your typical Social Credit gathering.

Nothing much happened until Vander Zalm arrived, leaping off his tour bus, which had only one police car as retinue. Because Esquimalt is so close to the capital, a few backroom Socred functionaries were cruising the hall, taking soundings of the crowd that numbered something less than 250. Big men with cruel mouths (scars in bloodless faces), they pranced around, obviously proud of their new boy.

Vander Zalm's smooth handling of what must have been the 419th stop on his four-week campaign, totally indistinguishable from all the others, was impressive. He has the rugged good looks of a safari guide in an old-fashioned jungle movie, with bronzed face, chestnut hair, and restless limb movements. Much has been written about his smile, and it certainly is no ordinary grin. The choreography of arched eyebrows, flashing dimples, pulled-back lips, sparkling cuspids, and crinkled eyes produces a Cheshire glow that envelops his audience.

Wife Lillian has a heart-shaped face (not much chin, lots of forehead for the obligatory headband), a perky, cheer-leading manner, almond-like nails trimmed short. Most noticeable is her smile, which seems wired to her husband's, so that they flash their ivories simultaneously, even if they're on opposite sides of a room and not looking at one another. They are not so much political cronies as lovers with an almost palpable flow of affection between them. Nice.

This campaign appearance, like all the others, has little to do with platform or policy. In fact, the party leader's mind hardly seems engaged with his vocal cords. But his nervous system is going full tilt. Suddenly the source of Vander Zalm's political magic becomes clear: he is the first Canadian politician who transmits his essential message entirely through body language. And it works.

It works partly because the body language of his chief rival, Bob Skelly, emits precisely the opposite signals. Throughout most of his campaign, the NDP leader betrayed the stance of an irresolute rabbit caught in the headlights of a moving car, soiling the air with his hesitancy and fear.

Before and after the election, Vander Zalm was being accused of being vague. Yet the message, at least that Saturday afternoon in Esquimalt, was as plain as the caps on his teeth: elect me and I'll worry for you. Sure, British Columbia may be on the verge of becoming the economic Manchuria of the Pacific Rim, but at least we'll all go down smiling. Somehow the notion is passed along that with Smilin' Billy and Smilin' Lillian safely ensconced in the Walt Disney pile of stones that passes for Victoria's parliament buildings, neither Ottawa, Washington, nor God will deal the province any more karate chops.

Vander Zalm's greatest asset – and the reason he won such a resounding mandate – is that he has a fresh way of approaching the province's problems. Instead of attempting to preach specific options or pretending that he has all the answers, he limited himself throughout the campaign to the pledge of changing the climate in which solutions might be negotiated. "We're open about what we propose to do for the people of B.C.," he said in Esquimalt that afternoon. "We'll develop a trust, and with that trust will come a confidence, and as people develop confidence in their province they'll want to invest in it, and when others see that investment they too will invest." In British Columbia these days that amounts to a major policy statement.

—1986

✳   ✳   ✳

WHEN THE COMMONWEALTH CONFERENCE was being held in Vancouver in the summer of 1987, Nathan Nemetz, then British Columbia's chief justice, hosted a formal dinner party for Lee Kuan Yew, most senior of the attending prime ministers, who has ruled Singapore with an iron fist since 1959. Much of the Vancouver Establishment was on the guest list, and Bill Vander Zalm had been asked to propose a toast to the distinguished visitor. As we stood outside the dining room, I watched the premier in action.

Despite his Great White Hunter good looks, his face somehow lacks definition, as if it were painted on a balloon, and his eyes seem as unfocused as billiard balls. What's remarkable is his body language – the semaphore signals sent out by his piranha-perfect teeth, always visible, the enigmatic duck of the head, and the arms parked akimbo, signalling that this man will not accept any assessment of himself except his own. Just before we were ushered in, the premier sidled up to me and whispered, as if to confirm a rumour he had once heard: "This Singapore – is it in the Commonwealth?" I allowed that it was. Aglow with this delicious secret (for which I was rewarded with a dazzling flash of molars) Vander Zalm took his place at the table and a few minutes later delivered a remarkably spirited toast to the Far East dictator, with whom he got on discouragingly well.

I was reminded of that performance as the B.C. premier, faced with a decisive challenge to his authority, tried to smooth away the wrath of his disillusioned followers with oily semantics. "I know a strong government will be challenged," he declared. "But I would rather have a strong government that gets challenged than a weak government that doesn't get anywhere."

That constituted a curious defence, because no one in the Pacific province is accusing Vander Zalm of being weak. Dumb, insensitive, certifiable – certainly. But never weak. The controversy over the resignations of Attorney General Brian Smith and former Deputy Premier Grace McCarthy has exposed to cold daylight the roots of Socred power. There are many misconceptions about the nature of the Social Credit movement (particularly outside British Columbia), none more prevalent than the belief that it is composed largely of marginal misfits, former and future talk-show hosts, used-up used-car dealers, and rednecks from bumper-sticker country who subscribe to the dotty dogmas of the party's official founder, Major C.H. Douglas.

That wasn't true when W.A.C. Bennett first used the Social Credit label to break the political deadlock that catapulted him into office in 1952, and it is even less true now. The party's followers include most of the province's mainstream voters. The common bond holding them together is a determination to keep the Socialist hordes out of office so that the 1972-75 NDP interregnum is never repeated.

But that is only the public face of the Socred phenomenon. Behind the scenes, the province's business establishment has up to now squarely supported Social Credit, providing party funds, contacts with the country's national power sources, and, above all, legitimacy. Vander Zalm was able to harness that support because, faced with the choice between the palavering left and the fanatic right, Vancouver's power-brokers swallowed the premier's nutsy excesses. What they asked for in return was a policy voice, which was expressed through the now departed ministers.

The real significance of the Smith and McCarthy resignations (and the firing of Highways Minister Stephen Rogers, the scion of a well-connected Vancouver family and a thirteen-year veteran of British Columbia's political wars) goes well beyond the fact that the cabinet has lost three of the premier's few ministers with any effective long-term experience in government. The move has irretrievably severed Vander Zalm's links with the province's business establishment. (And Vancouver itself. For the first time in its history, the city lacks representation in the provincial cabinet.)

Bill Bennett, Vander Zalm's predecessor, had established something called the Top Twenty Club, a closed circle of B.C. business elite, to hold private briefings with the premier. (There were actually sixty members; the club's designation represented the twenty swing ridings that the Socreds need to win.) The group, headed by Robert Hallbauer of Cominco and former MacMillan Bloedel chairman Jack Clyne, is now dormant. More significantly, Michael Burns, a former IBM executive who helped form the Top Twenty and was the party's chief fund raiser, has been replaced by Peter Toigo, Kentucky Fried Chicken King (he owns sixty-three franchises), who is as far removed from the B.C. Establishment as you can get. Vander Zalm's machinations on behalf of Toigo's bid to buy the former Expo 86 site for a gambling casino alienated Vancouver's business elite. Particularly put out was Canarim chairman Peter Brown, who headed the Crown-owned B.C. Enterprise Corporation, which held the disputed lands.

Whether Vander Zalm can (or wants to) heal the rift between his office and the business community remains an open question. Whether he will change his kamikaze style of government is not. He won't. He shows no willingness to alter his ways, even as most British Columbians begin to agree with Oksana Exell, the province's director for the Canadian Federation of Independent Business, who recently charged, "This government doesn't seem to have an agenda. It has pissed away its goodwill."

Ever since taking office, Vander Zalm has demonstrated the attention span of a squirrel, enunciating policies at the drop of a microphone with little benefit of forethought. This style of political surfboarding was best caught by former premier Dave Barrett, who once described Vander Zalm's operational code as: "Ready! Fire! Aim!"

Meanwhile, the province's button salesmen are being kept busy (one proclaims: "Gay Florists Are Against Vander Zalm"). The T-shirt merchants are flogging a model that has a smiling, hairy monster rising from a swamp, with the caption: "It came from Holland!" The premier appears unruffled, continuing to push his gardening video, host his Sunday radio phone-in show, market authenticated copies of his wife's headbands at his Fantasy Gardens gift shops, and lecture the survivors in his cabinet room, which has become an echo chamber. Hard days for The Zalm. Yet one achievement cannot be taken away from him: no one else could have made Bill Bennett look so good.

—1988

The Death of Mackenzie King

MACKENZIE KING DIED in Ottawa last week.

That was the subliminal message as I watched this latest in the round of permanent floating crap games, more officially known as constitutional conferences.

For years, the bush-league Tarzans who govern our provinces have been coming to Ottawa, beating their breasts, playing the great conciliators, yet accomplishing nothing. Their model – whether they realized it or not – was Mackenzie King, whose political vision never stretched beyond the point of regarding statesmanship as the accommodation of reconcilable differences. (He lasted as prime minister of Canada for twenty-two years by appealing separately to a variety of special-interest groups during election campaigns, then acting as a broker among them during the actual process of governing.)

This was the good, grey Canadian way. But last week's conference was different. Even if they were motivated by nothing more noble than fear of their electors, the conference's main participants betrayed the occasional sign of claiming the future instead of perpetuating past quarrels. Ontario's Bill Davis, who behaves on these occasions with the friendly officiousness of a corporate president attending his staff picnic, lurched to life and proposed the constitution's immediate patriation. It was an act of daring comparable to the declaration by a now-forgotten American senator who kept insisting that the only way to end the war in Vietnam was to declare that it had been a great American victory, then get the hell out.

That most unlikely of trios, Blakeney of Saskatchewan, Hatfield

217

of New Brunswick, and Bennett of British Columbia, came through all smiles and bonhomie, like the maître d' in a slightly run-down French restaurant hosting a convention of gourmets. In fact, it was only Sterling Lyon, that stately reincarnation of a nineteenth-century Manitoba village reeve, who ended up sounding mean and small. At one point, when he was declaiming against the entrenchment of language rights, he sounded exactly like one of those papier-mâché villains in films about the pioneers of American aviation who were constantly hectoring the daring young hero for believing that ''them goldurn contraptions'' could actually fly.

One of the conference's useful fringe benefits was to unmask, yet again, René Lévesque's true intentions. When it came time for him to prove that he might be willing to consider trying to make any kind of Canadian future that included Quebec into a workable reality, he scudded into intransigence. But it was the conference's host who provided its real surprise. Pierre Trudeau proved amazingly flexible. Perhaps he too has finally come to terms with the heretical notion that Mackenzie King is dead.

—1979

Patriating the Constitution

E VEN IF MOST CANADIANS find the very idea of constitutional reform a giant yawn, what's involved is the most fundamental of transactions in a democratic state. Constitutions define the relationship between citizens and their governments, setting out the powers of one over the other, prescribing the limits of collective and individual liberty.

The objective of the current conference of premiers is the first important step in giving Canada a contemporary constitution. We could do worse than examine the enlightened approach of the American constitution adopted at the Philadelphia Convention of 1787. That declaration underlined its own importance by beginning with an eloquent evocation of the republic it intended to establish: "We the People of the United States, in order to form a more perfect Union, establish Justice, insure domestic Tranquility, provide for the common Defense, promote the general Welfare, and secure the Blessings of Liberty to ourselves and our Posterity, do ordain and establish this Constitution for the United States of America."

In contrast, the British North America Act designed by our own Fathers of Confederation starts off with this descriptive parody of itself: "An Act for the Union of Canada, Nova Scotia and New Brunswick, and the Government thereof; and for Purposes connected therewith." The 147 sections that follow read like a badly written seed catalogue.

The U.S. constitution defines the relationship between federal and local governments with some sense of majesty: "Full Faith and Credit shall be given in each State to the public Acts, Records, and judicial Proceedings of every other State." An equivalent provision in the Canadian document drily states: "Canada shall be liable for the debts and liabilities of each province existing at the Union."

This difference in cadence and language accounts, at least in part, for the Americans' reverence for their constitution and the ignorant indifference with which most Canadians view the BNA Act. It's no accident that the one-sentence oath of office administered to incoming U.S. presidents pledges the aspiring occupant to "preserve, protect and defend the *Constitution* of the United States," while our constitutional provisions are regularly altered at countless federal-provincial get-togethers.

As a modest first proposal for the process of reform now under way, why don't our new Fathers of Confederation hire a poet to draft Canada's constitution? If we are to end this long, agonizing process with a document we can all live by and believe in, let's at least make certain its language stirs the blood and captures the excitement and potential of this wondrous land.

—1980

Ed Broadbent's Dream

A S THIS DISMAL ELECTION CAMPAIGN lurches toward its halfway point, with Pierre Trudeau and Joe Clark pawing at each other, displaying all the grace and inspiration of a pair of punch-drunk dancing bears, many voters are taking a new look at the third man: John Edward Broadbent.

A foxy pragmatist with brains, Broadbent is a very different breed from his NDP and CCF predecessors. Woodsworth, Coldwell, Douglas, and Lewis never could escape the notion that they should be loved for the enemies they made. They squandered their political lives demanding open-ended absolution for their utopian dreams from successive generations of Canadian voters. By turning their socialism into a religious faith, they became secular saints to the midnight philosophers who populate the Canadian left. But their righteous refusal to dilute purity of purpose alienated the mildly reform-minded political charmers and partisan carousers of the mainline parties. This left Canadian socialism striving to become the conscience of the country, yet destined never to govern it.

Broadbent's ideology has similar roots, but he has managed to put an impressive distance between himself and the kind of government we've had under Pierre Trudeau since 1968.

Broadbent grows more relaxed as the campaign progresses. A jealously private individual, he may be the only Canadian politician in living memory who has grown more cheerful on the stump. Not wittier, just more cheerful. (The difference is important. Wit is a device, cheerfulness an impulse.)

The source of Broadbent's optimism is his reading of current political realities, which he is certain will grant him parliamentary balance of power over Canada's next government. The NDP campaign has been a mixture of slogans ("a nation out of work can't work as a nation"), doctrinaire poses (advocating our withdrawal from NATO and NORAD), and extravagant pledges (such as the $150 million Broadbent wants to spend rehabilitating the steel mills at Sydney, Nova Scotia). Despite these tactics, the NDP hasn't been taken so seriously since Tommy Douglas left the Saskatchewan premiership to establish the party in 1961.

—1979

Rompin' Ronnie

AVING ACCORDED THE PRESIDENCY in turn to a grubby paranoid,* an interim successor who couldn't manoeuvre himself
gracefully down an aircraft ramp, and a peanut vendor whose
Sunday-school approach manages to link good intentions with inevitably abysmal results, America's voters seem bent on casting their
fate into the hands of Ronald Reagan.

As banal a politician as was ever nominated for leadership of any
major nation – much less of the free world – Reagan is a kind of poor
man's John Wayne, all profile and bromides, chasing the greatest
Oscar of them all (a prize that eluded him for all of his fifty films). A
used-up movie actor who peaked intellectually hustling General Electric deep freezers on TV's "General Electric Theatre," Reagan moves
into the fall presidential campaign with one overwhelming advantage:
he's not Jimmy Carter.

---

*My favourite story about Richard Nixon has to do with a tour of the Middle
West when he was Ike Eisenhower's vice-president, trying to boost the soggy
fortunes of obscure Republican congressmen, building up the party credits that
would eventually lead him to the presidency. As he landed at Toledo a crowd of
banner-waving Republicans surged up around the aircraft and Nixon responded with
one of his characteristic victory waves. Accompanied by a small press contingent,
he switched to the DC–3 of a feeder airline for a side trip to a place called Defiance,
Ohio, where he spoke about "all the old-fashioned virtues." It was late at night
when his party got back to Toledo, and the airport was deserted. Nixon, his face set
in a concentrated frown, strode up the ramp of the larger plane that would fly him
back to Washington. Then, just before ducking into the cabin, in pure reflex action
he turned around, flashed a smile, and waved at the empty tarmac.

The American presidency has always been a very special institution, combining within itself the regal imperatives of a chief of state with the awesome powers of the head of government. Its occupant's calling is to be the nation's spiritual leader. That's why it is Carter who gets most of the blame for the Keystone Cops mission to free the Iranian hostages and, worst of all, for inflation that continues to gallop along at double-digit levels.

Feeling cornered and increasingly insecure, many Americans are turning not so much against the system as against the habits of thought that have sustained it. The mood of impotence abroad, trouble at home, and ebbing faith in previously hallowed institutions are probably best symbolized by the drop in sales of U.S.-made cars. Driving a Chevy has become a patriotic act.

The animating credo of the conservative wave sweeping the United States dates back a couple of centuries. It's the original Jeffersonian notion that governments interfere with people's liberties and that only through the unhampered pursuit of individual initiatives can freedom and happiness be guaranteed. Precisely this mood has produced the Reagan phenomenon. His campaign exploits one of Hollywood's most hackneyed morality plays: fearless Ronnie has cast himself as the easy-lopin' cowboy who'll triumph over the bad guys in the last reel.

The overwhelming confirmation of his candidacy by the Republican convention places America's voters in an unenviable position. Their dilemma was best caught by Bob Hope while opening the Valley Forge Music Fair at Devon, Pennsylvania, earlier this month. He explained why he had been hired: "They figured this is an election year and you'd like to see a comedian who isn't running for anything."

❄   ❄   ❄

RONALD REAGAN'S ASTONISHING TRIUMPH has won him much more than an election. He has been granted a genuine ideological mandate by America's voters. A victory of this magnitude and diversity can be a revolutionary instrument: it confers on the candidate who gains it not merely the awesome constitutional powers of the U.S. presidency but the spiritual authority of the office as well.

This is the factor that has turned the former California governor into more than the leader of a reborn Republican party. He is – or must quickly become – an agent of the change. His constituency is what Anthony Lewis of the *New York Times* has called "the moral majority: those who believe that God favors a balanced budget and a U.S.-owned Panama Canal."

The campaign itself turned out to be a peculiarly dispiriting exercise; the Democratic candidate was trying to pit his mastery of the trivial against his Republican opponent's ignorance of detail. Reagan turned out to be superb at using body-English not only to propel his political ideas but also to dispel the Democrat-inspired stereotype that he was an urban-cowboy Dr. Strangelove, hot to nuke the Commies.

It's not Reagan's age that scares me – he would not, after all, be the oldest national leader; Ayatollah Khomeini is seventy-nine. It's what he represents. There exists a strain of thoughtful conservatism in the United States (and Canada) that can put forward a valid case against the kind of spendthrift liberalism that has come close to bankrupting the economies of both countries.

Reagan falls into a very different category. Back in the early Sixties, when the situation in Southeast Asia was turning against the Americans, the California governor proposed a solution noble in its simplicity: "We should declare war on Vietnam. We could pave the whole country, put parking stripes on it, and still be home by Christmas." Reagan still refers to the Soviets as "those monsters," and wants to expel the U.S.S.R. from the United Nations.

There is little doubt that Reagan's adamant advocacy of turning the clock back, trying to resurrect the simpler, more traditional way of life that once made America great, has caught the public imagination. The United States is going conservative and becoming militantly hawkish. Despite all the visible protests, more people believe in the use of atomic energy than are against it.

Except for his confession that he cries whenever he watches his favourite TV show, "Little House on the Prairie," not much is known about Reagan's thought processes. He doesn't like taxes ("the entire graduated-income tax structure was created by Karl Marx"), is against gun control, favours capital punishment, wants to outlaw abortion, and believes the way out of the energy mess is to allow the large oil consortiums unfettered freedom on pricing and distribution.

The Americans are a proud people, and it was the agony of watching their chief executive being manipulated and humiliated by the mad ayatollahs of Tehran that turned the voters against the incumbent. His indecision and weakness made patriotic Americans realize that their country was behaving more like a big Georgia than a world power.

The election results signal the most fundamental shift in American thinking since Roosevelt's sweep of 1932. Reagan's romp revives the simplistic credo dear to America's fundamentalists: that the essential role of government is to remove constraints on its citizens. This was the overwhelming sentiment that carried Reagan into office and that must now animate his deliberations and decisions. The perfectibility of the American Dream and inevitability of its triumph have been given a terrifyingly powerful new lease on life.

—1980

PART FOUR

Departures

John Lennon

HE WAS A MAN of invincible innocence. His lyrics could trigger your memory or desire and send you off in search of your own humanity. Yet his message was always simple: commit yourself to life and love – *but on your own terms*.

John Lennon, so senselessly gunned down in New York, was no ordinary troubadour. The songs that survive him are modern fables, thoughts and themes that transcend the sweaty domain of disk-jockey-dom. The philosophy of life he espoused may have appeared to lend itself better to T-shirt slogans than academic dissertations, but there was, in everything he wrote, an existential lustre that did away with poses and pat answers. It was the Lancashire in him. He was always out there right on the leading edge of things.

The mockery of Lennon's songs, his complex imagery, as in "Nowhere Man" ("He's as blind as he can be, just sees what he wants to see"), and evocative dirges like "Norwegian Wood" (my own favourite) pushed modern music into a new realm.

In that magic time when the young Beatles reigned, they sang the saucy anthems of change that told of a generation figuring out how it should behave, what it should believe about love, war, parents, drugs, sex, Christ, and haircuts. The kids lucky enough to grow up with the Liverpool foursome discovered that they weren't alone, that they no longer had to emulate their elders. Together they created the miracle of the Sixties counterculture – a welcome contrast to the crewcuts and bobbysoxers who preceded them and the self-absorbed me-decade complainers who followed.

John Lennon's most controversial claim ("We're more popular than Jesus Christ") may sound hollow now, but how many sermons have delivered a more direct or meaningful absolution than his "Give Peace a Chance"? The most independent and political of the Beatles, he never strayed from his well-honed sense of the absurd: when he wanted to be anonymous, he would call himself Greta Hughes or Howard Garbo.

The disillusioned graduates of the Sixties never gave up yearning for the Beatles to reunite, as if seeing them on stage again would affirm that all those brave dreams hadn't just been a fad or a costume party. Now it can never happen. "Yesterday" is ours to hear but not to have, and we'll never be that young again.

In his final album, househusband Lennon sings to his son Sean: "Life is what happens to you while you're busy making other plans." It's so true. Still, John Lennon's most fitting epitaph could well be Don McLean's "American Pie." His assassination marked the day the music died.

—1980

Stan Kenton

WHEN STANLEY NEWCOMB KENTON died in his sixty-eighth year at a Hollywood hospital, he was like a lion in winter – defiant in his going but well beyond his prime.

During the late Forties and early Fifties, Kenton's orchestra was the biggest jazz attraction in the world. Though he kept his sound evolving and his band travelling, Kenton spent the last decade of his life careering around the continent, still making converts but reduced to playing one-night stands at shopping-centre openings, musty night-clubs, and other neon snake pits on the American road.

He lived for thirty-eight years on a band bus, suffering the vaga-bond's indignities of little sleep and bad food, drinking a million cups of tepid coffee and eating all that stale Danish – dealing with the greedy souls of scruffy promoters while having to prop up musicians trying to dredge new sounds out of exhausted psyches.

His humour never deserted him. I was once aboard his big orange bus when he wouldn't allow it to start until "Cecil" was back on board.

"Who's 'Cecil'?" I asked.

"He's the giant horsefly who's been with us for months. Why, he's crossed the country on this bus."

"How do you know it's a male?"

"Because his name is Cecil. Did you ever hear of a chick named Cecil?"

What made his gruelling schedule bearable were the nightly con-certs when the old man would bound up on the bandstand, shout "Let's go!'' at his eighteen musicians, strike an imperious triad on the piano, and bring in the trumpet section with a chop of his right elbow. The bellow of that music would melt away the years and he would become a proud young buck cake-walking in the sun. The rich Kenton sound would descend on its listeners like a hailstorm.

What Kenton demanded from his musicians was that they broaden the harmonic, rhythmic, and structural boundaries of the band's arrangements so that each composition would trigger their ruminations. The best of them would grope for a melodic line, pursue it, then explore and soar with it, like astronauts dangling in the moonlight.

The Kenton band, which opened the 1941 season at the Rendezvous Ballroom in Balboa Beach, California, was a hybrid offshoot from the Jimmie Lunceford rhythm machine. But Kenton's own jazz charts moved quickly to the harmonic values and polyphonic inventions of Bartok, Stravinsky, and Darius Milhaud. London's Sadler's Wells Ballet choreographed some of his avant-garde arrangements, and several French and Italian art films were built around his music. Much of the thematic pseudo-jazz that now serves as background music for avant-garde films and television series can be traced directly to Kenton's influence.

The best of the Kenton scores sounded as if they might have been torn out of a late Dostoevsky novel, the bravura fanfares from his ten men of brass counterpointed by the deep-mouthed empathy of the smoothest saxophone section in the business. His own piano solos, all slides and whispers, had a smoky, three-o'clock-in-the-morning quality about them. He could transform Sondheim's ''Send in the Clowns'' into a lyrical comment about contemporary social values; his version of ''Here's That Rainy Day'' became a tone poem, its chord structure as poignant as the touch of lovers' champagne glasses.

Kenton's many critics claimed his concerts were about as spontaneous as a cathedral mass. The satirist Mort Sahl captured his tendency toward the pretentious with the line, ''When Stan Kenton spills a cup of coffee, he doesn't say 'Somebody help me clean this up.' He says, 'Look, I have created a mess!' ''

It certainly wasn't music to make love by, and it didn't always swing. ''There are many more emotions that can be portrayed and felt in jazz than just swinging,'' Kenton once explained to me. ''For some reason the critics haven't been able to communicate with my band.

But I don't worry about it. Most of that crap I just let go in one eye and out the other.''

The orchestra's final incarnation was a powerhouse of sound, pioneering time signatures seldom used in jazz to give the music hard-edged, unpredictable syncopation. In a number called ''Ambivalence,'' for example, the band switches from a complex 5/4 cadence to a goading 20/16 tempo, then back again. Kenton exploited the abstractions of his artistry – timing, harmony, phrasing – to define big-band jazz as a hot, existential music with a touch of class.

Kenton's followers were fervid in their loyalty, gladly driving five hundred miles to hear a concert, attempting to outdo one another with their knowledge of Kenton lore. They would revel in swapping such trivia as the name of the Catholic member of the trumpet section who crossed himself before taking the altissimo solo on ''Artistry in Boogie'' during the band's September 20, 1953, concert at the Theatre Royal in Dublin.*

Stan Kenton's main legacy is his 137 albums. They encompass just about every musical form known to man, including his version of such Wagner operas as *Lohengrin* and *Tannhäuser*.

The fundamental intent of jazz is to entertain and recharge the spirit with sensory awareness. No music depends so much on the individual player and his ability to improvise. Ideally, the jazz performer is a spontaneous, non-repetitive poet expressing himself through his instrument. But what Kenton demanded of his musicians was that they carry the spirit of his composers' ideas over into their own musical improvisations. That was the essence of his art, and that is why his music will survive.

But for those of us who followed his career and admired his music, the Kenton sound will never replace the Kenton presence. His passing marks not just the close of a musical era but a kind of death in the family. ''What we play is life,'' Louis Armstrong once said about jazz, and that was exactly the affinity we felt with Stan Kenton's music – its lustre and eloquence, its rage, and its unfulfilled promise.

—1979

---

*It was Conte Candoli.

Judy LaMarsh

THE QUALITY THAT ALLOWS most federal politicians to survive their grimy trade is a profound sense of detachment. Issues and principles dissolve into cynical responses to the call of each passing hour; private lives are relegated to a form of distraction. Eventually, their souls leak out of them, mixing with the comatose décor of the House of Commons' walls.

Judy was different.

Julia Verlyn LaMarsh, who died in Toronto at fifty-five, had that rare and terrible gift of natural rudeness. Loyal to her friends, merciless to her enemies, generous with herself (and her budget), above all she was gloriously gutsy, governed by the unvarnished dictates of her feelings.

She never tried to hide anything, least of all her emotions, existing within the tumult of her own making, as vulnerable as an open wound. She elevated honesty to a profound moral option. While some of her fellow lady politicians insisted that their formal photographs be taken through so many layers of cheesecloth they were made to appear as young as Ronald Reagan, Judy just stuck out her chins and told them to click away. When she landed at Eskimo Point in the Northwest Territories during the centennial celebrations, she introduced herself to a group of Inuit by patting her ample hips and exclaiming, "See, I brought my own supply of blubber!" After her helicopter landed on Steele Glacier in the Yukon, she just stood there and yodelled.

She lost her temper easily, once threw an ashtray at Senator Keith Davey, even though he was one of her most ardent supporters, and resigned (for two days at a time) on at least a dozen occasions from the Pearson cabinet. Her legislative achievements were considerable, but her behaviour in office often shocked the fastidious and discomfited the established. ''She was very democratic,'' recalls George Loranger, one of her former aides. ''She treated the office boy and the deputy minister exactly alike – she constantly gave them hell.''

The novels she wrote were her final passion, but she just couldn't get the sex scenes right. ''When you're engaged in a sexual act,'' she would explain, ''no one's there getting a bird's eye view. When I was trying to describe it, I kept giggling.'' It was typical that when she was granted the Order of Canada on her deathbed, as a kind of farewell gesture by a nation that had rewarded her contributions with remarkable stinginess, Judy's main reaction was to bitch about some of the people she thought were fools who had been similarly decorated.

She died with the raw courage and primitive dignity that exemplified her life, deciding late on the afternoon of Friday, October 24, 1980, ''Okay, no more medication. That's it.''

The reason Judy's death touched so many Canadians is that so few celebrities manage to preserve their real selves inside their public masks. Judy LaMarsh endowed each of her many careers with energy, intellect, and commitment. But, to the end, she never gave up her essential, gutsy humanity.

—1980

Walter Gordon

I T IS NOT EASY to write about Walter Gordon in the past tense. His death, at eighty-one, seems more like an interruption than an ending to his full life and impassioned quests. He was one of those pivotal individuals who leave their world very different from the way they found it. In his case, that meant bestowing a legacy of essential social welfare (including medicare) on future generations of Canadians; sounding the alarm about the debilitating effects of foreign investment; and turning the Liberal party upside down.

Although Gordon was a lifelong, card-carrying Grit, his ideology was difficult to categorize. Much more interested in the pursuit of ideas than of power, he saw history not as an orderly succession of events but as an accumulation of paradoxes in the midst of which anything could happen. The political game – which requires the bending of truth into so many shapes that it becomes hardly recognizable – was not for him. "If you have a too highly developed sense of the ridiculous," he once told me, "you can't get through daily political life in Ottawa without laughing, and that's not allowed."

He abhorred pretence of any kind. As finance minister during the early Sixties he frequently flew to Washington and made it a habit to phone ahead to request that no Canadian embassy officials meet him at the airport. He especially enjoyed that freedom from protocol when there was another minister on the plane and he could watch the vested flunkies bowing to, say, Paul Martin, then secretary of state for external affairs, while he climbed off the aircraft, his zippered overnight bag in hand, unattended and carefree.

236

Decent and gracious to the core of his being, Gordon had trouble getting the public to warm to him. The kind of man he was tended always to obscure the kind of man he seemed to be. Witty, intelligent, contemporary and humanitarian, he looked merely overprivileged – a Rosedale aristocrat in a bespoke suit and regimental tie. He was an intensely private person, and his language was that of his class, reasonable and cool. Although he preached policies that in Canada passed for revolutionary, he seldom appeared angry or strident, preferring to be a Garibaldi without a horse. Even his five books and his monumental 1958 Royal Commission on Canada's Economic Prospects, with their radical implications for Canadian society, read like manuals on beekeeping.

In the untidy jostling of our history, we have seldom been able to differentiate between pro-Canadianism and anti-Americanism, the one being all too often the mirror image of the other. Gordon had no such problem. Whether they were sending their hunter-killer teams into Vietnamese rice paddies or into Canadian boardrooms, Gordon saw most Americans as pushy imperialists who must be kept at bay.

In retrospect, he was probably right to hold himself back and preach without trying too hard to inflame the Canadian people. If he had insisted that economic nationalism be the Liberals' main policy plank in any of the four campaigns he ran – and if the voters had rejected it – the Americans could have assumed that Canada had repudiated economic independence as a viable option. That was a risk he never dared take.

When, with Professor Abe Rotstein and myself, he founded the Committee for an Independent Canada in 1970, we quickly discovered the danger of the independence issue. Because foreign investment threatens our collective rather than individual liberties, it is a hard policy around which to rally political support. But Gordon's initiatives significantly raised public awareness of Canadian sovereignty. At his final public appearance at Toronto's Massey Hall in the autumn of 1986, he attacked free trade as a betrayal of our future – and the country was listening.

Gordon always expected the worst from his encounters with the public. When he addressed the Canada Club in London on July 1, 1964, the great flag debate was just starting in Ottawa and Lester Pearson was still considering the semifinal three-colour three-maple-leaf design. But Gordon, who had no patience with symbols, had forgotten the colours and kept referring to the possible new Canadian flag as "red, white, and gold." Every time he made the mistake, voices in the audience would shout back "Blue!" In his self-belittling way, Gordon assumed they were yelling "Boo!" and the fifth time he was interrupted, he shrugged and said sadly, "I was afraid of that."

Whenever Gordon and I met for lunch, he insisted on going to Toronto's York Club, where the elite of Canadian business meet to exchange pleasantries and chomp passably fresh oysters and limp water biscuits. He would march defiantly in with the parade-square gait he first learned at the Royal Military College, and the assembled paladins of Bay Street would glare back at him. But in recent years they were actually greeting him, and so one day I asked whether they had come around to his way of thinking. "Oh, no," he said with a sad smile, "it just means that my company [Canadian Corporate Management] is doing so well they think I've been converted."

Walter Lockhart Gordon was never a convert. A true believer, not so much in his cause as in Canada, he possessed three qualities rare in politicians: courage, humbleness, and an original mind. During his long public service – he first went to Ottawa in 1935 as a researcher for the Price Spreads Commission – his presence enlarged all of us. We are diminished by his passing.

—1987

238

Jean Lesage

WHEN JEAN LESAGE, the dapper Quebec City lawyer who became a reluctant social and political reformer in his late forties, was elected premier of his province in 1960, he set off a political revolution that drastically transformed the pattern of French-English relations in this country. Not since France's dream of a North American empire was crushed by a British army on the Plains of Abraham had Quebec's destiny been altered so fast in so many new directions.

What it consisted of, this Quiet Revolution as it came to be called, was the essential separation of church and state. Lesage and the bright action-oriented politicians he brought with him, relegated the clergy to the spiritual realm, while the government took over the Roman Catholic Church's traditional control of education, health, and welfare institutions across the province. "The time when we wondered about our survival is over," Lesage declared. "We want to use our autonomy not as a sign of weakness and obstruction but of strength and action." By stubbornly implementing the fifty-three-point platform on which he had been elected, Lesage turned Quebec society inside out, establishing a left-leaning administration that eventually expropriated the province's private hydro installations and intervened in every aspect of daily life.

A graduate in law from Laval University, Lesage at twenty-seven became one of the youngest Crown attorneys in Quebec City's history and in 1945 went to Ottawa as a Liberal back-bencher. As chairman of the committee that devised a plan for old-age pensions without a means test, he so impressed Prime Minister Louis St. Laurent that he was brought into the cabinet in 1953 as the first minister of northern affairs and natural resources. He switched to provincial politics half a decade later and within two years brought his party, which had been in opposition since 1944, into office.

A smooth orator on the hustings, once in power Lesage transformed himself into a regal presence. His personal staff numbered twenty-eight, including a *chef de protocol* in morning coat, and his appointments schedule was mimeographed two weeks in advance. Three Montreal dailies once solemnly reported how the prime minister had been bitten by a mosquito on the middle finger of his right hand. I remember one interview we had in his majestic office, and how he bounded up from his desk, shaking my hand with the confident, over-the-net grip of a champion tennis player.

I tried to cool him down by asking a tough, and for any French-Canadian politician, unfair question: Did he consider himself a Quebecker or a Canadian first? His face flushed, his jaw worked, he glanced at my poised pencil; then he said, "Hell, I'm a Canadian. That's my nationality."

There was nothing anti-English about Jean Lesage. He kept a portrait of the Queen in his inner office and cried with emotion when Her Majesty came to Quebec City in the fall of 1964 to brave the hostile crowds.

When I brought up the Quiet Revolution and asked whether, in retrospect, he thought he had moved too fast, too soon, Lesage replied: "History will decide. But I had a cabinet of men of action. It was as though the gun had been fired for the start of a race. You had to run, otherwise you could count only on coming last. If Confederation fails, it will not be because Quebec separates from Canada but because the way to keep Quebec in Confederation hasn't been found."

It was a typical Lesage statement, pro-Canadian, yet based on no clear concept of the country's future. After his dramatic electoral victory of 1960, he made the mistake of trying to become a statesman before it was time for him to cease being an agitator.

Jean Lesage loved Canada and he loved Quebec, but his political philosophy was sustained by nothing firmer than a deeply felt instinctive response to the call of each passing political hour. At the end of his time in office, when his charm had been transformed into a kind of puffed-up arrogance, his ambition lost its direction, and he was no longer sure whether he wanted to become the next prime minister of Canada after Lester Pearson (whose choice he was for a time) or the first president of Quebec.

Despite his swashbuckling verbal assault on Ottawa, Lesage gained respect from most federal politicians for both his sincerity in representing the best interests of Quebec and his tendency to rescue himself at the last moment by agreeing to some complex compromise. The thirteen years he spent in federal politics before becoming leader of the Quebec Liberal party had left their mark. Even though he was leading a social revolution, Jean Lesage remained part of the Ottawa Establishment.

He had a direct hotline to Gordon Robertson, the clerk of the Privy Council, who often checked federal appointments from Quebec with the premier before they were made. He also had a special relationship with Pearson, whose parliamentary secretary Lesage had been for a while. After one memorable public row at a federal-provincial conference, when Lesage had denied the Supreme Court's jurisdiction over offshore mineral rights, the two men spent the evening at Harrington Lake, the prime minister's summer residence in the Gatineau Hills. At one point, Pearson caught Lesage's elbow and, pretending to be a federal policeman protecting offshore rights, said, "You can go to the edge of the lake, but no farther." Lesage drew himself up and with mock seriousness replied, "May I remind you that we are now in the province of Quebec." The vapid exchange broke them both up into gales of belly-pumping laughter.

On his home turf, Lesage virtually abolished patronage, brought into government service a cadre of brilliant young French Canadians (including an eager young minister of hydraulic resources called René Lévesque), and pioneered the notion that it paid to assault Ottawa's jurisdictions. Lesage was certainly a Quebec autonomist and indulged himself in some occasional excesses. On February 8, 1966, for example, his government introduced a bill known as the Official Time Act, which authorized the province to opt out of national time.

He also challenged the federal authority for a genuine sharing of fiscal powers. This was no ideological posture. Lesage needed the money. During his first three years in power he doubled the provincial debt. At one point in 1963, provincial finances became so desperate that Lesage ordered a temporary postponement on refills for fire extinguishers in government offices.

Though he was conservative by nature, Lesage quickly fell in love with the image of himself as the man chosen to lead his province out of its post-Duplessis backwardness. Many of the province's intellectuals dismissed him as *un homme de la situation* (a polite term for opportunist) and described him as a kind of Presbyterian Jesuit – a man who believes devoutly that the end justifies the means. But he was much more than that. In the early years of his regime, he brought to the government of Quebec a consummate honesty and momentum that for a time made it the most exciting and forward-looking administration in any Western democracy.

Pierre Trudeau commented on Jean Lesage only once. During a February 23, 1966, appearance on the Pierre Berton television show, Trudeau (then a parliamentary secretary to Pearson) said, "I personally think that Lesage is the sanest man in the Quebec government. He has kept on the evenest keel in regard to the problems of autonomy and nationalism. He's fighting for Quebec's autonomy, but he doesn't go off starting wars on Ethiopia every time something goes wrong. He just says, 'Well, we'll have to do it better next time.' He doesn't say it's the fault *des Anglais* or the Town of Mount Royal or anything like that."

History will probably relegate Jean Lesage to something of a transitional figure. But during the six exciting years he held power, he proved himself to be both a great champion of his people and a patriotic Canadian.

—1980

Donald Creighton

H ISTORY," DONALD CREIGHTON once remarked, "is the record of an encounter between character and circumstance." Canadians were fortunate that our circumstances – especially the epic of how Sir John A. Macdonald hammered out the compromise that became Confederation – were recorded by a character with as much integrity, insight, and style as Professor Creighton.

He was unique among Canada's academic historians. Unlike most of his milquetoast colleagues, he could write. "Mackenzie King," he once commented, "made both big words and small deeds serve his turn. There was at once more in him than met the eye, and a great deal less than filled the ear." He described General Douglas Mac-Arthur as "a mixture of Genghis Khan and Louis XIV" while Maurice Duplessis, the wartime Quebec premier, was characterized as "a short, spare French Canadian . . . who gained power by what was essentially a blatant electoral fraud and was to keep it through most of the remainder of his life by an organized system of electoral corruption."

Instead of subscribing to the clichéd portrait of Canada as some sort of harmonious mosaic, Creighton complained about "the large blotches, smaller blots and dabs of contrasted colours that make up the crazy pavement of Canadian society." His most passionate concern was the Americanization of the Canadian psyche. His angry facts were mustered with more skill than subtlety, and the message was very clear: in the process of turning ourselves from a colony of Great Britain to an economic satellite of the United States we had gone straight from having been bastard Englishmen to being bastard Americans and lost the chance of becoming defiant Canadians. He pounded home that theme with a kind of Captain Ahab intensity – his abhorrence of those dreamers of the American Dream who permeate these northern latitudes with their beguiling gospel of economic and political continentalism ever ready to engulf us.

Creighton's assessments were tough, but his instincts rang true. Alone among our established historians he championed Canadian independence, defying the old-line liberal internationalists who still form this country's political and academic establishments. It was a lonely battle, fought against soft men with soft ideas, with only the odd tough platoon sergeant and wise old whisky-priest for company.

Creighton's writing style bristled with wit and turns of phrase that transformed his dozen books into sources of pleasure and comprehension. Intensely aware of his craft, he believed that "history's closest affiliation is with literature and not with science." What separated him most boldly from his fellow historians was that Creighton had trouble remaining neutral about anything important. An ardent demonologist, he took every opportunity to joust – like some wise reincarnation of Don Quixote – with earnest defenders of the French Fact as well as apologists for the United States.

Creighton's strong streak of anti-materialism was reflected in his puritanical lifestyle. He spent the last two decades of his life (having retired as head of the history department at the University of Toronto in 1959) in a modest but cosy farmhouse in Brooklin, Ontario, with his beloved wife, Luella, writing the books, essays, and one novel that kept his ideas in circulation.

Probably Creighton's most controversial stand was his interpretation of Confederation as a political union between provinces rather than a cultural compact between the French and English ethnic communities. A storm broke following publication of a 1977 article he wrote for *Maclean's* in which he gave voice to the heretical notion that "while Quebec is undoubtedly dependent on English Canada, English Canada could get along very well without Quebec."

In mid-November of 1979, when the magazine was planning its new "Podium" feature that would open its pages to Canadians with strong, articulate opinions, we contacted Creighton to be among the first of our contributors. Although he was seventy-seven and mortally ill with cancer, the historian's narrative fires were still burning. He accepted the assignment, deciding to describe the corruption of our speech patterns by the pernicious influences from the south.

Then came the problem of a deadline. It was difficult, the professor confided; he really was very ill and could summon little sustaining energy. "Let's make it December 19, I'll have it finished by then," he promised.

That was the very day Donald Grant Creighton died and Canada lost its best historian.

—1979

Marshall McLuhan

ARSHALL McLUHAN and John Kenneth Galbraith are the two greatest modern Canadians the United States has produced,'' British novelist Anthony Burgess wryly observed, and he was right.

McLuhan, whose recent death we mourn, was an avid Canadian nationalist, not because he was that enthusiastic about homegrown culture but because he saw being Canadian as an escape. ''Canada,'' he lectured, ''has value as the DEW Line for the rest of the world. We have the situation of relatively small involvement in the big headaches. The Canadian has freedom of comment, a kind of playful awareness of issues that is unknown in, say, Paris or London or New York. Here you have a little time to breathe, to think, and to feel. It's because Canadians are protected from encountering themselves by layers of colonialism. I'm trying to alert them to the dangers of the twentieth century – so they can duck out.''

He was always interested in what the politicians were up to and once suggested that Richard Nixon should grow sideburns so that he wouldn't have to go on TV with ''just his bare face hanging out.'' And he insisted that Pierre Trudeau must be at least 40 per cent Indian because nobody could penetrate his tribal mask. Said McLuhan: ''Pierre has no personal judgment but he is always interpreting the whole process that he's involved in. So that when he slides down a banister or hops off a camel, it's not really a way of expressing what it feels like to be Trudeau – it's trying to express what sort of a hell of a hang-up he's in. He'll do anything to snap the tension.''

McLuhan was very concerned about Quebec's future, particularly after the invocation of the War Measures Act in 1970, because he felt that French Canadians would eventually drop out of Confederation: "I wondered during the debate on the War Measures Act if it would be possible to turn radios off in Quebec and just leave on the TV. Radio is hot stuff for such people as the French Canadians. It appeals to the ear, which for tribal cultures is their keenest sense, so it's like firewater to an Indian. It drives them mad. English Canadians are not nearly as prone to getting excited by radio because they have a much bigger backlog of literacy and visual culture to protect them and immunize them against the ear."

McLuhan was also a comedian of the first rank, and inevitably the first twenty minutes of our meetings were taken up with humorous musings, such as his story about the Scot who comes on the scene of a motor crash. The injured are lying around, and, poking one of the survivors in the stomach with his walking stick, the Scot asks, "Has the insurance adjuster been here yet?" When the reply is no, the Scotsman asks, "Do you mind if I lie down beside you?"

Even though he had dozens of attractive offers – and did leave temporarily to occupy such prestige-encrusted posts as the Schweitzer Chair at New York's Fordham University – he always came back. His dozen books, his countless lectures, and what he liked to describe as his "probes" turned McLuhan into a contemporary Aristotle. The province of Ontario declared him a "natural resource. The influence of the man's intellectual pyrotechnics was probably best caught in a *Financial Post* article by Alexander Ross: "There was a time when every university in Germany had a free period at eleven in the morning, because that's when Hegel was lecturing at Berlin. McLuhan is that kind of man, in our very own midst. So be proud."

Tom Wolfe, the tart-tongued New York journalist, once coquettishly inquired, "Suppose McLuhan is what he sounds like, the most important thinker since Newton, Darwin, Freud, Einstein, and Pavlov – what if he is right?"

To which Marshall McLuhan, with that Gary Cooper smile that signalled most of his sallies, replied, "I'd rather be wrong."

—1981

Nelson Davis

IT WAS SOMEHOW APPROPRIATE that when Nelson Morgan Davis died last week he was in Phoenix, planning a new "shack" that was to have been his third winter abode in the Arizona sun belt. I visited Canada's richest and most fascinating recluse there only once, during the early spring of 1976, and we spent a languid evening chatting by the side of his pool.

During the afternoon, Davis took me on a tour of Scottsdale, ending up at the private garage of his friend Tom Barrett III. There we clambered through half a dozen antique cars, including Rudolph Valentino's 1927 Isotta-Fraschini and Josef Goebbels's original Maybach-Zeppelin roadster, then returned to the Davis house. A rambling, six-bedroom villa of pink stucco and tile roofing, it had originally been built by Tommy Manville, the asbestos-fortune heir, who had lived there briefly with his eleventh wife. It was sold to Davis by Clare Boothe Luce in 1968.

"Nels," as he was called by his close friends, also owned a property at Sedona, a hundred miles north of Phoenix, but late in 1978 he started to get restless. At the turn of the year, he acquired another house just off the fourth hole of the Paradise Valley golf course and on the morning of his death had been arranging the transplant of a dozen large palm trees to his new domain.

His physician had examined Davis the day before, pronouncing him extraordinarily fit, the reward for a long life spent eschewing alcohol, tobacco, and excess in all its forms. But nothing could save him when his forehead hit the ledge of his pool after an afternoon dip on March 13; he sank to the bottom, his lungs filled with water. The gardener's punctured eardrums prevented him from attempting a rescue, and by the time Nelson Davis's wife, Eloise, was notified, it was too late. The Argus chairman was pronounced dead on arrival at St. Joseph's Hospital just after 5 p.m.

Nelson Davis's passing will not affect any of the existing hierarchies in this country's corporate boardrooms. The fifty companies he controlled can be ably operated by his son Glen and his brother Marshall. He had already retired from his most important directorship at the Canadian Imperial Bank of Commerce and was planning to leave the board of Falconbridge. Although he will miss his advice, Conrad Black holds impregnable control over Argus, so that no substantive changes can be expected there.

Yet it would be very wrong to deduce from all this that only his family will miss this unusual man and his quizzically materialistic outlook on life. Davis was probably Canada's shrewdest businessman. The Tudor mansion at the dead-end of Versailles Avenue in Toronto's York Mills area, from which he ran his many enterprises, was a cockpit of considerable corporate clout. "I get paid for what I know, not for what I do," Davis once astutely observed about himself.

His callers, who usually stayed for the Spartan lunches he offered, included some of Canada's most influential power brokers, seeking to draw him out on how best to negotiate the big-dollar deals. He was ever helpful, always polite, generous with his time and advice, asking only one favour in return: that his anonymity not be violated.

Secrecy became an obsession. His Toronto house had *five* unlisted phone numbers, and he seldom broke his self-imposed code against publicity of any kind. Nelson Davis was a keeper of distances. His strong sense of inner identity made it unnecessary for him to have a public *persona* to validate his success.

Much was made of the dimensions of his wealth – his five houses, six cars, eighteen servants, twenty power boats, and that private golf links. But less important than the extent of his fortune was its rationale. Most wealthy Canadians are much more interested in gathering money than in dispensing it, fascinated by the process of multiplying their investments through more and sometimes less immaculate transactions. But Davis unashamedly believed in spending his income of more than four million dollars a year. Unlike most of his contemporaries, he took pride and pleasure in his ceaseless search for perfection.

Unobtrusive and gentle in his demeanour, he had a permanent twinkle in his eye, but practical jokes were not his long suit. He remained vaguely puzzled and disturbed for thirty years after his friend Bud McDougald pulled a great stunt on him in 1949. Davis had visited Herbert Johnson, the famous London hatter, and with a typically grand gesture purchased two dozen models, one in every second shade the store had on display. When McDougald heard about Davis's buying spree, he promptly ordered the other twenty-four hats and asked for the bill to be sent to his friend Nels. Davis paid the account but seldom donned any of the forty-eight pieces of headgear and never mentioned the receipt of the extra hats to his pal Bud.

Still, it is probably his role as the agent who made McDougald's posthumous wishes come true that may be Davis's most lasting legacy. Before his unexpected death a year ago, McDougald had often discussed with Davis his intention of passing on the Argus reins to the Black brothers. He admired in particular the stretch of knowledge and ideological depth of Conrad, the younger, plus his record of turning the Sterling newspaper chain into a profitable enterprise. The problem was that with the optimism and disdain of common mortality so typical of him, McDougald never really planned to die and made no provision to ensure the Black brothers' succession.

It was during the crucial negotiations that followed Max Meighen's attempt to gain control of Argus that Davis stepped in to persuade Maude McDougald and Doris Phillips (who owned 47.2 per cent of the stock in Ravelston Corporation, the Argus holding instrument) that they should sign their shares over to the Blacks. In the process, he purchased about 10 per cent of the Ravelston stock for his own account and was named to the Argus chairmanship.

The death of Nelson Davis robs Canadian business of one of its last titans. His old-fashioned chivalry was no match for the computer-trained whiz kids now scrambling to the top of the corporate ladders. But he was a man to go tiger-shooting with. Once you earned his respect, he never let you down.

—1979

Bud McDougald

B UD McDOUGALD AND I were sitting in the sunroom of Green Meadows, his great Toronto house, with its Georgian stables, willow-lined drives, and thirty-car garage, discussing his death.

I had inquired about the provisions for succession at Argus Corporation as part of my research for the first volume of *The Canadian Establishment*, and he started to reply with the comment, "*If*, as and when I croak . . ."

The unfinished phrase hung between us. I ventured to ask, "How do you mean, '*If*'?"

He looked at me for a long, revealing moment, as if staring into the camera of history. Then he shrugged, raised his eyebrows, and waved his hand in a gesture of dismissal that seemed to indicate that both of us were well aware of the complexities of human existence, and what the hell was the point of adding to them.

We went on to talk of other things. But I vividly recalled our exchange last week when word came through from his mansion at Palm Beach that John Angus McDougald had died. Even though we'd had one terrible fight, we had grown fond of each other. He would telephone me every month or so to see how my next volume was progressing, offer advice on making *Maclean's* grow faster, use me as a listening-post to deride Pierre Trudeau's latest perfidies, and invariably tell me at least one new story.

My favourite anecdote concerned a large ranch he had recently acquired in Florida, which had housed a private zoo on its grounds.

Under the terms of his purchase, the animals were to be removed, and when he discovered that the crocodiles had been left behind, dozing in the sun, McDougald demanded to know why. The former owner informed him that it was because she had read in my book about his preference for alligator shoes.

McDougald thought this was all great fun but chided me for his now having to bear the expense of removing the animals himself, since he didn't wish to disappoint the previous landlord about the accuracy of my research. (He did have a penchant for alligator shoes, but only for the English bench-made variety that he would buy at a small shop near Claridge's in London.)

We all hate to get older, but it was typical of Bud McDougald that he would actually try to do something about it.* During the final two years of his life, he engaged himself in a private battle of documents with the archives of the 48th Highlanders, attempting to prove that he really was two years younger than his recorded age, vaguely maintaining he had faked his birth date in order to enlist as a youngster.

The few friends who were aware of the ploy realized it was all part of a half-serious attempt to extend past the compulsory retirement age his term as a director of the Canadian Imperial Bank of Commerce – an institution on whose board he had served since 1950.

But even though he died the day after reaching his seventieth birthday, it's highly doubtful if any official of the bank would have had either the nerve or the inclination to press the Argus chairman for his resignation. Hardly anyone treated him in accordance with the rules that apply to ordinary mortals. And with good reason.

Bud McDougald was the last of his kind. He was possessed by a kind of Henry James sensibility – a highly developed sense of the urbane, a limitless faith in manners, a deep respect for privacy and the proper order of things. He would no more question a man about his monetary worth than ask him about his favourite sex position.

In all his dealings – and he maintained an amazing variety of high-

---

*His strength of will did find at least one posthumous expression. When reviewing the arrangements for his burial, a thoughtful member of his family realized that Bud would have been appalled by the length of the hair on the young sextet of professional attendants supplied by Rosar-Morrison, the funeral directors. He telephoned the firm and requested they get haircuts. They did.

level contacts around the free world – he deliberately cultivated the absence of public visibility. He had such a strong sense of inner identity that he required nobody to remind him of exactly who he was.

He viewed the world with the undistracted gaze of a sentinel scanning distant fields through the battlements of his own castle walls. He had opinions on everything but hesitated to disseminate them, never once making a speech outside of his companies' annual meetings, refusing to appear on radio or TV. Discretion was best, anonymity better. It took me a full year to negotiate our first interview, but I gradually gained his confidence so that he would call me in for lunch-time sessions in his Argus office, both of us sipping Richmello Instant Coffee and munching Dominion Store vanilla cookies, speculating on the state of the world, discussing how fast the country was going down the drain, and tabulating who was moving up or down in the Canadian corporate power game.

Our only disagreement came when my book was done and McDougald asked to see a draft of my chapter about him. I pointed out that I never show anyone anything I write before publication and that he could be no exception. His blue-grey eyes flashed. He rose from his desk, expressed some not very complimentary thoughts about me, suggesting that his purchase of Maclean-Hunter was hardly worth the trouble of keeping me quiet, and finally calmed down when he recognized my position was not negotiable.

Our private lunch meetings continued into the fall of 1977, when he left Toronto for the last time. Once, he decided we should visit the Toronto Club together, "to show the flag a little." It was an amazing occasion. McDougald was ushered in with the punctilious flourish of a pope presuming worship, scattering small comments to favoured members like benedictions. Those he missed came over to his private table (reserved for him whether he was in town or not) to seek his glance or approbation.

He loved the insider's world he had created for himself but never really felt comfortable with the changing ethics of the society in which he prospered. The chairman of Argus lived by his own rules. He would probably have felt much more at home within the strictly defined hierarchies of the seventeenth-century England of Thomas Hobbes, who saw life "as a perpetual and restless desire of power after power that ceaseth onley in death."

Bud McDougald understood power very well and knew how to exercise it. He didn't need anyone to tell him precisely where he fitted into the Canadian Establishment's complicated structures. Right at the very top.

As he grew older he retreated into his various mansions and boardrooms, emerging to view the world ever more rarely, growling at the galloping imperfections of the liberal society he despised. That he paid personal income taxes of more than a million dollars a year accredited him in his own eyes as a roving commissioner free to criticize all government activities. He was never himself tempted to run for parliament, dismissing the idea "because of the sort of people you have to meet – all that terrible going to strawberry festivals and the like."

He considered all politicians suspect by definition, and when I asked him to name an exception, he couldn't. Finally, after torturous effort and the running down of long lists of possible candidates, he allowed that perhaps Abraham Lincoln wasn't all that bad. Then a look of pure mischief came over his face. He winked at me and said, "But, of course, I like John Wilkes Booth even better!"

—1978

Steve Roman

MY FAVOURITE MEMORY of Steve Roman, who has died of a heart attack at sixty-six, is of being at his castle overlooking his twelve-hundred-acre estate just north of Toronto, sipping a plum brandy known as slivovitz and talking about why he had never made it into the Canadian Establishment.

The house reflected the man: nothing flossy or phony, like so many of the pseudo-British country seats that mandatory decorators inflict on Canada's New Rich. Like the man, the house was large (seventeen rooms), tough (wall-to-wall marble), on the edge of vulgar (plush red sofas and crystal chandeliers) – yet functional and impressive.

Roman seemed to have it all. He was a farm-boy immigrant who had become controlling shareholder of a company worth nearly two billion dollars, a fervent Catholic whose confessions were heard by a bishop in his own private chapel. But Roman was obsessed by the fact that he had never been accepted by members of the Canadian business elite. They never granted him the right qualifying badges, never appointed him to a bank board, and they had rejected him for membership in the clubs that matter.

When I asked Roman what clubs he did belong to, the only one he mentioned was Toronto's Empire Club, which is no club at all but a Royal York Hotel luncheon group that sells tickets at the door. Still, he lived as lavishly as any of our wealthiest citizens, flying the world in his company's Gulfstream III and fervently pursuing the most elitist of hobbies, cattle breeding. (One of his three-year-old Holsteins made the *Guinness Book of World Records* when it sold for $65,000.)

Stephen Boleslav Roman was sixteen when he left the isolated Slovakian village of Velky Ruskov with his brother George in 1937. They bought a small farm on Scugog Island, near Port Perry, Ontario, and on one occasion, when George needed a plough horse, he traded his younger, tougher brother's services to a nearby farmer for use of the animal. Stephen later worked briefly at a munitions plant and as a guard on the Welland Canal; he joined the army, played the penny stock market, promoted a few cow pastures in his time, and, in 1953, purchased 900,000 shares of a speculative mining prospect known as North Denison. A year later he bought claims (for $30,000 and 500,000 of his treasury shares) in the Algoma district that turned out to hold the largest uranium ore body yet discovered. Roman's greatest personal achievement was to raise the $59 million required to bring the property into production without losing financial control. By the mid-Seventies he had amassed orders from Ontario Hydro alone worth $7.3 billion.

His company, Denison Mines Limited, quickly expanded into other mineral ventures, cement manufacturing, packaging, papermaking, potash mining, and, most of all, a world-spanning hunt for oil. Roman loved to boast about his wells in Marion County, Texas, in a basin off Louisiana, in the North Aegean Sea off Greece, in the huge Vega field off Sicily, and in the Casablanca basin off Spain. He owned three concessions in the Western Desert of Egypt and had built a pipeline to the Mediterranean. Other Denison crews were busy in the United Republic of Cameroon and in Senegal.

Roman considered such pursuits worthy of his talents but found himself instead having to deal with shareholders unhappy with Denison's record closer to home, particularly its disastrous foray into coal mining in northern British Columbia. The three-billion-dollar Quintette megaproject was a disappointment, and even though the federal and provincial governments poured in $1.5 billion, it will probably never be feasible. By 1985 Denison had to write off its entire $240.7-million investment, and two years later, for the first time in twenty-eight years, the company skipped its dividend payments.

Steve Roman had an evangelical faith in capitalism but no faith at all in politicians. He triggered violent confrontations with the Liberal government in 1965 (Prime Minister Lester Pearson, at the end of one discussion, told Roman that he was "fifty years behind the apes") and with Pierre Trudeau in 1970, when Ottawa tried to block the sale of Denison to a foreign firm. To counter Ottawa's influence on his company, Roman always kept a tame politician on Denison's board of directors. Among them were George Drew, the former Conservative leader, who kept falling asleep at board meetings, and Senator Keith Davey, who resigned on a point of principle when Roman refused to accept an Ottawa tax assessment. The current incumbent of the board's political seat is Mulroney confidant Sam Wakim.

Roman tried unsuccessfully to get himself elected, but his personal passions were much more closely tied with erecting the multimillion-dollar Cathedral of the Transfiguration, near his estate. The foundations of its twenty-storey tower and dome were consecrated by the Pope during his 1984 visit. "Everybody is put on this earth to perfect a divine plan," Roman told *Maclean's* writer Angela Ferrante in a 1978 interview. "Mine is to save my soul."

What made Steve Roman different – and important – was that, unlike the paper shufflers who inhabit the Establishment's roosts these days, he was a builder and a risk-taker on a grand scale. If that meant being a bit rough along the edges – and not being acceptable to the rarefied tastes of the country's Establishment – well, that was too damn bad, as far as he was concerned.

Still, Bay Street exacted its final verdict on Roman's primal ethic. News of his death began to circulate on the floor of the Toronto Stock Exchange within hours. At the end of the day's trading, Denison's stock had gone up a full point.

—1988

257

Donald Fleming

DONALD FLEMING'S POLITICAL MEMOIRS, *So Very Near*, are very hard to pick up, once you've put them down. During a quarter-century of active politics, Donald Fleming attained every office but the top, and the title refers to the fact that he came close to succeeding John Diefenbaker as prime minister, almost became chief justice of Canada, and did, in fact, achieve some remarkable accomplishments. But reading this political autobiography, published the year before he died, is a little like taking cod-liver oil: it's awful at each gulp, but the cumulative effect is vaguely beneficial.

Guaranteed to induce sleep in the most hardened insomniac, the twin volumes never let up in breaking the barriers of their subject's conceit. Fleming boasts that of the 826 Cabinet meetings he attended, he "never went to one . . . unprepared. Regardless of the hour I never took to my bed until every document . . . had been thoroughly studied." Then he asks himself: "How did I maintain this pace? How did I escape a physical and mental collapse?" Finally, he answers his own question with a resounding "I was serving Canada and the Queen!"

The veteran Tory portrays himself as the epitome of the Protestant ethic, as though hard work and denial of pleasure could absolve sins of omission and resolve every problem. Characteristically, Fleming seems to believe that enough suffering would produce a good book: "Every word of the text, numbering about 600,000 words, was written in longhand," he boasts in the preface. "My chair often felt hard, but I was driven by the thought that I was writing history." The poor man ploughed through ten thousand pages of Cabinet minutes and reviewed

120 volumes of Hansard, barely managing to reduce his notes to 125,000 double-column pages.

The memoirs cover every detail of a long life, from young Donald's first day in kindergarten to his retirement in Nassau. His budgets, which were not so much pre-Keynesian as Precambrian, are laid out in every boring, self-justifying detail. (It is a sign of how times have changed that Fleming's agony over spending too much federal money was based on the fact that in the seven budgets he tabled, the cumulative deficit amounted to about three billion dollars. We now go that deep into debt every month.)

During his five years as John Diefenbaker's minister of finance, Fleming beat off the assaults of political opponents like a Salvation Army major decrying the taunts of street-corner drunks. His book drips with the besieged righteousness he felt as he bowed to his prime minister's politically motivated spending habits, retreating ever farther from the fiscal orthodoxy that was his most cherished political belief.

The parade of details and statistics burdens the memoirs like lamentations on the stations of the cross. We are told, for example, that in 1978, during a typical year of his residence in the Bahamas, Fleming went swimming 1,309 times, played 208 tennis matches and 140 golf games (eighteen-hole). We learn about his favourite hymn when he was seven years old, the name and biography of his barber at the Royal York Hotel, how he once gave a ninety-minute budget speech with "not so much as a sip of water throughout," the identity of all his nominees who did *not* get Orders of Canada, a detailed breakdown of Canadian exports to Britain in 1960, and a record of every office he ever held in the Lodge of Perfection of the Scottish Rite.

Journalists' comments, the favourable ones, are not quoted as excerpts but as entire columns, while his critics of the time (including this one) are condemned for their perfidy. Part of the problem with these memoirs and their protagonist is that Fleming never admits to having been wrong about anything. "He doesn't just fight an issue," the late Austin Cross once wrote about him in the Ottawa *Citizen*, "he beats it to death. Then he cuts its throat, slashes its wrists, throws acid in its face, and sets fire to it." Exactly.

Yet there is a kind of hypnotic quality about Fleming's style, with descriptions inevitably tripping into the most awful clichés. Every friendly politician is a "stalwart" who "grasps the nettle," every unexpected event is "an untoward incident," every task quickly becomes "formidable," and Grits inevitably "blot their copybooks."

Somewhere in the welter of all this verbiage, an important book about an essentially decent man, trapped in the vortex of political expediency, is struggling to get out. A child of the most narrow kind of Orange-tinted Ontario Conservatism, Fleming not only learned to speak French but genuinely grew to understand the Quebec of his period. At the 1956 leadership convention he received almost unanimous backing from the Quebec delegation, and in the election that followed he was the PCs' pointman in French Canada.

His reconstructions of the manoeuvres within the department of finance during the Coyne affair and in the constant struggle to restrain Diefenbaker's extravagances are important, even seminal, accounts. He is at his best telling the inside story of the Tory Government's collapse. It is difficult not to sympathize with Fleming's verdict that, in terms of his treatment by the prime minister, Diefenbaker "was the most self-centred and self-seeking man I ever met."

His faithfulness to party and country does not require Fleming's elaboration; he was the ultimate loyalist, and it profited him not at all. Yet the dichotomy between his nature and his performance remains unresolved by these bulky volumes.

Although one exchange is not included in the memoirs, it serves to sum up the man and his bloated view of himself. At the end of his first financial statement, on December 6, 1957, Fleming flummoxed the House of Commons by blowing his own trombone. "May I say very humbly," he said not very humbly, "that seventeen to eighteen hours' work per day and one hundred hours' work per week are an insignificant price to pay for the high privilege of serving Canada." To which James Sinclair, then Liberal finance critic, whispered in reply: "If conceit is the small man's sword, Don's the best-armed man in Canada."

—1987

The Montreal Star

TO A JOURNALIST, the decision to close any newspaper is like a death in the family. This was particularly true for me of the *Montreal Star* because George V. Ferguson, its greatest editor, was one of my kindest mentors and most formative influences. It was Ferguson who turned the *Star* into a great journal of record, a tradition ably perpetuated by Frank Walker and Gerald Clark, the editors of the final edition.

The *Star*'s demise was, of course, only the most visible and most recent wound in the hemorrhaging of Montreal's influence. A survey published by the *Star* only two months ago documented the alarming defection of head offices that had moved out of the city since the 1976 election of the Parti Québécois. On top of such visible departures as Sun Life, RCA, and Bristol-Myers has been the secret and continuing transfer of the decision-making apparatus by key institutions whose chief executive offices only nominally remain in Montreal. The Royal Bank of Canada, for example, is still headquartered at Place Ville Marie, but its commercial marketing and international operations reside safely in Toronto. One federal study estimates that since René Lévesque came to power the number of people leaving Quebec has jumped by 33 per cent.

The trend certainly has accelerated, but Montreal's slide dates all the way back to the mining discoveries in the Canadian Shield during the teens of this century, when the Toronto Stock Exchange plunged into the mining boom while Montreal's investors delicately demurred, regarding the speculative fervour as "a bit undignified." Toronto's

Bay Street boys plugged themselves into the Wall Street money apparatus while their St. James Street counterparts continued to dream of a vanishing past, retaining their City associations with London. English Montrealers of the Thirties, Forties, and Fifties behaved with an imperviousness to change that Charles Dickens would have envied. They regarded Toronto as a place where only the vulgar nouveaux riches would want to live – and as for what lay west of Toronto, well, that was something no civilized person would even consider.

Ironically, Montreal's plight has deprived Quebec separatists of their main inspiration to expand their power through independence. This testimony to shift of authority from English to French is just the kind of story the *Montreal Star* was best at documenting. Now it has become part of the evidence.

—1979

PART FIVE

Business Watch

Giving Business a Bad Name

NOTHING REVEALS THE DARK SIDE of Canadian capitalism more clearly than the collapse of two wholly owned subsidiaries of Edmonton's Principal Group, whose chairman, Donald Cormie, now claims to bear "no responsibility whatever" for the mess he created.

Under this curlicue ethic, companies would be allowed to dupe their shareholders and investors by dumping speculations that turned sour into a basket-company, which could then be spun off into the bankruptcy courts while the balance of their portfolio remains unharmed. Cormie has not hesitated to proclaim this bizarre doctrine, boasting since the debacle that his Principal Group has current assets of at least $1.2 billion and is "the most liquid financial institution in the country." He has confirmed that more than two-thirds of the assets of the Principal Group's Principal Savings & Trust Company are "cash, short-term notes and government bonds" – and that the investors in his two bankrupt companies will not get any of that money.

Principal's most dubious real estate holdings ended up in the same two companies: First Investors Corporation Limited and Associated Investors of Canada Limited. And Principal's published documents state that "qualified assets in excess of 100 per cent" of the two companies' certificates were always held in a chartered bank. Even so, Cormie has washed his hands of the affair, telling the world: "Who, me? I had nothing to do with it!"

That's cold comfort to the 68,000 investors who had $550 million in the two companies because they took Cormie and his salesmen at their word. As more facts emerge about the devastating failure, the twin concepts of corporate accountability and responsibility, fragile at best, have been reduced to a bad joke. By paying his sales staff extra commissions to divert investors from Principal's other financial vehicles into the two now defunct subsidiaries, Cormie knew exactly what he was doing.

Apart from the morality of such an arrogant posture, his "no responsibility" claim doesn't ring true. Few if any Canadian companies have been run with greater daily hands-on management than the Principal Group – and Cormie holds 80 per cent of the ownership stock himself; his two sons and his partner, Ken Marlin, are on the books for the balance. Principal is essentially a one-man operation, and that man is trying to deny he is responsible for the fact that two companies, which held about a quarter of its assets, have gone under.

Cormie's solo operating philosophy extends even to his twenty-million-dollar, eighteen-thousand-acre ranch in the Tomahawk District west of Edmonton, where he runs the world's largest private bull-semen bank. In better days Cormie once boasted to me that he could monitor the sex life of every animal from a computer on his desk. His favourite critter at the time was a Swiss-born Simmental bull called Signal, which had already donated sperm worth $2,348,000 and was still corporately contributing, in its fashion. Right up there among the wealthiest of Canadians, Cormie owns two houses in Alberta (plus the province's third-largest legal firm) as well as a five-million-dollar spread at Brentwood Bay on Vancouver Island, which has on it two mansions with eleven bedrooms between them and the best view in the country. The residences are regularly rented out to provide lavish backgrounds for productions like *Five Easy Pieces* and "Love Boat" – yet Cormie is so small-minded he refused the previous owner's request to rescue garden bulbs she had left in the ground.

Whether or not Donald Cormie gets away with his self-proclaimed immunity from ethical standards will depend on the outcome of the hearings under way in Alberta and British Columbia. But the Principal debacle, which threatens the existence of Western Canada's last major independent financial institution, raises far more disturbing questions about Canada's whole financial industry. Cormie, who has always prided himself on being our ultimate free-enterpriser, may well be remembered as the man who buried Canadian capitalism.

—1987

Advice of a Beached Acquisitor

"I WANT TO GIVE YOU A MESSAGE," Peter Thomas is saying with that born-yesterday sincerity that allowed him to spin half a dozen mediocre franchising ideas into two personal fortunes. "We were victims of the King Arthur disease," the Victoria-based entrepreneur explains, referring to the high-flying Western Canadian acquisitors grounded by the recession but now timidly starting to fly again. "In those days, when somebody came to you with a deal, you'd tell your wife, your lawyer, and your accountant about it, and half the time they would try to talk you out of it. But you did the deal anyway, and made money. So after a while you didn't talk to anybody – you got too embarrassed to tell them about the crazy deals you were doing. You started getting these big lumps of cash and you felt invincible."

Thomas, who parlayed his real estate flips into a glittering thirty-nine-million-dollar fortune and a glitzy lifestyle, sounds defensive and retroactively hurt that he never got the Nobel Prize for his brassy triumphs. His tone reminds me of another West Coast entrepreneur-on-the-rocks who once complained in mock seriousness, "You think it was easy being the only kid in high school with clear skin?"

"I remember one deal," Thomas is saying. "It was in Eugene, Oregon, and the only reason I was down there was because my daughter, Liane, rated around tenth in Canada, was attending a gymnastics meet. I went down on Friday and had nothing to do, so I bought this building, the Atrium it was called, for $1.4 million. I sold it for $2.4 million without hardly seeing it. That's how you get King Arthur's disease. Then you fall on your face. I lost more than two thirds of my net worth.''

Typically, Thomas is now capitalizing on his fiscal downfall and, unlike many of the West Coast's onetime big hitters, is successfully reclaiming his particular branch of the money tree. ''I've developed a seminar I give business people on the King Arthur disease,'' he explains, ''telling them how to detect the symptoms.'' Some of Thomas's fellow predators are similarly employed, with Vancouver flipper Nelson Skalbania and Edmonton money-jockey Peter Pocklington also chairing occasional seminars. ''Peter and Nelson,'' Thomas laments, ''were carriers of the bug. They were contagious.''

Thomas, who left the Canadian Army in 1962, has always lived on the edge of his potential, first as a mutual fund salesman, later as the owner of a hotel, a construction company, and some resource and real estate investments. He made most of his cash as Canadian chairman of the Century 21 real estate franchise network and is still suffering the Great Recession's fallout. His net worth dropped by thirty million dollars, and times got so tough he had to sell his $800,000 Piper Cheyenne turboprop, his seventy-two-foot Stevens yacht, and his Harley-Davidson 1200. He did manage to hang on to his $120,000 Clenet convertible and still lives in his plush-lined Victoria hotel suite. If he has learned to sound humble, he reassures himself privately that the interference in his comfy-cosy lifestyle is strictly temporary.

Thomas's revival as a supersalesman is based on new franchise operations modelled on the success of the Century 21 formula. Last year the real estate chain, which now has 325 Canadian branches, sold three billion dollars' worth of houses yielding commissions of more than a hundred million dollars. That netted at least a million dollars for Century 21's chairman. Thomas has a small share of the Uniglobe travel franchises run by his Century 21 partner, Gary Charlwood, but most of his time these days is spent on expanding Mr. Build (home repairs) and Triex (used cars) franchises.

Whatever their pretensions, Thomas and his breed are essentially salesmen. It was this remarkable ability to market himself that prompted Peter Thomas's debut as an author. His recently published volume, *Windows of Opportunity*, is probably as sensible a distillation of the salesman's occult arts as has ever been put together in this country. ''I don't believe that salesmen are born,'' says Thomas.

"They are taught. We need to upgrade the calibre of people coming into the profession by opening up the gates and saying, 'Lookit, you too can be successful.'"

Thomas goes along with his own advice – that God gave us two eyes and two ears but only one mouth, and they should be used proportionately – by playing down the standard Willy Loman stereotype. "The basic requirement of a great salesman," he says, "is a subtle but genuine interest in other people and a lively curiosity. The old idea that you have to be a glad-hander, have a pot belly, smoke a fat cigar, and talk a mile a minute – that went out with the carnival."

Peter Thomas is living proof not only that his sales techniques work but that there is life after dropping $30 mill . . .

—1984

The Last Days of the Club

BAY STREET HAS ALWAYS BEEN more a synonym for greed and damnation to the rest of the country than just a handy spot to do business. That historical bias still applies, even though the Toronto Stock Exchange has long since moved off the Street, and 220 Bay is nothing more momentous than a Kentucky Fried Chicken franchise, across the street from a Double D variety store.

The reputation may endure, but the reality is changing. The financial community known as Bay Street, which once operated like a well-ordered club, with Wood Gundy, Dominion Securities, and A.E. Ames forming its Holy Trinity, is being transformed beyond recognition. Not very long ago the clans of money managers perpetuated themselves by pedigree, instinct, and fellowship—the line of succession ran directly from the "good" families into Upper Canada College and the Toronto Club, connections that were more than adequate to guarantee the beginner a pew in one of the major investment houses.

The first revolution against that established order of things was launched in the early Sixties by Bill Wilder, then executive vice-president and later president of Wood Gundy, who had gone to UCC and was a member of the Toronto Club but had also taken an MBA at Harvard and understood how the real world worked. Under his influence, modern management techniques and the first elements of competition were introduced to the club, and everything could no longer be taken for granted.

The next big shake-up came with the ascendancy at Gordon Securities of Jimmy Connacher, who finally broke the syndicates in 1983 when he introduced "bought" deals – the notion that new issues required no fixed rake-offs by brokers and should be guaranteed by the issuing house with its own funds. That permanently reduced the size of dealers' commissions.

Now, the third great upheaval is under way, and this time the club is not just changing; it is being replaced. The combination of rule changes by the federal and Ontario governments – which allow foreign participation in the investment industry and permit banks to buy directly into brokerage houses – with the introduction of negotiated commissions and the twenty-four-hour globalized securities market has turned Bay Street upside down.

The major house that first squarely faced the future and joined it was McLeod Young Weir, one of the Street's top firms that regularly turns over a 25- to 30-per-cent after-tax profit on its seventy-two-million-dollar equity base. The company sold 30 per cent of itself to the giant New York merchant bankers Shearson Lehman Brothers and another 19.9 per cent to the Montreal Bronfmans [and more recently sold out to the Bank of Nova Scotia] – but its daily operations remain under the direction of its chairman, Austin Taylor, and president, Tom Kierans.

Kierans qualifies as an ideal role model for Bay Street's man of the future. An MBA who became an important activator in two other investment houses (Nesbitt Thomson and Pitfield Mackay Ross) before joining McLeod's in 1979, he has crossed easily from the public to the private sector and back again. The tally of the financings he has managed includes participation in the world syndicate that floated the British Telecom mega-issue in November 1984.

"Competition on the Street is going to be brutal," he predicts. "We're basically running a national, not international, capital market, and the big international houses are going to be willing to spill a lot to access those of our issuers and borrowers who deal in the world markets. That's going to have an enormous impact on margins. The new players are also going to be willing to float some terrific loss leaders to obtain their share of market, and that's another reason competition will get so brutal."

At the end of the tumultuous transition period, Toronto will have been transformed from a dying manufacturing centre to a thriving financial capital. And Bay Street's once dominant clubs? "The clubs don't matter any more,'' Kierans insists, even if he remains a member. ''Who cares whether you lunch at the Toronto Club with some likely client? In the final analysis, his treasurer will call for tenders anyway.''

The most dramatic shift in the financial markets has been the jump in power of the institutional traders. It is the fund managers from the country's most careful financial institutions who most successfully manipulate the market these days. The other change is the introduction of a new generation of computers. The new machines can determine not only what a stock is really worth but what other investors might be planning to do about it. The ''smart money'' that was once able to multiply by playing on inside tips has been bested by electronic machines that can spot the first faint traces of stock accumulation. The secret unloaders are equally easy to identify because the new computers sound alarms when the acceleration in buying slows down, even though the price of the stock in question may still be rising. Not many ''sleepers'' can survive such electronic assault.

One way in which the Stock Exchange hasn't changed at all is that it remains one huge rumour mill, with stock tips and gossip wafting through the air like armoured butterflies. Inside information is the lifeblood of the trade, and traders seldom have to worry about assembly lines, capital investment, or depreciation allowances. Their product is money, and their objective is to turn as much of it as they can before the closing bell. Their time frame is split into the milliseconds it takes to record a trade: quickness of mind and a macho eagerness to invite risks is what separates good traders from great ones. The TSE's flashy new trading floor is populated by the same sharks and their pilot fish who have always thrived in the business. Despite its fancy trimmings, Bay Street is nothing more – or less – than Canada's most fashionable gambling casino.

—1987

The Fall of the House of Gundy

ECONOMISTS WILL IMMORTALIZE October 19, 1987, as the bottoming out of the five-year bull market. But for social historians, 1987 will be remembered as the year the Bronfmans had to bail out Wood Gundy.

The $137-million loan by one of the Peter and Edward Bronfman companies – at interest rates well above prime – helped to stave off the latest crisis threatening the financial integrity of the once-great investment house. The transaction also carried a much deeper meaning, because it signalled the final transfer of power from the old-line WASP Establishment to a feistier group of entrepreneurs more concerned with playing by their own rules than in obeying the hoary edicts of Bay Street's old boys' club.

The Montreal-born Bronfmans, once dismissed as minor players (because Sam Bronfman's branch of the family inherited the controlling block of Seagram stock), have emerged as Canada's most imaginative capitalists. Meanwhile, the credibility of the eighty-two-year-old firm of Wood Gundy, which once ruled Canada's financial roost, boasting the most prestigious imprimatur in any underwriting syndicate, took a tumble.

Gundy's negotiations with three prospective partners – Gordon Capital Corporation, the Royal Bank of Canada, and now First National Bank of Chicago – collapsed. Then it was rumoured to be close to an agreement with [and was finally bought by] the Canadian Imperial Bank of Commerce. But as he lurched from one unsuccessful rescue mission to the next, Ted Medland, the embattled chairman of

Wood Gundy, was haunted by his own statement that his company would "wither and die" if it did not find a partner. The problem was always the same: because he assumed that Wood Gundy still retained its former prestige and dominance, Medland's demands of any potential partner were unrealistically high.

The Royal Bank's Allan Taylor, for example, was ready to close his intended purchase of Wood Gundy with a favourable pre-crash offer, but Medland's self-valuation pushed the price out of reach. Taylor later bought Dominion Securities at a realistic 2.1 times its book value. The now defunct arrangement that Medland originally negotiated with the First National (trading 35 per cent of his firm's equity for a cash injection of $270 million) called for a premium of about five times book value. (At one point Medland also flatly refused to accept the terms of a potential purchaser who insisted that Medland's resignation be part of any deal.)

Before the Bronfman loan, Wood Gundy's working capital had been reduced to critical levels. Gundy had to absorb losses on an unsuccessful $125-million Saskatchewan bond float and suffered severely in the market downturn. But the worst single blow was the insistence of Medland's company on taking up half of the $770-million Canadian share of what turned out to be the disastrous privatization issue of British Petroleum. That decision cost Gundy an overnight loss of about fifty-five million dollars and threatened to drag its ratio of retained capital to contingent liabilities below levels required by the Ontario Securities Commission. That's where the emergency loan came in. (The Bronfmans also came to Gundy's rescue by parking one hundred million dollars of an unsold Australian preferred issue.)

At the same time, Wood Gundy was embarrassed by the departure of many of its best retail salesmen to Walwyn Incorporated. And the internal chaos was not helped by Medland's cost-cutting edicts. In mid-December, for example, he let 150 staff members go in Bay Street's largest post-crash layoff. That was an understandable move in the circumstances, except that most of the people fired were at the operating end, leaving the executive floors hardly touched.

Wood Gundy's fall from grace is only the most dramatic of the events that have recently shaken Bay Street. The big change, of course, has been the internationalization of the Toronto financial community. As part of that trend, sixteen Canadian investment houses have sold majority or minority shares in themselves. In one of the largest deals, Security Pacific Corporation of Los Angeles doubled the capital of Burns Fry to $300 million in return for one-third ownership. The result of all that dealing is that during the last six months of 1987 total capitalization of the Canadian securities industry jumped to about $4 billion from $500 million.

The catalytic agent driving most of the reforms was Jimmy Connacher's Gordon Capital, which in 1981 became the TSE's dominant block trader, eventually breaking Bay Street's cosy fixed-rate commission arrangements. Two years later Connacher successfully challenged the underwriting syndicate monopoly of such firms as Wood Gundy by undercutting inflated overhead costs. Under that scheme, which is now common but at the time seemed revolutionary, Gordon Capital by-passed most of the expensive and time-consuming formalities by buying stock issues on its own account.

What isn't generally known is that Connacher could afford to break the existing syndicates only because he found ready partners from whom to rent the considerable capital required to purchase billions of dollars' worth of equity issues. The source of those funds was – you guessed it – the Bronfman brothers, the new kings of Bay Street.

—1988

PART SIX

Diversions

Wall Street on Film

W ALL STREET IS LESS A PLACE than a metaphor. As the world's leading financial centre, the seven-block alley of skyscrapers on the seaward tip of Manhattan Island determines the price of money. But in recent years it has also determined America's ethical standards – or rather, the lack of them.

In *Wall Street*, a flawed but powerful film, Oliver Stone, director of the Academy Award-winning *Platoon*, attempts to define Wall Street's gutter ethic that climaxed with the October 19, 1987, fall from grace. He comes so close to succeeding that at times his film ventures dangerously close to being a documentary.

Stone's portrait of moral decay within the upper reaches of U.S. capitalism suspends disbelief without ever becoming preachy, and it is this gritty quality that makes it so compelling.

The 125-minute film is a lightning-paced morality play in which an ambitious but weak young stockbroker named Bud Fox is ensnared by a Boesky-like mogul, Gordon Gekko, who had an ethical bypass at birth and "was on the phone thirty seconds after the Challenger blew up selling NASA-related stocks." The youthful Fox courts the wily Gekko, is quickly seduced into providing illegal inside information, is betrayed, and in the end incriminates his corrupter.

The new Stone release concentrates on mental rather than physical violation but is as effective as his classic *Platoon*. The dominant theme of that Vietnam film was that the first casualty of war is innocence; the motif here is that every dream has a price tag - and that most people are willing to pay it.

The two notions converge in Stone's decision to film downtown New York as a battle zone, so that Wall Street's spiritual tundra becomes less a backdrop than the movie's main theme. People spend their days transfixed by the eerie glow of computer terminals, frantically dialling for dollars as they try to con their equally greedy customers into buying shares in some company that is "in play." The shouting never stops. Like jumped-up cocaine addicts, the big shooters are in it as much for the game as for the gain.

Using hand-held cameras and the best of current cinéma vérité techniques, Stone is able to capture not just the action but also the killer instinct of the participants. "If you need a friend," one stockbroker tells a complaining colleague, "get a dog." Another dismisses a beautiful and reputedly sexy analyst at a competing firm with the cutting comment, "Having sex with her was like reading the *Wall Street Journal*."

Even nature turns malignant. The New York sunsets and sunrises have the same ominous quality as the day changes in *Apocalypse Now*. They create a mood of foreboding that can break at any moment into a shark-feeding frenzy.

Under Stone's direction, the camera becomes a predator, probing the film's characters for vulnerabilities of the soul and skin. The most devastating aspect of the screenplay, written by Stone and Stanley Weiser, is that insider trading is accurately portrayed, not as a crime, but as a natural outcome of the value system in play here. "Come on, who really gets hurt?" is the question. "It's ridiculous to have laws that regulate the free market while muggers waste old ladies in the street. We can buy our freedom. There is justice higher than the law."

Although *Wall Street* has seventy-nine speaking parts, at least three of the main characters play considerably below the potential of their roles. Hal Holbrook is ineffectual as a vaguely idealistic broker. Daryl Hannah tries hard to turn herself into a sort of Hertz bimbo (for rent if not for sale) but ends up portraying only a pouty indifference meant to reinforce her boyfriend's contention that "money's the sex of the Eighties."

The worst casting is Charlie Sheen (Martin's boy) as the corruptible stockbroker. At twenty-two, he lacks the face and body language to portray pathos, and his upward mobility is about as interesting as an elevator ride. Apart from Oliver Stone's sensitivity as a director, what turns *Wall Street* into a fine film is the performance of Michael Douglas as Gordon Gekko. Exuding an irresistible field of force, he is a rat-fink poet with a quip for every occasion. "I bought my way in. Now all those schmucks are sucking my kneecaps," he complains. "Love is a fiction invented by people to keep them from jumping out of windows." "Lunch is for wimps." Such bons mots aside, Gekko brings to life the twisted ethics of Wall Street. His creed is simple: "I create nothing. I *own*."

His best scene occurs during a successful takeover of Teldar Incorporated, a faltering New Hampshire wood products company, when he rises from his seat during a shareholders' meeting to answer the incumbent management's charges that he is solely motivated by greed. "The point is," he insists, "greed is good. Greed is right. Greed works. Greed clarifies, cuts through and captures the essence of the evolutionary spirit. Greed, in all of its forms – greed for life, money, love, knowledge – has marked the upward surge of mankind. And greed, mark my words, will save not only Teldar but that other malfunctioning corporation called the U.S.A."

That tirade may serve as the quintessential explanation for the Wall Street crash. When men and women equate their net worth with their self worth – not just in a movie but in real life – the social contract is burst asunder and the system explodes.

—1987

The Old School Tie

A FEW CHRISTMASES AGO, the thorny problem facing the poobahs who run Upper Canada College, the Canadian Establishment's Finishing School, was how to celebrate its 150th anniversary. After considerable brow-furrowing, they found the obvious answer: Why not invite the Duke?

Edinburgh *is*, after all, the school's patron, having enjoyed a long association with Toronto's – and arguably Canada's – most prestigious private school.

The ensuing festivities were mobbed by so many graduates that the Automotive Building at the Canadian National Exhibition had to be rented to accommodate their black-tie dinner. A grand time was had by all, and everyone thought it only proper that genuine royalty should take time out to salute one of Canada's most regal institutions.

It's not the oldest of the country's seventy-odd private schools (that honour belongs to King's Edgehill School in Windsor, N.S., founded forty years earlier, in 1788), but UCC commands the respect of generations of Canadian *prominenti* in business and public service. It's a family affair. One out of five of the approximately two hundred day boys and eight hundred boarders enrolled in the school is the son of an Old Boy. (That, of course, is how the "Old Boys' network" got its name.)

My own stay at the College (1944-49) was the result of my father's wisdom in realizing that as an immigrant from war-torn Czechoslovakia, I would learn better English being immersed in a private school than by attending daily classes in more mundane surroundings. The other boys teased me endlessly, mimicking my peculiar mixture of German, French, and Czech. I must have learned English in six weeks flat. I also discovered that UCC really does instil a collectivist approach to life – the notion that if you're part of something, you have to carry your share of the load. All in all, Upper Canada was no academic Valhalla – but I did learn to play the drums.

The school worships its long traditions, such as the time when, during the Fenian Raids of 1866, a company of lightly armed UCC boys provided Toronto's only military garrison. In the Second World War, an astounding 75 per cent of the Old Boys won commissions, twenty-six of them attaining General rank. Roughly a third of Canada's most influential corporate directors are private school graduates – half of them from UCC

Perhaps because their influence comes so early, when personalities are still being formed, the private schools are essential in instilling Establishment values. Youthful impressions absorbed through willing pores set lifetime priorities, presumptions, and even partnerships. Even though private schools in Canada are only slightly tainted by the snobbishness characteristic of their British equivalents (which, according to one of their critics, perpetuate a race of languid duchesses and intrepid deer-stalkers), they still manage to instil the idea that privilege exists on this side of the Atlantic and that rebellion, however fleeting a temptation, is ultimately self-defeating.

The schools are run with spiffy discipline more than a little foreign to the Canadian character. The strictness is imported. "I am prepared to give the boys more liberties," famed Eton headmaster Michael McCrum once declared, "providing they do not take them."

The major shortcoming of the private school is that its boys and girls emerge from puberty isolated from life's realities – and from one another. They are trained for a world that doesn't exist. This can be only a temporary obstacle to some, curable by a couple of years in a job or at university. But for a surprising number of the alumni, their time in residence turns out to be the emotional high of a circumscribed adult life. In retrospect, they glory in the days of gowned masters, midnight high jinks, rustling rhododendrons, the common-room's red leather chairs, the bullying prefects, and that cold glass of morning milk said to have saltpetre in it.

It's a tidy, taut world, and there is that problem of meeting head-on afterward the sloppiness of life on the outside; but the men and women who have attended private school are probably the better for it. There is a good deal of truth in the rationale for this style of rarefied education given by Patrick Johnson, an Oxford graduate and former captain in the 9th Gurkha Rifles, who spent ten years as principal of Upper Canada College. "Many educational theorists," he said, "believe that comprehensive education is a panacea, because all students will then have equal opportunity. Unfortunately, the egalitarianism they seek is the equal opportunity to be mediocre. If equality is what we're after, I would be happier with the proposition that equality means equal opportunity to develop *un*equally. . . . I see nothing wrong – and much that is right – in competing to be excellent at the level of excellence at which an individual student can perform."

Perhaps that sums up the ultimate justification of the private school: it tests and stretches potential early, pushing students to discover that the hardest limits to overcome are those that are self-imposed.

—1983

Private Clubs

E VEN IF THEY HAVE BECOME faintly outdated and eminently spoofable, private clubs still matter in Canada.

Belonging has become at least as important as actually attending club functions, but membership in these select institutions continues to be a badge of social certification. While the new-breed wheelers are dealing in the posh watering holes that pepper most of Canada's city centres, the older crowd can still be seen ducking into the unmarked oak front doors of the major downtown lunching clubs. Their adherents may be playing out superannuated rites of privilege, but the conviviality they feel, the sense of *belonging*, of being cherished for what they *are* instead of what they *do* – that's what club life is all about. That, and sipping those marvellous screwdrivers made with real orange juice.

There was a time, not so long ago, when many of the commercial, charitable, and political liaisons that mattered were negotiated over *consommé madrilène* or those inevitable wrinkled baked apples featured on club menus. The processes of decision making have become much too complicated for that, but the old-boy network remains powerful and the social leverage of membership in certain clubs can make a difference. At the same time, the really good clubs provide their members with islands of calm in a troubled world. A British duke once noted that White's, then London's most uppity club, was "an oasis of civilization in a desert of democracy."

Club life was born in eleventh-century Britain when a circle of lunching companions organized themselves into *Le Court de Bonne*

Compagnie. The idea was transplanted to this side of the Atlantic in 1785, when the first Beaver Club was established in Montreal as a private gathering place for the adventurers who garnered fortunes from Canada's early fur trade. Most of Canada's clubs were founded in the days when the worship of all things British heavily influenced Canadian social behaviour – especially among the very rich. The institutions flourished through most of the Fifties and Sixties, but by the early Eighties some of the less prestigious clubs were in decline. For one thing, the 1971 federal budget disallowed membership fees as a legitimate business expense. (Royal Trust once claimed tax deductions for seventy-eight executive memberships.)

At the same time, it stopped being *de rigueur* for fathers to enrol their sons in these clubs as part of any young gentleman's proper upbringing. (Conrad Black was given membership in the Toronto Club on his twenty-first birthday.) The younger generation makes a beeline for the swanky commercial restaurants (Black himself splits his lunches between Winston's and the Toronto Club). They also like to have the option of enjoying the company of women, still forbidden in most of the clubs' dining rooms. (Until recently, for example, the Ranchmen's Club in Calgary allowed women to be present only on New Year's Day.)

In most Canadian cities, there are at least a pair of lunching clubs, such as the Mount Royal and the Saint James's in Montreal, the Vancouver Club and the University Club in Vancouver, the Manitoba and the Carleton in Winnipeg, and the Rideau Club and Le Cercle Universitaire in Ottawa. Toronto has half a dozen entries. The Toronto Club, founded in 1835 and housed in a downtown Victorian heap on Wellington Street, has the best summer buffet and the longest waiting list; the York Club, a former Gooderham mansion in uptown Toronto, has the most distinguished membership but is half deserted most noon hours – it serves tough roast beef and fabulous peppermint-marshmallow sundaes; the National Club, a kind of bullpen for the Toronto Club, was founded by Goldwin Smith in the 1870s and tends toward slightly intellectual members not afraid to admit they read slightly avant-garde publications, such as *The New Yorker*; the Albany (Tories), the Ontario (Grits), and the University (jocks) make up the balance of the roster.

Apart from these eating establishments, Toronto boasts an increasingly important group of sports-oriented clubs – the Badminton and Racquet, the Royal Canadian Yacht, the Granite – as well as various golf, squash, and hunt clubs. Farther afield, and probably most exclusive of all, are the fishing clubs, such as the Ristigouche in New Brunswick and the Long Point Company on a peninsula jutting southward into Lake Erie. On Georgian Bay there are the Madawaska, the Tadenac, and the Griffiths Island hunting preserve, in which membership costs seventeen thousand dollars. They say twelve thousand pheasant, a thousand partridge, three hundred quail, and a hundred deer are gunned down every season. Ontario's most exclusive ski clubs are Osler Bluff and Craigleith, both situated in Collingwood.

Gaining membership in these and other private clubs isn't quite the same as gaining acceptance: the few Jews and selected ethnics who belong are occasionally made to feel their tokenism. The clubs operate by exclusion, and a blackball at voting time is still considered a bitter social slap in the status-ridden society of Upper Canada.

Such rejections occur infrequently because most nominators and seconders of potential joiners are careful to sound out enough members to assure a favourable vote before proposing any outsiders. Few clubs practise outright sexism or anti-Semitism as they once did, but many women and Jews prefer to join their own organizations.

A generation from now, many of the private clubs will have vanished; some will manage to survive only by becoming business conference centres or catering to other nonexclusive functions. Montreal's once-hallowed Mount Stephen Club, for example, turned a few extra dollars by renting its premises for the CBC's "Empire Inc."

Though that may be the route for some, the future of other clubs depends on their ability to retain the strict exclusivity that has become their hallmark. This can be carried too far. In the early nineteenth century, the Duke of Portland, an eccentric British landowner, decided that the clubs he belonged to were populated by the wrong kind of people and that he would start his own. He purchased luxurious new premises, staffed them, and then set himself up as a committee of one to screen new applicants. No one measured up to his rigid qualifications, however, and for the next twenty years until his death, the snooty duke remained the club's only member.

—1983

Canadian Style?

ARE WE FOREVER CONDEMNED to remain colonial in our tastes – caught somewhere between California Patio Slick and Brideshead Revisited? Will there ever be an authentic Canadian style of living?

Now that we have become a country mature enough to have its own constitution and can boast of the independence we have been so assiduously seeking since 1867 – having all that, surely it's time for us to start developing a truly Canadian approach to décor and architecture. Apart from such obvious regional expressions as the Erickson aviaries set into the cliffs that ring Vancouver and the impeccably reconstructed Maria Chapdelaine farmhouses where Westmounters summer, we have almost no original style to call our own. (There is pine, of course, restored or created, but it's hardly enough to hang a lifestyle on.)

In the search to fill this vacuum, the country's taste-setters have reversed the normal tradition, in which banks took their cue from the formal but comforting parlours of the rich and the powerful. Members of our moneyed elite now have done a turnabout. For inspiration on how to furnish their homes, they look to the offices of their favourite bankers.

This curious reversal in house décor requires a word of explanation. The offices of the chairmen of the Big Five banks (father-confessors to the Establishment) reflect their wish to reassure their treasured mega-account customers by making the fiscal big hitters feel at home. The banks' corporate inner sanctums are furnished to resemble upper-class British drawing rooms: subdued colours, Adam sideboards, and paintings of anemic hounds chasing exhausted foxes. If they could manage it, the bankers would probably play "Rule Britannia" over their Muzak systems, with the interspersed high howls of vanquished Argentines. This is the real world, after all.

The bankers seldom step outside their head offices even for lunch, preferring to entertain clients in the banks' own executive dining rooms, which serve discreet cocktails and hors d'oeuvres followed by meticulously prepared meals. (Quiche Lorraine is the specialty at Commerce headquarters, which also features a special drink made of apple juice and ginger ale with a touch of Angostura bitters; the Royal's resident chefs in both Montreal and Toronto roast the best salted almonds in the country.) It is here, away from the noise and confusion of everyday commerce, over silver platters and escutcheoned china, that the chairmen solidify contacts that lead to the big decisions.

It is no surprise, then, that the country's ruling clans have responded in a typically Canadian way: they have – subconsciously, perhaps – furnished their living rooms to resemble bank chairmen's offices. John A. "Bud" McDougald, who until he died on the ides of March, 1978, ranked as the Canadian Establishment's dean, was a prime exponent of this discipline. The front hall of his stately Toronto home, Green Meadows, had a fireplace, blue-and-white wallpaper, a huge bowl of "seasonal flowers" on an Adam table, and a grandfather clock made by Robert Macadam of Dumfries. The sunroom had been done up in white wicker with pink chintz. The pale green and gold hues of the drawing room provided an elegant setting for the rich patina of the Queen Anne furniture; the dining room's Sheraton table was well-doilied during dinner with ecru lace mats.

The banking trend in Canada's homes of the superprivileged (and the slightly less so) has gone far enough. Banks are for borrowing; living rooms should be lived in. The day when functionalism was unimportant and families used their prime space mainly for special occasions is long gone. One of the most pleasant legacies of the Sixties has been the practical use of a home as a series of areas in which to do enjoyable things, rather than being a showplace for visiting aunts and uncles.

The new approach to designing and furnishing a home should take advantage of this trend by reflecting the individual tastes and priorities of those who own and occupy it. Form should follow function so that we plan our spaces not only by what we do but by who we are. What better way to celebrate this happy use of space than by creating a genuinely Canadian approach? Only a truly indigenous style will allow us to get away from merely copying the borrowed culture of our mother society.

Anyone for Precambrian Modern?

—1982

The Unknown Element

WE HAD DROPPED ANCHOR at Whaletown and my sloop, the *Indra*, tugged softly on the chain, her mast trailing across the sky in the slow arcs of an indolent summer afternoon. We sat in the cockpit watching the intertidal ballet – the alternating sequence of beaks and upturned duck bums, the whiskered snout of a curious harbour seal, gulls bleating derision at a preening bald eagle. Whaletown is a tiny notch in the rocky southwest coast of Cortes Island, three days' hard sailing north of Vancouver. In 1869 and 1870, the Dawson Whaling Company's harpoon masters set off from here into Georgia Strait aboard the schooner *Kate* and came back with catches large enough to produce thirteen thousand gallons of whale oil. Ever since, the little outport has been rehearsing to become a ghost town.

There was another vessel anchored near us that afternoon. We watched its owner, who looked as though he surfed for a living, washing his deck. He in turn watched us. He said nothing for a long while, studying our stern and the white lettering – *Toronto* – that had stayed on the transom even after we changed home ports to Cordova Bay, B.C. Amused, he finally shook his head and said, "Must have had a hell of a time getting through Rogers Pass."

We had trucked the *Indra* across the country, but the remark was not as outlandish as it sounded. I was deep into research for my history of the Hudson's Bay Company at the time and had discovered that except for Rogers Pass, it is indeed possible to cross most of Canada by boat – if not aboard the *Indra*, certainly in a canoe. The early fur traders of both the HBC and the North West Company developed water transcontinental highways from the Mackenzie River through the fur-rich Athabasca region down into Lake Winnipeg, and then out to Hudson Bay and the North Atlantic or, through interconnected lakes and rivers, into Lake Superior and on to Montreal and the St. Lawrence.

While the three-thousand-mile journey entailed many portages around rapids, waterfalls, and beaver dams, it had, incredible as it may sound, only one sizable land gap: the twelve-mile hike at Methy Portage in northern Saskatchewan, at the watershed between east and west. It was this intricate network of water-roads that maintained the fur trade as North America's dominant commerce for two hundred years and that first created the notion in its travellers' minds that what later became Canada was possessed of a natural geographic unity.

We have, in the intervening years, come to believe that the prevailing gene of our nationhood is possession of land, claiming citizenship by right of having stood up to its vastness and its chill. A.R.M. Lower, the great Queen's University historian, raised the worship of soil to near theology with his cri de coeur, "From the land . . . must come the soul of Canada." And Mordecai Richler's Duddy Kravitz whined that in this country, "a man without land is nobody."

Maybe. But I suspect that water has been at least as important to our psyche, and the evidence isn't hard to come by.

During the ten dozen years since Confederation we have auctioned off major chunks of our resources and our real estate – our land – to the highest bidders, first the British, then the Americans. At the same time, our culture has been subverted and just about pecked dry by Madison Avenue; militarily, we have become a client state of the Pentagon; the majority of enterprises that turn a profit in this country have been taken over by foreign-owned multinationals. This massive sellout raised so little concern that back in the early Seventies, when Walter Gordon, Abe Rotstein, and I started the Committee for an Independent Canada, we could barely gather a quorum and received virtually no help. While Brian Mulroney was dismantling the remains of the Foreign Investment Review Agency and the National Energy Program, most of us were too preoccupied with rancid whiffs of *thon politique* to mount an effective protest.

It is not much of an exaggeration to suggest that selling off the land-based assets that are supposed to be the sacred repository of our identity, our very soul, ranks just below curling as a national pastime. We have casually allowed outsiders to reduce us to squatters on our own land, and anyone who dares object is either ignored or relegated to the status of a marginal kook. But let an American icebreaker point its reinforced bow into the North West Passage, let a Portuguese fisherman dip his nets in *our* waters, or let anyone suggest that we export a drop of the stuff, and this country is up in arms. Mention that the Americans are poisoning our lakes with acid rain and Canadian urbanites are ready to march on Washington.

Simon Reisman, our free-trade negotiator, who has been charged with every Canadian sin except not knowing the words to "O Canada," formally defended himself in public only once. Accused of having advocated the sale of water from James Bay as the ultimate "sweetener" in any deal with the Yanks, he could smell the lynch mob and dashed off a letter to the *Globe and Mail* denying any intention of even considering such a devilish idea. Although he had been actively associated with the Great Recycling and Northern Development (GRAND) Canal Company, which may have this objective in mind, Reisman swore the basic loyalty oath of patriotic Canadianism: not even if whipped with beaver tails would he trade away our water.

In his emphatic denial, Reisman was voicing a common reaction. The late General A.G.L. McNaughton, former chairman of the Canadian section of the International Joint Commission, the body charged with regulating cross-border flows, let loose a flourish of rhetoric against American attempts to grab Canadian water that still stands as the basic doctrine on the issue: "This is a monstrous concept, not only in terms of physical magnitude, but also in another and more sinister sense, in that the promoters would displace Canadian sovereignty over the national waters of Canada, and substitute therefor a diabolic thesis that *all* waters of North America become a shared resource, of which most will be drawn off for the benefit of the midwest and southwest regions of the U.S., where existing desert areas will be made to bloom at the expense of development in Canada."

Just about every federal politician charged with shepherding our natural resources has since made a similar affirmation. The Pearson administration's northern affairs minister, Arthur Laing, flatly declared that "diversion of Canadian water to the U.S. is not negotiable.

There is no such thing as a continental resource. We own it." The Mulroney government's environment minister, Tom McMillan, has gone even farther. Not only is he opposed to the export of water, he is on record as also being against transfers between domestic watersheds, including those designed solely to meet Canadian needs. Even one of Canada's most parochial provincial politicians adopted the same protective attitude. W.A.C. Bennett, the B.C. premier who treated the sale of his province's resources like loss-leader barbecue sets in his Kelowna hardware store, was enraged at the idea of bargaining away our liquid dowry. "British Columbia," he declared, "will sell the U.S. hydroelectric power, but not water. Even to *talk* about selling it is ridiculous. You do not sell your heritage."

Indeed, water is one of the few commodities not being sold across the 49th parallel at the moment. The only exceptions are a few local arrangements between border communities, such as the daily twenty thousand gallons that Coutts, Alberta, pumps to Sweetgrass, Montana. Water is such a heavily charged emotional issue that merely introducing the topic into the current free-trade negotiations could scuttle the whole exercise.

None of this makes sense. We not only enjoy a clear domestic surplus, but per capita we have more usable water than any nation on earth. Seven of the world's fifteen largest lakes are in Canada; we have so many bodies of inland water, in fact, that no complete inventory is feasible – although 563 lakes with a surface of at least thirty-eight square miles have been tallied. Estimates of our renewable fresh water supply range as high as 10 per cent of the planet's total. And unlike the other raw materials we sell, water is a renewable resource. (One factor that reduces the value of our water is that so much of it is in the wrong place. Nearly two-thirds of our rivers drain to the north, away from the population; and uneven flows in the prairies can create droughts and floods, sometimes in the same season.)

Obviously, water is much more than just a tasteless liquid when it comes to quenching our psychic thirst. The novelist Clark Blaise has spoken about "the parenting effect of water on the Canadian imagination." Dr. Peter Pearse, the University of British Columbia resource economist who chaired the recent Inquiry on Federal Water Policy, has attempted to understand this strange mystique. After touring the country listening to scores of witnesses, Pearse concluded that for most Canadians, water – and more particularly its inviolate retention within our borders – has become a moral more than an economic issue. ''We tend to think that it's an opportunity when foreigners want to buy our other natural resources, even when they are not renewable,'' he told me. ''But the talk of exporting water raises all kinds of apprehensions. Perhaps it reflects a cultural perception that water is the essential element within the Canadian ambience. We identify water as a critical part of our mental and physical landscapes.''

''Water is very special to Canadians,'' I was told by Dr. Derrick Sewell, a leading expert on water usage who taught geography at the University of Victoria. ''There is no Indian word for wilderness because while we may regard it as something separate from us, for them the wilderness is everything – their dwelling place and source of food, part of their being. To some degree, Canadians view water with that kind of internal attachment.''

Certainly, our affinity for water has deep historical wellsprings. The first visitors here were after fish, not empires; as they worked the Grand Banks off Newfoundland they gradually began lengthening their sojourns by setting up camps ashore. Canada was first explored by water instead of land travel because horses, even when available, could not move easily or find enough nourishment in the Precambrian Shield. How the continent was explored by various navigators pushing up the St. Lawrence and elsewhere in search of the North West Passage is a familiar story, but even the academic history of this country had watery beginnings. As early as 1686, in Quebec City, the Jesuits held classes in hydrography for professional St. Lawrence River pilots.

The first water-driven grist mill was built on the Lequille River in Nova Scotia as early as 1607. The technology spread steadily westward. By 1836, there were six hundred grist mills in Upper Canada. Lumbermen pushed in on the heels of the fur trade, using many of the same waterways to float their logs to market, down the basins of the St. John, the Miramichi, the Saguenay, and the St. Maurice, and along the lush tributary valleys of the Ottawa. The chief market for most of the timber was Britain, cut off by continental wars from its traditional Baltic sources of supply. One imaginative provisioner to the Royal Navy, Charles Wood, of Port Glasgow, Scotland, decided to evade the English import tax by building huge wooden vessels at a shipyard near Quebec City, sailing them across the Atlantic, then breaking them up to sell their timbers. The first of these behemoths, the 301-foot barque *Columbus* (3,690 tons), launched on July 28, 1824, was the biggest ship of her day. In 1825 the even larger *Baron of Renfrew* (5,880 tons) hit the slipways, but she was wrecked in the English Channel through pilot error.

That was long ago. Now that we have no merchant marine it's easy enough to forget how deep this country's nautical traditions run and what a dominant maritime power we once were. During the second half of the nineteenth century, Canada ranked fourth among the world's shipbuilding and ship-owning nations. The tidal terminals of every river and nearly every creek that empties into the Atlantic were crowded with angular silhouettes of the great wind ships. During the late 1870s Canada built and manned a fleet of 7,196 salty thorough-breds (with a total of 1.3 million tons) that made their owners so rich they formed their own banks and insurance companies. Yarmouth, a sleepy harbour in southwestern Nova Scotia, boasted more per capita tonnage than any other centre on earth, with two thousand ships, most locally built, on its registers.

These early nautical adventurers were not limited to the East Coast. Paddle-wheel steamships provided the first mass transportation across the prairies (even the battle of Batoche was partly a naval engagement), and the Great Lakes swarmed with so many vessels that there may be as many as ten thousand shipwrecks on their sandy bottoms. In one year alone, 1869, 121 ships went down. The prodigious inland ship-building effort required to back this armada included construction of major tonnages in some highly unlikely places. The *St. Lawrence*, launched in Kingston in 1814, for example, was larger and more powerful than Lord Nelson's flagship, *Victory*. Boasting 112 guns and manned by a crew of a thousand, the full-rigged ship established British control of Lake Ontario in the later stages of the War of 1812. (She was later sold for twenty-five pounds as a floating wood-storage shed.) Except for a temporary upsurge during the Second World War, when Canadian shipyards built 878 naval and merchant vessels and the Royal Canadian Navy swept the North Atlantic, not much except residual memory now remains of our nautical past.

Water intrudes into Canada's economic history in more subtle ways. The four main developments that allowed this country to con-solidate its political control over the northern half of the continent –

the canoe-based fur trade, construction of steam-locomotive railways to the Pacific, the application of steam power to ocean navigation, and the wave of industry-related canal building – were water-based technologies. Growth of the pulp-and-paper industry, the milling processes that allowed large-scale mining to become economical, and, above all, the generation of hydro-electric power that industrialized Canada's agricultural base – all depended on adequate water supply.

During the first two decades of this century, Canada fought the United States when the Americans diverted water from Lake Michigan to flush organic wastes from Chicago's huge abattoirs down through the Mississippi River system, and we raised hell again during the First World War when Buffalo and Syracuse demanded more than their share of the electricity we developed on our side of the Niagara River. The export of water in the form of hydro power has since become a routine transaction, with about forty million gigawatt hours (10 per cent of our output) now surging across the border. With the impending collapse of the U.S. nuclear industry, American utilities are looking at our electrical sources with renewed envy. At least three projects worth a total of eight billion dollars (additions to Quebec's James Bay installations, completion of Manitoba's Limestone project on the Nelson River, and the building of the Site C dam on the Peace River in British Columbia) are early development possibilities.

But it is the debate about exports of raw water that sets off most of the howls. The grandest and dumbest of the half-dozen schemes hatched by American engineers to drain our lake and river basins was the North American Water and Power Alliance (NAWAPA) project dreamed up in 1964 by the Ralph M. Parsons Company, a Los Angeles consulting firm. That $100-billion undertaking would have involved diverting Alaskan and northern Canadian waters into California and the eastern United States through a five-hundred-mile Rocky Mountain trench and a ditch across the prairies. Despite initial murmurings of approval by some American congressmen, the plan collapsed under its own weight.

NAWAPA's Canadian equivalent is the GRAND Canal Company's proposed $100-billion diversion of fresh water from James Bay into the Great Lakes system, to stabilize water levels and irrigate crops in the United States and Canada. Tom Kierans, the visionary Newfoundland engineer who conceived the idea, believes it's technically feasible. So far, despite a grant from the National Research Council, it has won few supporters. Kierans (Eric's cousin) is realistic about the Canadian aversion to exporting water but warns that we should negotiate while we still have the option. "Of course, the United States will not simply come and grab our water," he explains. "They'll find another rationale – like saving us from the Russians."

When set against most estimates of future fresh water requirements south of the border, that prophecy makes sense. The impending crisis in U.S. water supplies has to do with inadequate conservation and antipollution control (a quarter of that country's sixty-five-thousand community water systems are seriously contaminated); depletion of the Ogallala aquifer (the chief underground water source that stretches from Texas to South Dakota); and huge jumps in home and industrial consumption. A presidential task force has predicted that one fifth of the United States will face a chronic water shortage by the year 2000, when obtaining adequate water will become a critical American issue. Unlike energy, which can be obtained from many sources, water to fill critical gaps in U.S. water supplies can be got only by importing it from Canada.

Few Canadians have grasped the implications of this apparently irreversible trend. One of the few politicians who spoke out on the issue was Alvin Hamilton, the agriculture minister in the Diefenbaker government. The most articulate voice has been that of Roy Faibish, once Hamilton's executive assistant, who has since advised three Canadian prime ministers and is now a television executive in England.

"I have been trying since 1956," says Faibish, "to alert parties and people in Ottawa to how important water is and will become in the context of U.S.–Canadian economic and military relations, particularly during the last decade of this century and the first decade of the twenty-first. The U.S. South and Southwest will not be able to develop without it. In addition, there will be a large new requirement for cooling water for the defence missiles that may go up in the next ten years in Utah.

"It will be impossible for Canada to say no to the export of fresh water when it is needed to sustain human life. It may be easier to say no when it is used for industrial and military purposes, but I doubt it. When Reagan talks about a United States/Canada/Mexico arrangement, what he has in mind in the long run is not Canadian energy, although that's part of it, but essentially water."

Faibish sets the problem in a global context: "Canada will only be able, in the long run, to say no to water export if it fills up its empty spaces with forty or fifty million people. The strategic planners sitting in Peking, Moscow, Washington, Paris, and London are looking at Canada – with our space, fresh water, energy, minerals, protein, wood fibre, and so few people. Either we start exporting our water or else! From 1900 on we said we'd never export electricity. Eventually we did. And so it will be with water."

—1987

Margaret Trudeau's Last Fling

THE HORDE OF PAPARAZZI who stalk the doings and undoings of those pigeon-breasted popinjays of all sexes who flit along the world celebrity circuits have a new darling. She is Canada's former "first lady," the most mixed-up graduate of the Sixties who ever slouched across the land.

Like the second prize in some huge raffle, she exhibits her bum, along with her emotions and her indiscretions, for all the world to see. For a while, especially when she went electioneering with her husband in 1974, Margaret Trudeau seemed a refreshing change from the dutiful matrons who had previously occupied 24 Sussex Drive. At the start of that campaign, she went on record as casting her ballot for Pierre because "in the three years we've been married and for a few years before that, he taught me a lot about loving."

That seemed as good a reason as any to support the Liberals, even if it didn't rank with constitutionally entrenched language rights in the prime minister's own lexicon of policy pledges. But as soon as their marriage broke up, Margaret began to measure the currency of her life by inches of type in the gossip sheets, becoming a composite of headlines instead of a real person.

If her pre-publication revelations are a representative sample, the Margaret memoirs that are about to hit the bookstores are neither crippled by common sense nor governed by good taste. She has forgotten that she is no disembodied spectator of the events of her own life, that every act must have its consequences and every confessional tidbit will claim its victim. As Richard Gwyn, the *Toronto Star*'s perceptive columnist, has noted: "It's gushy to go on and on about her innocent vulnerability. Sure she's naïve – but shrewd enough to get a prime minister to marry her by the nervy device of asking him, and to be able to flog parlormaid confessions for half-a-million-plus."

The tumult of her own devising now enveloping her seems to have robbed Margaret of the basic decency that should survive even the unhappiest of marriages: that its joys, passions, and torments must remain the private property of the partners who shared its enchantments and played out its final tragedies.

Some Liberal strategists feel that if it weren't for her intriguing anatomy, there ought to be a bounty on her scalp. But it seems to me that it is not an issue that should influence voters. There are plenty of better reasons to cast ballots for or against Pierre Trudeau than the uncontrolled prattling of a woman who is about as much a flower child as Bette Midler.

—1979

By the Time You Get to Phoenix

B Y THE TIME YOU GET TO PHOENIX, the paradox of the changing American power structure takes on heightened reality. A very different country is being born here, and few of us who study the United States at a safe distance (tied into the dreary demonology of picking over the actions and pronouncements of our involuntary conquerors) are aware of the delicate yet astonishing transformations in train to the south of us.

It is simple enough to sit about in the bureaucratic lodges of Ottawa or the penthouses of Toronto cursing the saturating force of American civilization, gloating a little over the nightmares of Vietnam and Watergate, smugly mourning the long evening of the American Dream. But even if the complex struggle among its countervailing constituencies has left the United States disturbed and divided, out of the confusion is emerging a novel configuration of people and forces, restructuring the republic.

The placard carriers and card burners of the Sixties have long vanished. Martin Luther King, Malcolm X, Jimi Hendrix, Janis Joplin, and Phil Ochs are dead. Rap Brown is in prison. Tim Leary has turned informer. Tom Hayden is a legislator. Neil Armstrong, first man to walk the moon, is back in Cincinnati teaching school. Vietnam is forgotten, Watergate absorbed. The only new political force winning significant converts is a riptide of hostility against Washington as the symbol of extravagance, corruption, and good intentions gone sour.

But, at the same time, there's a fundamental metamorphosis under way, permanently altering the social, cultural, and economic geography of the U.S.A. Not too long ago, Phoenix, San Francisco, Los Angeles, Tulsa, Fort Worth, Houston, and New Orleans served as distant outposts of the New York–Boston–Chicago–Washington power axis, with the real wealth and influence flowing from the manicured estates of Newport, Grosse Pointe, and Greenwich, Connecticut. Now the action that counts has moved into Texas, the Carolinas, Georgia, Florida, Tennessee, Arkansas, Oklahoma, California, and Arizona – big-sky Baptist states that average three hundred days of sunshine a year and place few limits on a man's potential.

The tight-lipped, Ivy League patricians of the East are being displaced by open-collared Westerners who don't give a damn for family background or Harvard and prefer humming Johnny Cash to Stephen Sondheim. Their philosophy is a kind of Whig populism, returning to the roots through self-enrichment – a revival of the Protestant work ethic dressed up with flourishes of Mexican *machismo*.

AS THE TRADITIONAL METROPOLITAN AREAS of the North continue to decay, the Southwesterners are inheriting the country. During the past decade eight million Americans have moved into the Sun Belt. Every night the fourteen-wheel furniture vans push south down the interstate freeways, then race back, high and empty, to load up again. According to Kirkpatrick Sale, who has studied the region, the gross national product of what he calls the fifteen "Southern Rim" states is about $500 billion – larger than that of any country except the whole of the United States, and the U.S.S.R.: "It has more cars (43 million), more telephones (38 million), more housing units (22 million), more TV sets (25 million), and more miles of paved highway (1.1 million) than any nation except the Soviet Union – in short, it is a superpower on a world scale." The area contains most of the major growth industries and especially the country's energy sources – Texas, Louisiana, California, Oklahoma, and New Mexico account for 82 per cent of the U.S. domestic oil and 88 per cent of the national gas production. While 82 per cent of the new manufacturing jobs in the United States since 1970 have been added in parts of the Southwest, New York has lost sixteen major head offices in the past twelve months alone.

The Southwesterners have even moved into New York to grab

some of its surviving profit-centres: Bergdorf Goodman, the best department store on Fifth Avenue, has been bought by the Carter Hawley Hale organization of Los Angeles; Time Inc. is controlled by Temple Industries, a Texas investment company representing the family of lumber millionaire Arthur Temple; Hebrew National Kosher Foods Incorporated, Manhattan's largest delicatessen supplier, has been taken over by the Riviana Corporation of Houston. Major-league sports franchises have been moving south. Tourism is booming, with twenty million people clicking through the gates of the Disney fantasy lands in Anaheim, California, and Orlando, Florida. Nashville, Dallas, and Georgia are grabbing more of the entertainment industry.

The future of America somehow seems most visible in Phoenix, where the arid wind comes howling in from the parched moonscapes of Utah, raising the temperature thirty degrees in one hour. Life here combines the self-determination of the nation's new conservative spirit with the open optimism of a last frontier and the big-buck ostentations of men and women who no longer recognize their own beginnings. The good burghers of Phoenix regard their nation's recent misadventures strictly as Washington phenomena, little connected with their own sense of propriety or guilt. They are a very different breed from that honourable and sometime benevolent meritocracy of Eastern Establishment liberals who have had the run of American affairs since the first inaugural of Franklin Delano Roosevelt – all those swift young men, ever graceful under pressure, at home among the elegant nuances of finding any issue's exact centre of gravity, old hands at choosing among the least of any number of evils. (Their epitaph came from Gene McCarthy, himself once an honoured example of the species, when he defined a liberal as one who helps a man drowning forty feet from shore by throwing him a thirty-foot rope while shouting: ''I've met you more than half way!'')

The new paladins of wealth who run Arizona – and are decisively tilting the U.S. power structure toward the south and the west – bear few of the burdens of liberal doubt or compassion. They are proud and rigid in their self-confidence and, like most WASPs with principles, tend to scowl at strangers. They all seem to have closely cropped hair, which leaves their ears exposed and abnormally prominent, giving their faces a cast of perpetually tentative candour. (They love gimmicks. The latest gadget – for $29.95 – hooks into the back of a car and flashes "You're welcome" at the automatic "Thank You" signs on toll gates.) They no longer pretend to Stetson hats or pear snaps on their cuffs; only black string ties with turquoise clasps remain of the Western motif they once affected. Their conversation, strong as horseradish, is devoid of the IBM words and mid-Atlantic cadence that still bedazzles them in the button-down East. No talk here of viable thrusts or incremental contingencies.

"Got good security at your place, Arnie?"

"You bet. Tighter'n a bull's ass in fly time."

During Arizona's territorial days (it didn't become a state until 1912) free enterprise was defined by the noisy end of a shotgun, and things haven't changed a whole lot. Most people here distrust questions that reach beyond life's reckonables. A radical is someone who frequents bookstores. (Most folks are suspicious of anything that's printed except dollar bills.)

The streets of Phoenix are lined with palm trees, their frowzled heads slanting east as they bow to the same wind that still dances the odd tumbleweed across the wide boulevards. The city has the confectionery feeling of a Mel Brooks mirage. There is cactus, astonishingly beautiful, blooming everywhere. Arizona's jump in manufacturing employment is the United States' fastest, with an increasing number of large corporations (Ramada Inns, Greyhound) making Phoenix their national headquarters.

Last May, when Rolls-Royce was looking for an appropriate spot to launch its new Camargue (retail price: $90,000) for the American market, it picked the Mountain Shadows resort in Scottsdale, one of Phoenix's richest suburbs. Scottsdale's most important watering hole is the Paradise Valley Country Club, where the centurions of the Phoenix Establishment meet to fondle tumblers of Cutty Sark or bourbon on the rocks, compare golf scores, rail against "that gang" in Washington, and point at a bungalow on the side of Camelback Mountain where Jack Kennedy is supposed to have spent a dirty weekend with Angie Dickinson.

"Can't help feelin' a bit poorly these days, Jason."

"What's the matter, Otis? The mail slow getting your dividends out?"

During the long, languid evenings, with the smell of jasmine and the cooing of sweet doves flavouring the night air, Arizonans visit each other, driving their cinnamon, air-conditioned Sevilles or sky-blue Broughams with Episcopalian grace across the iridescent desert. On the far horizon, like giant fireflies, executive jets land at Phoenix's Sky Harbor International, the country's busiest private airport. The moonlight glints off their silver wings and the sky is alive with their roaring.

In the new Southwest, spending money is a way of life; wealth equals status. On a freeway leading out of the concrete canyons of Houston, the city's commuters get up-to-date flashes from an electric billboard of fluctuations in the daily Dow Jones Industrial Average. When Jack Randall, a millionaire oilman who lives in Liberal, Kansas, heard that 1976 was to be the last production year for Cadillac Eldorado convertibles, he ordered eight new models. ("I figure I got me enough ragtops to last a lifetime," he explained, not bothering to mention that he is seventy-two years old.) There is another story about a rancher who ordered two Rolls-Royces, one with right- and the other left-hand drive – so he could get an even tan on *both* his elbows.

—1976

Hollywood Madness

IT'S STILL LOS ANGELES – and particularly the glitzy suburb of Hollywood – that best distills the American Dream. The city explodes with nervous creativity. Every conversation has an encounter-group atmosphere with egos in primal combat for that "big break" that means everything. The airport cabdriver, one of Hollywood's 10,000 unemployed actors, strikes up what he imagines to be probing small talk, giving his sincerity a morning workout, just in case his fare might have a vague connection with some obscure branch of The Industry. "*Maclean's*?" A blank look – then the big smile. "Oh, yeah. Great toothpaste."

There's a story going the rounds about a pushy Hollywood writer who is receiving cobalt radiation for cancer. Asked by a competitor at a party about his treatment, the writer spreads his hands in a gesture of triumph, and says: "Treatment? Hell, we're into script!"

Having left high school sweethearts or husbands in the dental supply game far behind them, the self-styled starlets still frequent Schwab's drugstore (where Lana Turner was discovered in 1935) and parade along Sunset Boulevard, their lip gloss, coy glances, and spit curls at the ready, threatening to return at any moment to the Jaqueline Susann novel they're re-enacting.

They view the world with a kind of failed Okie shrewdness, their eyes uncomprehending and unafraid. Eventually, they return home or become department store salesladies, smiling beauties who dare not frown in case they fracture their makeup.

The prancing men of uncertain sexual persuasion who put the

Hollywood deals together strut around in fifty-dollar mussed-look haircuts, peasant body shirts, and contact lenses that blend eye colours with their pre-faded Paris denims. They're constantly on the move, like beagles in heat, the blood running through them, testing all the possibilities, rehearsing their Oscar acceptance ad libs in their tuxedos with the wine-red or royal-blue lining. When a deal gets hot, they rent a white Rolls at sixty-five cents a mile.

Sex and religion are both big business. On Sundays, the Bible-bangers recruit choirs of freshly bathed boys and girls to croon the background as they claim the conversion of any showbiz personality they can conjure up, right down to Lawrence Welk's drummer. Hollywood's sex shops advertise "air-conditioned torture dungeons," obscene phone calls from "a guaranteed nude girl," and reproductions of sex organs that "plug into the cigar lighter of your car."

People come here to divorce their past. But they seldom become total Californians. Six thousand corpses are shipped out of the Los Angeles airport every year, listed on airline manifests as boxes of HR (Human Remains) for that final journey *home*. This doesn't mean that departing Californians don't appreciate great scenery. Nearly all of the 555 people who've jumped off San Francisco's Golden Gate Bridge since it was opened in 1936 took the leap from its eastern side.

The view is so much better.

—1976

Resolute Bay

PERCHED ON THE SOUTHWESTERN TIP of Cornwallis Island in the Eastern Arctic, hugging the 74th parallel and barely five hundred kilometres from the North Magnetic Pole, Resolute Bay in the Northwest Territories has the worst climate and the worst economy in the country. Signs of abandoned hope include boarded-up houses, burned-out cars, and dead Skidoo carcasses.

This is a land of ice, not snow, and what snow there is (thirty inches a year) falls in relatively moderate July and August. Mean temperature (and it *is* mean) even during April, when I flew in for a brief stay, was −36°C, but it has been known to drop below −50°C. The sky is an eerie whiter shade of pale, and the permanently frozen ground has the texture of pitted pewter. Except for the black dots of ravens hovering over the garbage dump and the thick-furred dogs huddled in the curves of snowdrifts, there are few signs of animal life. Walking about Resolute can get tricky because ice storms can instantly obliterate the sight of your own boots as you stumble from one over-heated habitation to the next, sucking breath out of the dry polar air. The social highlights of the year are the High Arctic Dive in early August, when hardy locals swim off ice still floating in the harbour (last summer a cavorting walrus joined the festivities), and the annual Sunrise Party, held in the first week of February to celebrate the end of the twenty-four-hour winter darkness that pervades the tiny community from early November.

Resolute is an accident. In the summer of 1947 the U.S. icebreaker *Edisto* was escorting a merchant ship assigned to unload material for a weather station at Winter Harbour on Melville Island, but the ice closed in early that year. The ships dumped their cargoes where they were stuck – which happened to be Resolute Bay. Within three weeks U.S. Navy engineers had bulldozed a six-hundred-foot gravel airstrip and erected the weather station. The Canadian government eventually took over the installations, determined to turn the tiny outpost into the transportation hub of the Eastern Arctic. With the bravado that only Ottawa bureaucrats who have never been north of Kingsmere can muster, a town planner from Sweden named Ralph Erskine was hired to design a townsite for three thousand. He produced elegant drawings of three-storey apartment buildings in a horseshoe shape to form a windbreak for the single-family units in the middle. He planned a shopping centre complete with domed indoor park. An underground sewage disposal system was actually built; it promptly froze solid, as did its accompanying water pipes, but not before the territorial government spent hundreds of thousands of dollars trying to fix them. The first unit of the apartment buildings was finished on schedule for $1.2 million and was furnished with luxurious Scandinavian-design accoutrements. It was occupied off and on for several years before all the plumbing gave out; this was mainly because its citified architects had installed all the pipes in the north wall, which is the most exposed to the elements. The complex has stood there, empty, ever since.

Another Ottawa brain wave was to populate the settlement with Inuit from Port Harrison, Quebec, and Pond Inlet, N.W.T. The move was supposed to improve their trapping prospects, but that particular directive never got through to the animals, and the newcomers have been scratching around for a living ever since. (In the 1979-80 season, the last figures available, Resolute listed thirty trappers; only seventeen of them earned more than six hundred dollars.) The main cash crop is the "grey market" in hunting muskoxen and polar bears, both semi-protected species. Native hunters are issued tags for a limited number of kills, and they in turn sell them, for more than ten thousand dollars apiece, to outsiders who consider stalking these magnificent animals a great blood sport. This season Resolute Inuit have a quota of thirty-eight bears, and two German hunters have already paid $20,000 to local guide Sam Idlout and his dogs to take them on the trail. A pair of American hunters paid $18,000 for a muskox expedition.

Resolute's mayor, George Eckalook, was not available for comment during my visit because he was out driving the settlement's only garbage truck, but I talked to Elizabeth Allakariallak, a bright and articulate Inuit who is the local social welfare officer. She estimates that more than a hundred Inuit have left Resolute and that only a third of the 190 who remain can find work. Only one Inuit (Simeonie Amarualik) is still carving soapstone. "The back-to-the-land movement is very strong here," Allakariallak told me. "We want to go where there are fish and caribou. We still don't know why we were moved here – probably to provide cheap labour for local mining operations, but those jobs never materialized either."

She is as puzzled as the visitor about the empty government apartments that dominate the Resolute skyline, a massive monument to the proposition that even crime wouldn't pay if the government ran it.

Despite the high unemployment rate and the increasing loss of skills needed for surviving in a most inhospitable climate, the Inuit remain proud and independent. Only seven families are currently accepting full welfare. A couple of years ago the local Bay store burned down, and its credit records were destroyed in the blaze. Within hours every Inuit at Resolute had reported his debts to the store manager – and the total tallied with the company's estimates.

The Inuit are there to stay. "Resolute *has* to survive because it's our home," says Allakariallak. "When you're born here, you stay with it. I tell you, we don't have much choice."

—1974

Sailing The County

EVERY SUMMER, FOR A FEW STOLEN WEEKS, I head for that very special realm of rural Ontario called Prince Edward County, or, as its natives prefer, The County.

Named in honour of Prince Edward, father of Queen Victoria, The County is an island in Lake Ontario. Until 1889, it was connected to the mainland by a narrow Indian portage known as Carrying Place. Completion of the eleven-kilometre Murray Canal made the area into an island, though it is well connected to the shore by ferries and bridges.

Only a couple of hours' drive from Toronto (or three days' boating), The County in summer weaves a spell of rural land and coves, bays and islands. Apart from such obvious land-plus-water attractions as Sandbanks Provincial Park, which has a decided flavour of Cape Cod without the hotdog stands, the twenty villages and towns slow the racing urban heart to something approaching normal and create a mood that is not so much nostalgic as calming.

The United Empire Loyalists, in 1784, chose The County as a refuge from the American Revolution. Their physical presence is long gone (except for the burying ground at Adolphustown), and few families can trace their roots back into the eighteenth century, but the quality of the people hasn't changed. County folk are tough, honest, unaffected, and kind. Visitors are welcomed, and land-buying newcomers are tolerated but carefully watched for a generation or two.

Picton, the largest community, was once a centre for commercial boat construction. Except for Wicked Point, say, or the shoals around the Ducks and False Ducks, most of the bays and beaches in the area are protected and hardly qualify as a Bermuda Triangle, but forty schooners, fifteen steamboats, and eight barges have been wrecked within Quinte's predictable waters.

Maritime tradition was revived in the late Twenties, when running rum (and beer) across Lake Ontario became a major industry. George Miller's eleven-metre speedboat would haul three hundred cases of beer to Main Duck Island, where the contraband was repacked into burlap sacks and transferred to small cruisers for the run to hotel-keepers and their thirsty customers in Oswego, New York.

Boat life congregates around Brighton and Bath (on the mainland) and Picton's Prince Edward Yacht Club – as friendly and informal a sanctuary for boaties as any I've yet encountered. I've been a PEYC member for more than a decade and was taken aback only once – when the club's mimeographed newsletter contained an item pretentiously headed "Protocol." Not having been aware that the club had any, I was much relieved to read the item that followed: "Effective immediately, no one will be admitted to the Saturday night dances unless they wear shoes."

In Picton there still stands the District Court House and Gaol (built in 1833 in the Greek Revival style) where Sir John A. Macdonald, Canada's first prime minister, began his career as a lawyer. The Regent in Picton looks from the outside like any small-town movie house. It isn't. It's a full-scale vaudeville theatre, originally built in 1922 to seat eleven hundred, with a stage area comparable to that of Toronto's Royal Alexandra. Still belonging to the Cooke family, which built it, the Regent is one of only four independent theatres in the province.

Wellington, the second-largest community, is a sleepy hamlet that boasts one bank, one drugstore, a bait-and-tackle shop, one lawyer, and fourteen antique shops, selling everything from vintage marine hardware to Japanese lustreware, from 78-rpm records to Depression glass in sparkling blues, pinks, and amber. Wellington once had a great harbour where seines 1,828 metres long were hauled in by hand; one remarkable catch in 1856 netted 47,000 whitefish. The nets will never again reap that much, but the white floats marking seine nets are still set out by County men to harvest the deep waters of Adolphus Reach and Prince Edward Bay.

The County has some fabled fishing holes, with pickerel, rainbow trout, bass, and muskies in abundance; the coves along the eastern edges of Picton Bay are particularly good. John Waddingham, the local taxidermist, will immortalize "the big one," if the proud fisherman is so inclined. Black River on Road 13, just past Milford, has one of the few cheese factories in the free world not yet owned by Kraft; it makes and sells that wonderful crumbly cheddar you rarely find any more.

At Glenora, where Highway 33 ends, The County operates two free ferries across Adolphus Reach. Beside the southern landing dock, a mill once owned by Sir John A. Macdonald's father sits solidly at water's edge below the cliff. On top of the cliff is a turquoise, stone-rimmed lake. Adolphus Reach – long, wide, and deep – has been picked by *Yachting* magazine as one of the world's best sailing areas.

Non-boatie visitors to The County rave about the homemade chicken dinners at the Maple Inn in nearby Bloomfield. But the most delicious culinary treat of all, by my sights, is a plate of the blueberry pancakes Maria Scheidthauer whips up at the Picton Bay Motel.

The Bay of Quinte Yacht Club in Belleville was founded in 1877, and four years later had attained the grand position of sponsoring its own entry in the America's Cup race. And the *Belleville Intelligencer*, now swallowed up in the mediocrity of chain journalism, once was owned and edited by Sir Mackenzie Bowell, who was Canada's prime minister from December 1894 to April 1896. Trenton, on the edge of Quinte, during the Great War housed a huge munitions plant, which blew up on October 15, 1918. The town then briefly became a Hollywood North. Parts of *All Quiet on the Western Front* were shot here, as were *Carry on Sergeant* and several other early films.

Nearby Presqu'isle Bay is still known for its wire-strong weeds, tough enough if not mowed by weed-choppers to jam the propellers of sizable trawlers. Yet an inspection closer inshore yields other flora, including fourteen varieties of orchids, cinquefoil, and the profusion of pussy willows and cattails Gordon Lightfoot sings about.

The land is bountiful, the accommodation comfortable, the farmhouses unpretentious – and the general stores still sell one-cent candy. As I travel, I meet kindred souls by the dozen who hesitate before divulging their addiction to this therapeutic island and the communities that fringe it but who return again and again from the capitals of bustle and frustration to the soothing alchemy of The County.

Here, in the peaceable kingdom of Quinte's Isle, sailing my own sloop, the *Indra*, I annually rediscover a postcard paradise inhabited by rural philosophers such as Bob Davis, who spent four years hand-crafting an exquisite twelve-metre ketch called *Kindly Light* but seldom sails her out of Picton Bay. Blue heron and tern the colour of burnished brass patrol the luminous dusk as we tie up for the night. I notice a sharp-bosomed American tourist, aboard a large Chris-Craft, aim her cleavage at a couple of snickering boys down from Trenton to pick raspberries at Meadowcrest Farm.

Just how quintessentially Canadian Quinte really is was particularly noticeable this season, because Camilla and I had crossed Lake Ontario to spend July 4 at Sodus Bay, a tiny harbour-resort in northern New York State. A squad of legionnaires presented arms with real rifles as the assembled picnickers sang "America the Beautiful." Frank Horton, the local congressman, then delivered a rousing, Reagan-like harangue, ending with the assurance that "the people are strong. If we can just get the government off our backs . . . that's all we need." Picton's July 1 celebration had been much more subdued, including such traditional country pastimes as a taffy pull and a strawberry festival – eat all you can pick.

There is nothing quite like the ambiguous urgency of a sailboat at anchor, its mast sweeping the sky in insolent gestures. Its bow shudders as the wind balloons the great white triangle of the mainsail and the boat takes the wind like a dolphin at play. One magic day when the sun was spreading silver across Adolphus Reach, with sailboats dotting the horizon like white asterisks, I realized the appropriateness of Joseph Conrad's definition of sailors as "the grown-up children of a discontented earth."

My favourite moment of any outing inevitably comes when the day finally folds into itself and I'm heading home, the crew members hugging themselves against the chill of a cool westerly. It is only when the boat is tied firmly back to earth that I realize why sailing means so much to me. I always return with a heightened sensitivity. I see the world anew, freshly and vividly, with a surge of inner excitement that the best of urban existence can never match.

—1980

Sundown Serenade

O NE OF SUMMER'S PLEASURES is to attend the folk festivals, large and small, that liven up various parks and meadows across the country. Along with my daughter Ashley, I spent a July weekend at the eighth annual Winnipeg Folk Festival, held at Birds Hill Park, thirty-two kilometres northeast of Manitoba's capital. Staffed by Rosalie Goldstein's 420 volunteers (she could mobilize the Normandy invasion) and inspired by musical director Mitch Podolak, the Winnipeg event has become North America's largest annual sing-out, with thirty-five thousand folkies crowding the grounds.

Folk music is different; it knows no absolutes. There is no "best" arrangement, tune, or chord. Alone among contemporary musicians, the folk-singer plays in search of his own humanity and, if he's good, his message is as magical as the imprint of a starfish washed up on the seashore. Folk songs are important. Their themes serve as a kind of tuning fork of the country's mood. We listen to great folk-singers and see inside ourselves. Their melodies are pitched to the nation's vibrations. If the Winnipeg performances reflected such folk wisdom, we may be in better shape than the Gallup polls indicate. Certainly, we're a long way from the Sixties, when folk-singers blew angry radical messages through their moustaches.

Today's troubadours deal with the old virtues of faith and compassion, the notion that the only true journey of knowledge and experience is from the depths of one being to the heart of another; that love, at least in one way, is like money – you can't give it away if you've never had it. And that love is as good as it gets.

The only political message I saw all day was a yellow T-shirt with black lettering imprinted on a map of Sterling Lyon's Manitoba, which read: "HAPPINESS IS NEVER HAVING TO SAY YOU'RE TORY."

The concert's climax was the set by Steve Goodman, who flew up from Chicago for a four-hundred-dollar fee. He started out singing "Good Morning, America. How Are Ya?" – the song NASA played to wake the astronauts dozing on the surface of the moon in 1972. Edith Butler, an Acadian version of Buffy Sainte-Marie, lit up the proceedings with her mesmerizing mischief and pathos. Valdy, Canada's most underrated performer, tugged at the soul with his tough tribute to John Lennon, "Thank God He's a Stranger." The Celtic artistry of Na Cabarfeidh reminded me of Norman Mailer's comment that bagpipe music is "a warning of the fever in the hearts of the WASPs." Jim Post's humour, Peter Alsop's wisdom, and the Battlefield Band's lyricism were some of the many other highlights.

But the best moment of all came one evening when a Cajun bluegrass plucker noticed that behind us nature was staging one of those magnificent firestorm prairie sunsets. He stopped the music, pointing silently at the sight. We turned around – then broke into spontaneous applause.

—1981

Taking Maclean's *Weekly*

A N IMPORTANT CHANGE WILL TAKE PLACE in the ongoing evolution of *Maclean's* with our October 6 [1975] issue. We plan to double our frequency of publication to become Canada's first indigenous newsmagazine.

By coming out every second Monday and drastically reducing the interval between when copy is written and when the magazine reaches our 3.4 million readers' hands, we will, in effect, be creating a second career for a publication whose pages have shaped the collective imagination of Canadians since the turn of the century.

The new magazine will look, feel, and be different, but its basic purpose will not change. Since Maclean-Hunter launched this publication seventy years ago, its stated aim has been to document the excitement and the problems of being – and staying – Canadian. Distributed free of charge to our troops in the Second World War, *Maclean's* has provided the platform (and occasionally the talent) to pull together for a national audience the essential interpretations of what it really means to live and work in this country, chronicling the lives and times of those men and women who helped form our image of ourselves.

Any successful magazine has to build a sense of identity for its readers to share. The notion that first made *Maclean's* possible was that Canada consisted of a series of unconnected communities – large and small – and that the magazine might provide a vital, if fragile, east-west link across this unlikely hunk of geography: a platform for the nation to speak to itself.

It has been a successful experiment, but now we feel that our mandate needs to be renewed.

The world is changing as we walk in it. No one is isolated any more. *Maclean's* must assume a more contemporary identity. Instead of trying to shape collective perceptions, we are planning to publish a twice-monthly magazine that will define what's happening across this country and in the world outside. Instead of emphasizing, as we have in the past, what Canadians are *thinking*, we intend to concentrate on what they are *doing*. We also plan to report foreign news, always through Canadian eyes.

The twice-monthly *Maclean's* will attempt to touch much more directly the lives of our readers, describing as objectively as possible some of the less obvious dimensions of the news they see on television, hear on radio, or read in newspapers. Our ambition will be to work toward weekly publication, as soon as the special conditions of the Canadian magazine industry make that a practical option. Meanwhile, we will stay as close as we can to the surge of events, covering the arena where the news is made, where reputations flourish and die, where the interaction between challenge and response decides the course of history. Our objective will be to penetrate the complexities of each situation and connect its various components to their origins.

The magazine will perpetuate *Maclean's* continuing concern for Canada's fundamental problem – that we belong to one of the few countries in the world that became a political unit before it became a community. We believe that a truly indigenous newsmagazine that opens up channels of communication across this nation is bound to help pull it together.

Hopefully, the new *Maclean's* will reflect the sense of adventure and excitement, the curiosity and the passion that we, its editors, feel about Canada. Any successful magazine must be treated as the property of its readers. We certainly will remain accountable primarily to those of you who care about this magazine – and this country – as much as we do.

—1975

WITH THIS ISSUE *Maclean's* becomes a weekly newsmagazine. Like human beings, magazines possess their own life cycles. *Maclean's*, which dates back to 1905, is permanently woven into the memories and dreams of this country. As a general-interest monthly it earned a proud place authenticating the Canadian experience. The bimonthly that replaced it in October of 1975 provided a worthy transition.

Now, at last, we can widen our purview to reporting the ebb and flow of events as they actually happen, conveying not only information but understanding. By attempting to make sense out of the barrage of news that avalanches into most Canadian living rooms on a daily, almost hourly basis, we plan to provide our readers with a rough working-draft of history. We will be much less concerned with publishing a tally of events on the run than with describing the kind of times those events add up to.

The transition will not be simple. The sixty-four talented full-time editorial staffers plus fifty-three part-time contributors who have come together to produce this magazine share two emotions as we put this inaugural issue to bed: the exhilaration of being embroiled in an exciting new journalistic venture, and the terror of not really knowing exactly where it will take us or how we can best get there.

Still, there exists a floating consensus among the staff about the kind of magazine we want. Our tone and content will continue to be strong, reform-minded, and irreverent. We will interpret, assess, and define, trying always to separate the authentic from the contrived. We will not – except in signed opinion columns – advocate, prescribe, or moralize. We'll never be stuffy, treating the enemies of laughter with the same contempt as the enemies of truth.

In an age of nuclear power blocs, megacorporations, and mammoth bureaucracies, it is our intention to humanize the endless flow of decisions that govern our lives from a point of view that no newsmagazine has ever attempted before: an authentically Canadian perspective. Yet what we are launching here is not only Canada's first newsweekly but also a fresh instrument of communication that may change the way this country sees itself. According to present projections, *Maclean's* will be read by nearly three million Canadians a week; our subscribers and newsstand readers will be buying thirty-three million copies annually.

As the editor of *Maclean's* for the past seven years, I have held the slightly heretical notion that despite its deep regional division this country is made up of fundamentally decent people with not dissimilar aspirations, hopes, and promises to keep. I believe that what we will share and care about in common is more vital than the economic, social, political, and linguistic forces trying to divide us.

My hope is that *Maclean's* will eventually become a national sounding board, recording in print the events that shape our history and give Canada its sense of continuity – a way of defining our collective and individual lives, fifty-two times a year.

—1978

❋   ❋   ❋

MACLEAN'S EIGHTY-YEAR EXISTENCE, celebrated in this issue, has been an essential life cycle. The magazine has not always provided a wholly luminous view of Canadian life, but the view it did provide was often the only national focus available.

When you travel across the sparsely occupied areas of this country, as I did while trying to reconstruct the lives and times of the Hudson's Bay Company fur traders, that point is driven home hard. In those geographically marginal regions of the country where our future growth must take place, American television is creating the images that become the prevailing world view – the way local residents see their country and themselves. There is nothing wrong with American television as entertainment, but if we ever begin to believe that the tube reflects reality we're all in trouble. The very essence of popular television is to reduce complexities, homogenize feelings, and in the process blunt intuitions.

Every revolutionary junta in the Third World realizes how important television is in shaping the mind-set of the people, and that is why TV transmitters rather than national treasuries or arms depots have become prime targets for early capture and control. (There was an in-between stage when it seemed as if every coup d'état was directed at the local radio station so that its leader could telephone Barbara Frum on "As It Happens" and tell her how things were going.) The Americans are now saturating our airwaves to an extent that has reduced Canadian TV, no matter how good or relevant, to a minority taste and audience. Fully 98 per cent of the drama and 75 per cent of *all* programs available on prime-time English-language television are beamed up to us from the United States. It may be too late to dilute such an overdose, although I hope not. Nothing less than a rewriting of the Canadian Broadcasting Act will be needed to make any substantial impact on the status quo.

But drastically altered broadcasting regulations will not be enough. What the pulse-takers of public opinion have found is that even if most formative impressions and images are derived from TV, viewers still seek confirmation from the printed word. They look to newspapers which, with their new technology, can react to events nearly as quickly as television. What newspapers very seldom achieve, however, is a national viewpoint and the ability to synthesize news as well as report it. Magazines, though they cannot offer hour-to-hour immediacy, do not suffer from that limitation; they can and do place events in perspective and allow readers to form comprehensive opinions.

That self-serving observation is worth making because *Time* magazine is once again exploring the possibility of launching a full-scale "Canadian" edition. The New York publication's precise plans remain secret, but the fact that *Time* has retained the services of Tom d'Aquino, head of the powerful Business Council on National Issues and Ottawa's most influential lobbyist, indicates that this could become a serious incursion. It is an old battle. It was fought – and won – in the Seventies when the Trudeau government passed Bill C–58, which had the effect of allowing American magazines into this market for what they were instead of what they pretended to be. By adding a few pages of Canadian news and hiring a posse of smooth-talking publicists, they could masquerade as "Canadian editions" that were basically fancy ad traps.

I have always been fascinated by the fact that in the official history of Time Incorporated, Henry Luce, its founder, describes the magazine's Canadian edition as "our best baby." Luce may have been a cultural imperialist, but at least he was honest about it. During the 1960-61 hearings of the Royal Commission on Publications, Lawrence Laybourne, then the managing director of *Time* Canada, had pleaded that his magazine be considered "in all essential respects a Canadian periodical, having regard to the character and quality of its contents and the nature of its publishing operation.'' But that application for Canadian corporate citizenship was rudely demolished by no less a witness than Luce himself, who appeared before the commission on January 17, 1961. Said Luce: ''I may be in some disagreement with my colleagues, but I do *not* consider *Time* a Canadian magazine.''

The Mulroney government should not allow C–58 to be reopened. American newsmagazines – along with all other foreign publications – must retain unhampered access to this country. They have that now, and *Time* is making good use of it, with a profit of six million dollars showing on its Canadian balance sheets for 1984.

The return of *Time* into this market would probably not destroy *Maclean's*; this magazine's subscription base, advertising support, and editorial authority are too well established for that. But the re-entry of *Time* and the dozens of other American magazines sure to follow might hamper the ability of *Maclean's* to continue evolving into an even more vital, world-class publication. Equally seriously, it would prevent new Canadian magazines from starting.

—1985

❄ ❄ ❄

AFTER NEARLY TWELVE YEARS, I have decided to resign the editorship of *Maclean's* as of September 1, 1982.

When I came to this magazine in the winter of 1971 I had a clear idea of what I hoped to accomplish – to put together a publication for which the best writers, editors, illustrators, and photographers would be proud to work and to provide a creative atmosphere for them to practise their craft. The doing of it turned out to be more difficult than I could have imagined. Still, having myself laboured in the trenches of daily journalism for many years, I believe *Maclean's* has granted its staff more freedom, more breathing space, and more stylistic licence than any other mass medium in the country.

At its best, *Maclean's* was a mirror in which Canadians glimpsed one another and recognized themselves. We attempted to refine the country's image of itself, and, in the process, Canada's self-anointed national magazine realized new potentials. During my stewardship we have grown from a jitney staff of eleven trying to stay afloat on a yearly editorial budget of less than $400,000 to the vibrant group of nearly one hundred listed on the masthead, spending more than five million dollars in the gathering and presentation of news. Our weekly readership is nudging 2.5 million, and the magazine's financial outlook has never been healthier.

It has been a joy giving magazine reporters the chance to practise a new style of uncompromising journalism – an approach to reporting that attempts to make sense of the moments that endow history with its excitement and meaning.

I have always felt that what makes any periodical special is that its editor is possessed of a strong sense of audience that touches the readers' genuine concerns and emotions. This is not so much a matter of dictating a magazine's contents, or even of presiding as chief arbiter over any particular editorial mix, as of trying to fathom its audience's collective frame of mind. The mark of any editor worth his salt is that he never knows precisely what he should publish. There is no formula. More eager to capture the mood of his time than to advocate any specific set of ideas, he must have a constantly renewable curiosity. The trick is to report not so much *what* has happened as *how* and *why* it is happening. That remains the quintessential difference between daily and magazine journalism. At *Maclean's*, we have also tried to think nationally, to take into account the subtle differences in sensibilities that separate Canadians from Americans.

I am hoisting anchor at *Maclean's* because I feel that my mandate has been fulfilled. I was a writer before I became an editor and I am returning to what I enjoy doing most. My stint here has been exhilarating, and I thank the magazine's readers for sharing a slice of their time with me.

—1982

Billy's Bounce

BACK WHEN TV EVANGELISTS had private sex lives and Billy Graham was still a prime news-maker, he decided to launch one of his religious crusades in Canada. For reasons that now escape me, I was assigned to cover his Toronto visit for the American edition of *Time*.

Being even the temporary representative of a major U.S. newsmagazine allowed me access to the Graham entourage, and I dropped in after the first night's activities were over. The Canadian National Exhibition Coliseum, which had been turned into a makeshift place of worship for the occasion, was still reverberating with the echoes of Graham's slick salvation-machine's performance; but backstage, the mood of the Bible-thumpers was one of annoyed puzzlement. The crowd response had been much better than they had expected; there had been more converts per capita than at any other first-night revival meeting. Encouraged by local churchmen co-operating with Graham, more than a thousand Canadians had stepped forward to ask for Billy's blessing, displaying the familiar, loose-limbed symptoms of evangelical ecstasy.

The problem was that when it came around to collection time, the crowd had responded with nickels and dimes instead of the more substantial contributions the Graham people had always received stateside.

"What can we do?" they kept asking, and since I happened to be the only Canadian behind the curtains with them, the question was eventually directed at me.

"Simple," I said. "This is Canada. Before you ask for money, just make it clear that donations will be acknowledged with tax receipts. Even when they're saving their souls, Canadians want to be sure it's deductible."

"Bless you, Brother," several of the Graham operatives mumbled, and next evening the appropriate announcement preceded the passing of the collection baskets.

Hallelujah, how the money rolled in.

But it still bothers me that I gave away the secret route to Canadians' pocketbooks that long-ago night at the CNE.

What if Billy tells God?

—1982

EPILOGUE

The View from Cordova Bay

THE QUEST FOR CONTENTMENT is a subtle and precarious process. In some ways, each of us is the sum of the people we have known, including, in my case, the five dozen or so men and women who have been profiled in this book. Genuine contentment has as much to do with intensity of feeling as banishment of alienation. (Alienation in its many forms denies us clear access to our own needs and desires; it makes us not true to ourselves.)

Equally essential in stemming this sense of isolation is to discover and develop some sensible rhythm to one's life, in the same way nature draws its seasonal bounties from the earth. That might help explain why in 1983 I moved to Canada's West Coast, living first aboard my sloop in Tsehum Harbour and now at Cordova Bay, a village on the shore of Vancouver Island's Saanich Peninsula. Life here is full of thrust and sky, a proving ground for the soul. From these wildflower cliffs it seems appropriate to lament that so many urbanites have opted for the frantic gavotte of trying to "get it all," thus abandoning the ability to be excited by anything less. Detachment pervades urban life. Natural instincts are smothered in the clanging cities as men and women forget the eternal faring of the tides and the magic grace notes of the sunsets.

Savouring the sights, scents, and sounds of the turning days and seasons on these Pacific shores creates an alluring fourth dimension of shared silences and flashes of understanding, as mysterious as the midnight scurry of alley cats across a balcony. "The world is not respectable; it is mortal, confused, tormented, deluded forever," according to Spanish philosopher George Santayana. "But it is also shot through with beauty, with love, with glints of courage and laughter. In these, the spirit looms timidly and struggles to the light amid the thorns."

Parading our well-nourished grievances and corroded sensibilities like medieval knights brandishing shields, most of us get through life by pretending to develop bulletproof psyches, but we end up instead sporting a kind of loose amiability that hides the wounds of loneliness. Loyalties fragment; the human spirit becomes dry and brittle. The theologians trumpet a crisis of faith, the secularists a crisis of reason. But atonement and redemption are not for everybody. Still, every act bears its consequences and eventually we must possess our own pasts.

When the mad knight in Miguel de Cervantes's *Don Quixote* achieves one final moment of lucidity and recognizes how ridiculous he has become, he refuses to wallow in self-pity. Instead, with the unalloyed mischief of a man who has explored the far side of his being, he inquires whether the reader would like to join him in "casting off the melancholy burden of sanity." Most of us would prefer to travel less hazardous routes to salvation, but it is only in compassion – in love and in faith – that true contentment can be achieved.

The credo that has animated my work and my life is that Canada is the world's luckiest land – that to be a Canadian imposes obligations of thanksgiving not to take our individual freedoms and collective opportunities for granted. If in this collection of journalistic fragments I have seemed too idealistic, it is for one reason: I have always believed that although it may be absurd to advocate innovation and reform, it is far more absurd not even to try.